Youth Community Inquiry

Colin Lankshear and Michele Knobel
General Editors

Vol. 68

The New Literacies and Digital Epistemologies series
is part of the Peter Lang Education list.
Every volume is peer reviewed and meets
the highest quality standards for content and production.

PETER LANG
New York • Washington, D.C./Baltimore • Bern
Frankfurt • Berlin • Brussels • Vienna • Oxford

Youth Community Inquiry

NEW MEDIA
FOR COMMUNITY
AND PERSONAL GROWTH

EDITED BY
BERTRAM C. BRUCE,
ANN PETERSON BISHOP,
AND NAMA R. BUDHATHOKI

PETER LANG
New York • Washington, D.C./Baltimore • Bern
Frankfurt • Berlin • Brussels • Vienna • Oxford

Library of Congress Cataloging-in-Publication Data

Youth community inquiry: new media for community and personal growth /
edited by Bertram C. Bruce, Ann Peterson Bishop, Nama R. Budhathoki.
pages cm. — (New literacies and digital epistemologies; vol. 68)
Includes bibliographical references and index.
1. Community and school. 2. Inquiry-based learning. 3. Technology and youth.
4. Transformative learning. 5. Democracy and education.
I. Bruce, Bertram C., editor of compilation.
II. Bishop, Ann Peterson, editor of compilation.
III. Budhathoki, Nama R., editor of compilation.
LC215.Y68 2014   370.11'5—dc23   2013026108
ISBN 978-1-4331-2404-4 (hardcover)
ISBN 978-1-4331-2403-7 (paperback)
ISBN 978-1-4539-1201-0 (e-book)
ISSN 1523-9543

Bibliographic information published by **Die Deutsche Nationalbibliothek**.
Die Deutsche Nationalbibliothek lists this publication in the "Deutsche
Nationalbibliografie"; detailed bibliographic data is available
on the Internet at http://dnb.d-nb.de/.

Cover design concept by Iván M. Jorrín-Abellán

The paper in this book meets the guidelines for permanence and durability
of the Committee on Production Guidelines for Book Longevity
of the Council of Library Resources.

© 2014 Peter Lang Publishing, Inc., New York
29 Broadway, 18th floor, New York, NY 10006
www.peterlang.com

Printed in the United States of America

Contents

Section 4: Evaluating and Making Sense of Youth Activities

Preface

When we imagine young people today, we often see them glued to cell phones, mobile media devices, digital cameras, or handheld games. Or, they may be sitting with a computer, sharing music, photos, and videos, podcasting, web surfing, playing video games, or interacting on social media sites. Their experience of the world seems markedly different from that of their parents, or even older siblings (Alvermann, 2010; Coiro, Knobel, Lankshear, & Leu, 2008; Ito et al., 2010; Jenkins, 2006). This digital realm offers many benefits. Words such as *adventure, learning, connection, social,* and *global* have become commonplace in descriptions of so-called "digital natives." For some, their experiences are liberating and integral to the development of identity and social relations, but they can also be excessively individualized, aimless, and isolating. Moreover, living in a digital environment does not entail being digitally competent (DiMaggio & Hargittai, 2001; Li & Ranieri, 2010).

Another image for young people and technology involves their use of social media for political change. Through cell phones, YouTube, Twitter, Instagram, Facebook, Google+, Wordpress, etc., young people around the world are seen to protest and organize resistance movements. Studies of such social action (Earl & Kimport, 2012; Loader & Mercea, 2012) are underway to determine who participates, what they accomplish, and how these online activities relate to offline life (Haythornthwaite & Kendall, 2010).

There are other possibilities for how youth relate to digital media, including embedding technology use in a community-focused context (Warschauer, 2003). The use of new media for active citizenship, beyond protest per se, is receiving increasing attention (Benson & Christian, 2002; boyd, Palfrey, & Sacco, 2012; National Writing Project et al., 2006; Ross, 2012). A broad range of practices from mapping community assets to writing community history has the potential to bring the facility with and attraction to diverse digital media together with the drive for social change. Young people can build upon their actual or latent abilities with digital photography, audio and video production and editing, Internet search, GPS, databases, Internet radio, and more. They can go beyond individual use and beyond social media in a narrow sense to make a difference for their neighborhoods and their communities.

What does that look like? What could they accomplish and what challenges would they face? Can learning and technology use become more integrated and connected to community life? Can young people be allowed, indeed expected, to become responsible participants in the public sphere and to address problems such as economic injustice, racism, alienation, illness, or environmental degradation? Can they become active sustainers of their own communities? Can they use their facility with new information tools in a way that helps connect and build community, rather than leading to further isolation?

Our book brings a new perspective in three ways: (1) It shows how youth energy and facility with new media can address community needs in a concerted way, rather than simply describing existing youth practices with new media. (2) The use of new technology goes beyond social media per se to include building geographic information systems, designing community technology centers, hosting Internet radio, and other extensions of typical use. (3) It brings in the perspective of community members in the selection of problems, design of activities, and the interpretation of results. Many of the coauthors are non-academic, community members.

This Book

This collection addresses questions about youth, community, and new media through the theory of *community inquiry* (Bruce, 2008a; Bruce & Bishop, 2008; Bruce & Bloch, 2013) and by means of a detailed look at how young people use new media to help their communities thrive. The examples come from Youth Community Inquiry, a large-scale collaboration among diverse urban and rural communities, schools, public libraries, community centers, a public media station, 4-H, and the University of Illinois. Chapter 1 develops the theoretical and historical background.

Succeeding chapters tell the stories of work with young people engaged in community building using new media. The settings range from a small farming town to an inner-city neighborhood of Chicago, and with youth from ages 8 to 20. Going beyond works on social media in a narrow sense, the projects involve the use of varied technologies and media, such as GPS/GIS mapping tools, video production, use of archives and databases, podcasts, and Internet radio. The chapters present extensions of theory, the inquiry-based activities, the technologies, the experiences, and what has been learned.

Each chapter addresses questions such as the following:

- What are the participants doing?
- What are they learning?
- How are new literacies employed to enhance community inquiry?
- To what extent is the experience a good model for informal learning and community development?
- What role can and should adults play in youth-oriented community-based projects?

You will discover a variety of purposes, perspectives, and styles in the chapters. Some are more scholarly in style, often displaying a critical perspective on community activities. Others emphasize pedagogical goals; still others, community building. The authors include teachers, community activists, students, university staff, and others. Most of the projects have changed in some ways since the writing—coming to an end, expanding, shifting direction, generating spin-offs. The chapters discuss those changes during a segment of time, but you would need to follow up with particular sites to know what they are doing today and planning for tomorrow. We deliberately chose to preserve that variety as a manifestation of the diverse ways that the Youth Community Inquiry (YCI) ideas were realized. In each case, the projects embody the goals of learning about the world in a connected way, acting responsibly in the world, and transforming the world, which are ultimately inseparable.

We hope that these chapters will be useful for communities. They should also help professionals who work with youth in educational settings. These include K–12 teachers and media specialists, youth services librarians in public libraries, education directors in museums, and youth development specialists and program directors in agencies such as Boys & Girls Clubs, 4-H, and summer youth programs. In addition, they should help university staff and students whose work involves connecting communities and higher education, fulfilling the promise of public engagement. Finally, they provide insights for anyone interested in the meaning of new media in a diverse and changing world.

Bertram C. Bruce
Ann Peterson Bishop
Nama R. Budhathoki

Acknowledgments

This work was enabled by generous volunteer work across many communities, by libraries, schools, and community centers, by individual community-focused grants, and by the U.S. Institute of Museum and Library Services (Grant No. RE-03-07-0007-07). It would not have been possible without the support of the Graduate School of Library and Information Science and 4-H Extension at the University of Illinois. In addition to the authors of chapters in the book, many other individuals contributed in important ways to the project, including Moustafa Ayad, Naomi Bloch, Christy Brinkley, Susan Bruce, Lynn Carter, Jon Gant, Carol Inskeep, Sharon Irish, Chera Kowalski, José López, Sandra Mitchell, Alejandro Molina, Matthew Rodríguez, and Claudia Şerbănuţă, and XiaoXiong Xu.

1. Community Inquiry

Bertram C. Bruce

The concept of *community inquiry* highlights the ways that people come together to establish common ground and to work toward common purposes. The process is an essential aspect of building a larger democracy (Williamson, Alperovitz, & Imbroscio, 2002; Longo, 2007). It might also be called participatory democracy. But the usual terms fail to capture the process we envision. *Democracy* is often reduced to a particular form of government, such as having a constitution or a parliamentary system of representation. *Participatory democracy* sometimes means little more than having the right to vote. *Community inquiry* could be similarly reduced in scope. But for the purposes here it emphasizes inquiry conducted of, for, and by communities as living social organisms. It implies support for collaborative activity and for creating knowledge connected to people's values, history, and lived experiences. The inquiry entails open-ended, democratic, participatory engagement. Community inquiry is thus a learning process that brings theory and action together in an experimental and critical manner.

Engagement in Community Life

The word "community" has many meanings (Cohen, 1985). As used here, one we do not accept is that of uniformity or consensus. Uniformity in beliefs, values, or aims is in fact a barrier to community growth, because it precludes the dialogue that is necessary to achieve things in common. Clark (1994) argues that most idealized views of community share a belief that "the concept of community cannot be separated from the demand for agreement" (p. 63). If the discourse of community instead is to function in support of democratic engagement, it must not only allow, but insist upon valuing difference and change:

> If the political function of an ethical discourse of community is to constitute and maintain a democratic collectivity, then participation in that discourse must be guided by an ethics that directs people to value their differences because that is what enables their cooperation as equals (Clark, 1994, p. 62).

The chapters in this book reflect the valuing of difference. We made no effort to disguise or pass over differences between university and community, or among any of the participants. Indeed, the story in many of the chapters starts with conflict, or at least, different assumptions about how to achieve some goal. Community is seen here as a process, one in which acceptance of difference can lead at times to the recognition of common values (or not). That recognition in turn may need to be reconstructed upon encounter with new participants in the community.

Kendzior (2011) describes an extreme case, that of the online Uzbek dissident community. Participants there disagree about history, methods, responsibility, and virtually every other aspect of their enterprise to resist oppression in Uzbekistan. They appear to agree only on the idea that they are not part of the same community. Nevertheless, they attend to what each other says, they care about the same issues, and they write with the others in mind as a crucial audience. The communities described here rarely exhibit that degree of divergence, but all of them reveal different perspectives within and interesting approaches to working with difference. This is a key ingredient for enabling growth of both communities and the individuals within.

Recognizing both the challenges and the possibilities of the dramatic changes in science, technology, and social relations he observed, John Dewey saw growth as the essence of that learning process. Individual and social development are two sides of this one phenomenon; the individual requires a supportive society to thrive and society depends on the health of all its members. Participatory democracy for all in a learning society follows: Young people need to be engaged early on in active citizenship, while adults need to be lifelong learners. From this perspective, "[t]he idea of education as preparation and of adulthood as a fixed limit of growth are two sides of the same obnoxious untruth" (Dewey, 1920, p. 185).

> Moreover, all institutions in a democracy have a purpose, namely, to set free and to develop the capacities of human individuals without respect to race, sex, class or economic status. . . . Democracy has many meanings, but if it has a moral meaning, it is found in resolving that the supreme test of all political institutions and industrial arrangements shall be the contribution they make to the all-around growth of every member of society. (p. 186)

Thus, there is a two-way obligation: The larger society needs to guarantee full opportunity for individual participation and growth and the individual needs to contribute responsibly to society, to help it develop as well. Jane Addams (1915) developed this idea of emphasizing the duties as well as the rights of citizenship. Moreover, democracy must be extended "beyond its political expression" to make "the entire social organism democratic" (Addams, 1892/2002, p. 15). But as Dewey (1927) warns, the public itself can become eclipsed and no longer function as the venue in which people can work together toward shared understandings and common good.

Along this line, Addams (1912) also stressed that women had a civic duty to become involved in municipal affairs as a matter of civic housekeeping. At Hull House, these duties involved reform efforts regarding poisonous sewage, impure milk (which carried tuberculosis), smoke-laden air, and unsafe factory conditions. Addams saw this as crucial for the emerging democracy of her time but also essential to develop an enlarged role for women in the public sphere (Calhoun, 1992). The youth projects here represent a similar impulse, essentially extending the civic housekeeping idea to all citizens, including youth. (Note that "citizen" here includes all who participate in community life, regardless of documented status.) Although the communities the youth inhabit have underappreciated assets, they also have serious needs, many unfortunately persisting since Addams's day. By working to improve those conditions and to help their communities thrive, there is the potential for young people to learn more, develop themselves, and expand their role in the larger society.

Youth and Their Communities Today

Jonathan Kozol's classic *Savage Inequalities* (1991) highlights the gross inequalities across schools for different classes and races in America (including one of the communities discussed in this book). During the intervening two decades, those inequalities have only worsened. What Kozol saw in schools is coupled with similar inequalities across communities. Meanwhile, even in good schools, many students find that their schooling is increasingly irrelevant. In *The Teenage Liberation Handbook*, Grace Llewellyn (1998) offers what some would call the outrageous claim that our school system is so bad that dropping out has become a rational alternative. Society's response has been to ignore the underlying inequalities and simply impose more rigorous testing of students and teachers, even though narrowly focused, decontextualized testing is itself a significant part of the problem.

There are outstanding teachers making a real difference in the most difficult circumstances. But the educational system as a whole has not served many youth well, a fact that has consequences beyond individuals or their families. It certainly affects the economy as a whole, but more importantly, it undermines the premise of a democratic society: that all citizens have the opportunity to become informed and to participate fully, while simultaneously developing the capacity for civic responsibility.

For example, as discussed in Chapter 10, one community partner related how many African American youth from low-income families simply won't cross the major street that separates their neighborhood from the university. It is effectively gated; it doesn't belong to them. The general problem was noted by Benson, Puckett, and Harkavy (2007) in their book on the role of universities in a democracy. Other community members have expressed similar concerns about public libraries, museums, city-run activity programs, and other activities that purport to be open to all. There is clearly a need for more meaningful dialogue across institutional and cultural boundaries (Linden, 2002, Meyer Reimer & Bruce 1994). We also need to recognize that schools are not the only site for learning:

> Throughout our nation's history, education has been linked to the promise of democracy. Yet over the past century this connection has too often been narrowed to the school as its sole vessel. This is harmful to education—it puts too much pressure on a single institution. It is also harmful to democracy—it ignores the role of the many

institutions that educate, along with the connections between these institutions. (Longo, 2005, p. 2)

Reinforcing the broader view of sites for learning is a growing recognition of the untapped and unrecognized funds of knowledge (Moll, et al., 1992) in every community. But these funds of knowledge, as well as outside sources, often fail to connect with issues of health, education, economic development, and community building. Better and more appropriate technologies are needed to promote learning, knowledge sharing, literacy development, and democratic engagement. Better ways to document community situations, to access information sources, to connect with knowledgeable people and organizations, to communicate problems and successes, and to form collaborations are also needed. This implies the need for new kinds of information professionals (Bruce, 2003; Kapitzke & Bruce, 2006), who can work with an increasingly diverse, multilingual population often disenfranchised from full participation in society.

It sometimes requires considerable ingenuity on the part of universities and community partners to integrate community and campus life. A deeper understanding of community life within academia could help community engagement move beyond traditional outreach or service learning concepts, in which the focus is usually on university achievement rather than community empowerment (Bishop, Bruce, & Jeong, 2009). The usual conception of community outreach needs to be complemented by a notion of institutional inreach, in which communities take the lead. There are models for education and community development when people from diverse backgrounds are able to learn together and from each other (Bruce & Bishop, 2008; Ginwright, Noguera, & Cammarota, 2006; McKoy & Vincent, 2007; Nam, 2012; National Writing Project et al., 2006; Oakes, Rogers, & Lipton, 2006). Collaborations among community members and university people on projects that use information and communication technologies for community building show both the challenges and what is possible.

The Youth Community Inquiry (YCI) Project

The John Dewey Project on Progressive Education (2002) identifies two key aspects of progressive education. There is first the imperative of fostering a respect for diversity throughout society, including within universities, professions, and among interacting communities. Each individual and each community needs to be recognized for their own abilities, interests, ideas, needs, and cultural identity. Second, the goal of participation is not simply learning technical skills or accumulating isolated knowledge, but the development of a critical, socially engaged intelligence. Thus, progressive education entails not only progressive methods for individual learning, but education for a progressive society (Bruce & Drayton, 2013; Bruce & Pecore, 2013; Hogan & Bruce, 2013).

At the Graduate School of Library and Information Science (GSLIS) at the University of Illinois, we wanted to find ways to show young people the diverse ways in which information science professionals work, but also to prepare them as leaders to expand the definition of the field. In previous projects, youth had participated in the delivery of training and refurbished computers to hundreds of low-income, predominantly African American families (Bishop et al., 1999). Later, we had involved students in setting up numerous technology centers and teen tech teams across Illinois, particularly in economically disadvantaged communities such as East Saint Louis (Choksi, 1997). This activity provided a learning opportunity for our students, addressed the information technology needs of low-income and minority communities, and provided an ongoing opportunity to better understand the needs and appreciate the assets of these communities.

Work at GSLIS complemented that of the University of Illinois Extension, which serves many thousands of youth across the state under of the umbrella of 4-H clubs and activities. 4-H is the largest, nonformal, public-funded youth development program in the country. It offers a broad range of hands-on, project-based curricula in areas including communications, computers, geospatial technologies, robotics, and citizenship. The 4-H club, especially the project group, is a form of experiential education based on John Dewey's (1938) principles of interaction and continuity. Its motto of Head, Heart, Hands, and Health is a living model of Dewey's pedagogical ideas (Enfield, 2001).

Bringing these organizations and learning from previous community-based projects together, our Youth Community Inquiry (YCI) project (also called Youth Community Informatics) engaged university students and faculty in work with diverse underserved communities to help young people learn about new technologies and to develop academic potential through self-expression and community building (Bruce & Bishop, 2011). The young people did research in their communities, produced video documentaries and podcasts, used GIS/GPS technologies, explored social issues through protest songs and oral history, and more.

We assumed that they needed to be involved in active learning related to information science and to experience the field in ways that are truly meaningful to their lives. This included having opportunities for significant interaction with professionals and pre-professionals in the field. Given the larger goals about engaged citizenship and equitable participation, we knew that the focus should be on community involvement, not just on individuals. Moreover, there must be democratic and equitable engagement of participants in design, implementation, and evaluation. This recalls Tully's (2008) theory of agonistic freedom, according to which power must always be exercised over subjects who are in some ways free. Oppressed people thus always have ways of thinking and acting other than they do, not just playing within the game, but of changing the rules. This means responding actively, not passively, to complex and changing, often difficult, circumstances. In diverse ways, the project sought to enlarge the set of tools that people had for this game changing.

The progressive education movement offered various ways to integrate learning across disciplines, such as the integrated learning units (Urban & Wagoner, 2009), project learning (Tenenbaum, 1951), or theme studies (Gamberg, Kwak, Hutchings, & Altheim, 1988). That idea of integration can be extended beyond schools, to community centers, after-school programs, 4-H clubs, libraries, museums, and informal collaborations. One can then couple learning per se with the aspect of social transformation, seeing the purpose of inquiry as not only to interpret the world but also to change it. Change in turn can lead to deeper understanding, in a cycle, or spiral, of inquiry.

Ethos of Inquiry

While learning about new digital media creation provides a significant incentive for youth to participate within proposed projects, the project sought to embed an ethos of inquiry into the entire process. As described in the field notes of one of the university students working on the project, youth need to be

> encouraged to begin "thinking outside the box." We have grand ideas about working with these [teenaged] students, but we have to realize that they may not be used to exploring, questioning, and thinking in the ways we are hoping these activities will play out. In fact, school systems may squelch these kinds of expansive behaviors. We can give them a safe space to explore their own thoughts and ideas.

The challenge of introducing inquiry-based pedagogy not only applies to the youth but also to their youth leaders, and perhaps most of all, to the university partners. Helping to foster new ways of learning within the community itself becomes an activity using the strategies of community inquiry. As such, we view our implementation of the project as a meta-inquiry cycle as we join together within new communities of inquiry at each of our focal sites across the state. Such practice requires that we suspend disbelief and open ourselves to new ideas and evidence; communicate with an emphasis on listening; act to effect change; and use discussion and reflection to assess and learn from each experience (Shields, 1999).

Steps to build these communities of inquiry centered around new digital technologies would not be possible without the rich background of experiences already shared between professionals and youth leaders. Work in the urban community of East St. Louis, for instance, is grounded in the activities of the East St. Louis Action Research Project, a university-based community engagement activity with a 20-year history. At its core, these participatory activities require strong relationships that arise out of shared experiences of action within the community.

For pre-professionals just coming into the project, though, it can be difficult to connect with this rich history of relationships that might be experienced by seasoned professionals and their community partners. For instance, one writes:

> Personally, I have long been interested in service learning, but my concern is that service learning has mostly a uni-direction from the outside of community: Students (mostly from white middle class) go into the others' community, meet with others' needs, learn about others, and empower others. Although much research advocates the reciprocal relationship between the community and the participating students, I could still see in many cases the community people (minorities, underrepresented people, those in poverty) are regarded as an object/a client for student learning. I have wanted to look at the other side of a story, which is from the community.

Inquiry in the project implied a close connection between understanding and action, as in Dewey's example of what it means to know an automobile:

> An individual may know all about the structure of an automobile, may be able to name all the parts of the machine and tell what they are there for. But he does not understand the machine unless he knows how it works and how to work it; and, if it doesn't work right, what to do in order to make it work right. . . . Understanding, by its very nature, is related to action. (Dewey, 1937, p. 184)

Youth in the project sought understanding in the sense of learning "how things work" but also action in the sense of "how to do things." An example was to study the problem of alcoholism in the community, then make a book about it, such as *This Is the Real Me* (Nam & Bishop, 2011). The understand/act distinction is not absolute; it's hard to come up with a good example in which the two roles are not blended and mutually supportive. But it can still be useful for reflecting on our work. Understanding as enacted here goes well beyond what often occurs in school in terms of relevance, connectedness, and community base. Dewey saw the more limited learning as imparting information, but not understanding. Thus, the action rarely happens at all.

Supportive Environments for Inquiry

David Hawkins (1965) describes his work in a fifth-grade class teaching about pendulums. He identifies three patterns, or phases, of school work in science. These phases induce different relations among children, materials of study, and teachers. If we substitute *mentors* or *colleagues* for *teachers*, we see that they apply fairly well to science work itself and to other kinds of learning. That's not so surprising, given that the essence of the phases is that general patterns of inquiry recur across diverse situations of life, work, and learning. In fact, Hawkins prefers the term *work* over *play* even though it might appear that he's just arguing for allowing children to have time to play.

He has in mind the kind of work one might do on a boat, citing the famous passage in *The Wind in the Willows*, by Kenneth Grahame (1913):

> "Believe me, my young friend", said the water rat solemnly, "there is nothing . . . absolutely nothing . . . half so much worth doing as simply messing about in boats. Simply messing . . . nothing seems really to matter, that's the charm of it. Whether you get away or whether you don't; whether you arrive at your destination or whether you reach somewhere else, or whether you never get anywhere at all, you're always busy, and you never do anything in particular.

Hawkins discovered that in order to learn in science we need ample time to explore or "mess about," which he symbolized by the circle (**O**). In the pendulum study, the messing about was far from chaotic or undirected, because the materials provided a structure to the investigations. In fact, as students messed about they began to generate the very questions that the lesson was intended to address, but in a way that was more involved, and connected to their direct experience. He also saw the need for two other phases, the triangle (**Δ**), which involves "multiply programmed material" to support work that is "more externally guided and disciplined" (p. 72) and the square (**□**), for "discussion, argument, and the full colloquium of children and teacher" (p. 74). The phases are unordered, and all are important. Learning requires the opportunity to experience all of the phases in a connected way, and to move easily among them.

Franz and Papert (1988) build on Hawkins's ideas in a paper about students learning how to measure time. They argue that using computers well for learning requires

> open-ended projects that foster students' involvement with a variety of materials; . . . activities in which students use computers to solve real problems; . . . [connection of] the work done on the computer with what goes on during the rest of the school day, and also with the students' interests outside of school; . . . [recognizing] the unique qualities of computers; . . . [taking advantage of] low-cost technological advances . . . , which promote integration of the computer with aspects of the students' physical environment.

In a typical, short-term Youth Community Inquiry project (see Chapter 2), middle school students made podcasts of stories important in their lives. They needed time to explore, experiment, and become comfortable with the technologies and each other, to mess about (**O**). They selected images from the web, scanned in family photos, created graphics, downloaded appropriate music, created audio files, edited audio using Audacity, and created presentations. Through guided inquiry (**Δ**) they learned about copyright and citing sources, as well as about design and storytelling. Curricula in the form of inquiry units (see next section) were a means to support this guidance and the collaborations. The students also used the podcasts as a way to connect with and talk about their families and their lives outside of school. That colloquium (□) was extended for many youth in community meetings, our YCI summer forums, conferences, and other venues, as well as online.

In doing all of this the young people made technology part of their lived experience, not something divorced from it. More importantly, they made themselves more engaged citizens in their community. In this and in more complex, longer-term projects, community inquiry provided a framework for youth to mold and shape the activity, the inquiry unit, and the technologies to their needs. Through their inquiries, they were able to engage themselves in positive, meaningful work toward community goals. The chapters in the book show many other examples of this community-based work and learning.

Inquiry Units: The Community Is the Curriculum

A key goal for the project was to develop *inquiry units* to support community action (Figure 1). These allowed for a broad range of topics to be similarly structured based on the concept of the Inquiry Cycle (Bruce, 2009; Bruce & Bishop, 2002): *Ask, Investigate, Create, Discuss, Reflect.* The activities were facilitated through an array of hardware and software technologies we developed or appropriated (Eglash, Crossiant, Di Chiro, & Fouché, 2004; see also Chapter 13). The *inquiry units* were incorporated into a curriculum, developed through use in different settings (see Chapter 14). We brought these aspects together through both online and face-to-face forums for interaction.

An example *inquiry unit* is *Information Spaces in the Community.* The activity makes use of diverse new technologies, but the focus is on learning about the community, asking questions, and sharing findings with others, not on the technologies per se:

Ask. How do people in the community get the information they need to learn, solve problems, and conduct their daily lives? This leads to the question: What are the information spaces in the community? And from that, how can new digital technologies be used to investigate communities and to share what is learned?

Investigate. Participants go out into the community in small groups (6–10), each with a group leader. Each group visits between one and three information spaces. In each space, they meet with people involved, listen, and discuss. They explore the space, make a video about it using a video camera, and determine geo-coordinates using a handheld GPS receiver. This investigation takes at least 30 minutes per site but could be extended to a half-day or multiple visits. At each site, the participants ask questions such as the following: What do we see in this information center? How do we like it? What is this center about? What do we want people in our community to know about the center? How can we give others a clear idea about the center through watching/hearing our report?

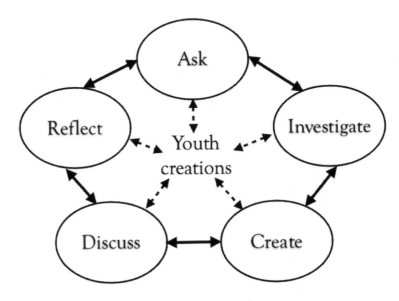

Figure 1.1. The inquiry cycle

Create. Participants return to a computer lab, where they make a GIS site using Google Maps and mark the coordinates of the places they visited. This could include the path they followed. They upload their video, music, and text. In some cases they might make a podcast or slide show about their findings.

Discuss. Participants share their findings and the product they create with others. Discussion may lead to new questions (Ask), new actions (Create), and so on.

Reflect. Participants think about issues of journalism, democracy, careers, technologies, etc. Some questions they consider include the following: What were the unexpected events, the surprising findings? How do different information centers compare (based on the presentation and discussion)? Do all community members have equal access to these information spaces? What kinds of information are available? What kinds are missing? How useful are the digital technologies for recording our findings? What other features might be helpful?

Through activities such as this, young people learned about their community and generated new questions about it. Discussions led to issues of freedom of speech, poverty, diverse lifestyles, and more. In some cases this investigation of community led to political action.

For example, a group of African American teenagers realized that many people, both within and outside their community, thought that their neighborhood had nothing to offer, especially for youth. They saw few opportunities for jobs or even for volunteer activities. Working with community youth leaders, the teenagers interviewed their friends and took notes on needs and known resources. They then wrote a flyer and distributed it to 6,000 homes, asking for ideas. They identified a number of businesses and community organizations, including, for example, the Boys & Girls Club and the local community college. They developed an interview protocol and spoke with key people in each organization. They edited the interview footage and added a narrative as well as metadata, such as the types of services or number of people served. They used a geographic positioning system (GPS) to identify locations and entered all of this into a Google map: http://go.illinois.edu/e2ymap.

The work done by these young people addressed a real community need. The product they developed provides information for youth service providers, the youth, and their parents. It also helps everyone understand the community better, in terms of both its assets and its needs. Meanwhile, the youth learned about new literacies, video editing, GIS/GPS, interviewing, project management, and writing. Moreover, they did this, not simply to learn for themselves but to help their own community. From a pedagogical perspective, this is what we call community as curriculum. Inquiry in the sense of learning more was coupled with inquiry for action.

Communities of Inquiry

In his development of a theory of inquiry, Peirce (1877) emphasizes its social nature: "Unless we make ourselves hermits, we shall necessarily influence each other's opinions; so that the problem becomes how to fix belief, not in the individual merely, but in the community." This leads to the idea of communities of inquiry, which are prerequisites to community inquiry as defined above.

Communities of inquiry offer a framework in which people can come together to directly address community needs. During a summer forum, youth engaged in the Information Spaces in the Community unit described above. At another, it was Music as the Message. Participating teens investigated political and socially charged songs such as Marvin Gaye's "Inner-City Blues" and Catpower's "Names." They researched the issues addressed in these protest songs, then created multiple forms of media, such as zines, videos, and slideshows, to share what they learned and felt about these issues (see http://youtube/XU62fXl2n3A).

A highlight of the forums was the opportunity for youth to interact with others from diverse backgrounds. For example, white youth in a rural school and African American youth from an urban setting were able to interact with each other, with adults, and with university partners who hailed from Nepal, South Korea, Japan, and other countries. At the international 2010 iConference, those youth worked together to guide adult participants in a full-day workshop. Community groups also connected with other university departments or public organizations such as the public radio and TV station and the Planetarium.

The first summer forum provided an example of how bringing together youth, youth leaders, and university personnel from diverse sites provides both unique opportunities and also unique challenges. Community inquiry happens best when plurality and differences are understood using a hermeneutic process while also maintaining focus on the larger context (Bruce & Bishop, 2002). Discussions among participants provided opportunities to explore their similarities and differences. Indeed, as a result of bringing together youth and youth leaders from a variety of underserved communities, one youth leader stated:

> I believe, in the not too distant future, that this conference will be seen as a landmark in developing a new perspective as part of the partnership between those marginalized sectors of civil society and the university in bridging the digital divide.

Also, since its inception, YCI participants played a central role in the Puerto Rican Cultural Center's (Chicago) annual Community as Intellectual Space symposium. Focusing on a different theme each year, the symposium brought together community members, artists, educators, librarians, activists, and students to address social justice issues and support community-building efforts. Youth in other communities participated in Dialogues in Methods of Education (DIME) meetings. The DIME group includes teachers at all levels, students, community members, and others who gather to discuss various issues related to teaching, learning, and community inquiry. One such workshop involved place-marked digital video. In another, middle school youth presented their community asset-mapping project to DIME participants. These workshops helped DIME members to learn new technologies that they could use in their work, but more importantly, called on the young people to develop as leaders in community change.

The project had an impact on the GSLIS curriculum and on similar programs at other universities. The most important impact was on the students and university staff themselves, as is evident in the chapters. Within GSLIS, several different community informatics courses used YCI projects as case studies, including inviting youth and community partners from various sites as guest presenters. Youth librarianship faculty incorporated community informatics into their curriculum. In a course on networking systems, students explored equipping community programs with the hardware and software tools they needed. Experiences, findings, and issues were incorporated into a "Community Informatics Studio" course, which looked at design issues.

Students drew from readings in community building, digital storytelling, community media, and participatory journalism to develop and execute a plan for integrating community media and citizen journalism into established public computing spaces.

Finally, although based primarily in Illinois communities, the YCI project had impact beyond its borders, even internationally. For example, through work at the Puerto Rican Cultural Center (PRCC) in Chicago, Sarai Lastra and others at the University of Turabo in Puerto Rico now collaborate with GSLIS and the PRCC around community inquiry. XiaoXiong Xu, a professor at Ningbo University, is creating bridges among high schools, universities, and the community to address the educational and employment challenges currently faced by Chinese youth. The project aims to provide youth with hands-on experience using new technologies to help prepare them for employment, and to respond to the needs of underserved communities. Iván M. Jorrín Abellán has started a project in Miranda de Ebro in Spain with youth leaders with the aim of mapping different social elements that affect youth, such as youth participation, youth leisure and entertainment offerings, youth and outdoor activities, and training for youth leaders. They use tools such as wikis, blogs, and mapping to promote and engage young people in community initiatives.

Section 1

Learning About the World in a Connected Way

We used *inquiry units* as a structure to organize activities and to show possible roles for youth, community leaders, teachers, and others. As communities engaged in specific projects, they revised the units and created new ones based on their experiences. The units thus served to record what we learned. In a more general sense, the units supported a *social justice youth development model* (Ginwright, Noguera, & Cammarota, 2006). This was to help young people—indeed, all members of a community—address three interrelated aims, to understand the world in a connected way, to act responsibly in the world, and to use what they know to transform the world.

The first of these aims corresponds generally to inquiry-based learning. That inquiry was closely tied to action, not simply to gain knowledge in an abstract sense. The second goal might be glossed as civic engagement, or developing a critical, socially engaged intelligence. The third is a social justice imperative. These goals pervade the project as a whole as well as the examples in the individual chapters. We grouped the chapters in terms of which of the three aims they most strongly exemplified, even though none of them fit entirely within one.

Some chapters focus more on the learning about the world aspect. In Urbana, Champaign, and Joliet after-school programs, middle school students conducted Internet research and used multimedia formats such as podcasting to investigate and share findings of youth-identified research topics. These topics included the U.S.-led war in Iraq, obesity, children in Africa, the history of the local Mexican American community, survival tips for immigrant students, and multicultural literature. Ching-Chiu Lin and Karyn M. Mendoza discuss some of this work in Chapter 2, "Youth Interests and Digital Media: 4-H Podcasting Program in Urbana Middle School."

Alex Jean-Charles takes that learning in the direction of learning about technologies used *against youth* in Chapter 3, "New Media Technology: Tools of Expression/Repression in Communities." That chapter discussed video surveillance of urban youth, and then the use of video *by youth* to portray and take charge of their own lives.

In Chapter 4, "Beyond Human Sensors: The Learning Instincts of Youth Using Geospatial Media," Nama R. Budhathoki, Bertram C. Bruce, Jill Murphy, and Kimberly Rahn discuss the use of geospatial tools to learn local history. At a rural Illinois middle school, students conducted several community mapping projects, such as the one shown at http://wp.iwest.k12. il.us/maps/.

In Chapter 5, "Now I Am College Material": Engaging Students Through Living Reflections of Self-Identity as a Form of Pedagogy, William Patterson and Shameem Rakha relate experiences in the Youth Media Workshop, a project of a public media station with community youth to learn about their own history. The Youth Media Workshop was developed in 2000 as a form of pedagogy using indigenous knowledge, media, and popular culture to enrich the education and social development experiences of African American youth. The pedagogy used by this oral history and media creation project is informed by Patterson's notion of "living reflections of self-identity," which suggests that through the use of media and local living history, students' educational experiences and beliefs about education can be changed. The authors explore the impacts of the Youth Media Workshop on the social capital of its participants.

2. Youth Interests and Digital Media: 4-H Podcasting Program in Urbana Middle School

Ching-Chiu Lin
Karyn M. Mendoza

In an after-school project we explored how inquiry learning (Bruce & Bishop, 2002; Bruce & Davidson, 1996) using digital media could support expression and communication for middle school youth. Our goal was to foster both personal growth and community engagement. Audio and audiovisual podcasting became a means for learners to explore creative and critical inquiries using their existing literacy skills along with new understandings of technology. They would investigate topics of interest through digital media and further their participatory citizenship by activities that address community needs.

Overview of the Program

4-H Podcasting was one of the many classes offered in an after-school program, SPLASH, at Urbana Middle School (UMS) in Central Illinois. The project followed SPLASH's schedule and structure, with five classes per session. Classes took place each week on Mondays from 3:30 to 5:30 p.m., and there were five sessions total throughout the semester from August 2007 to May 2008. It included educational activities that integrated library and information science (LIS) curriculum modules on the Internet, multimedia and podcasting, and ethical issues around youth engagement in multimedia production. Concepts and practices related to copyright, Internet safety, community inquiry, and media consumption were introduced and discussed through interactive dialogue with the group.

Building on a partnership between GSLIS and the Extension Statewide 4-H Network, we worked with middle school students using multimedia as a tool to investigate youth-identified research topics. Specifically, the students chose a topic representing their personal interests, researched the topic online, and then made a 1-2 minute audio or/and audiovisual podcast by using editing software applications such as Audacity, iMovie HD, and GarageBand. As for student background, three to seven students, including African American, Latino/Latina, and Caucasian youth, attended each session, mostly because of their interest in computers. Among the 26 student participants we had over the five sessions, there were only four girls, two joined us only for 2–3 classes while the other two dropped out of the project due to other after-school commitments. Very often students dropped in on the class without registration; for those students, we provided program overviews on a one-to-one basis and encouraged them to begin with identifying and researching topics of interest.

Student Vignettes

We present two vignettes here to convey an idea of the experience of students in the program. The students attended at least one session (five classes); they produced drafts or finished media work during the classes, and they expressed interest in learning through and about digital media.

Alex. Alex, a sixth-grade boy, has a passion for making videos. He signed up for the project because he did not want to wait to learn computer applications until eighth grade, when the computer courses are offered in the school. He attended all five sessions throughout the year with the clear and persistent goal to make a video that would teach youth his age how to make a video. Alex's motivation drew from his frustration at not being able to find youth-friendly video-making tutorials. He believed that documenting his learning experience would benefit other youth like him.

Although Alex was focused on his goal, initially he was impatient with the long process of creating his final product and was eager to operate the video camera right away. It took a while for him to realize that video production is composed of multiple components, such as planning, storyboarding, script writing, and soundtrack development. He conducted a school survey on his peers' interests in learning new media; learned to use search engines and find online resources; made an audio podcast on his opinions about the fun of making videos; created a PowerPoint slide presentation on an introduction to video equipment; and produced a short video that provided a step-by-step guide to video creation.

Eli. Carlos was a seventh grader who participated in our pilot study involving Latino/Latina youth and digital media (see Bruce & Lin, 2009, for more details). He invited Eli, an eighth-grade participant in the fifth session. Eli made it clear that he wanted to compose a soundtrack as a music podcast by using GarageBand. Fascinated by his one-time experience of playing with GarageBand during a school computer class, Eli wanted to use this after-school opportunity to learn more about it. During the classes, Eli came in with a "ready-to-work" attitude, putting on his earphones and messing around with GarageBand by trial and error and self-practice. He composed a piece of electronic music through GarageBand's software instruments, mostly electronic guitar, built up his song using loops, remixed and recorded his audio piece, played it back with iTunes, and sent it to his iPod.

Eli would ask the class to be quiet, asking the instructors and students to listen to his music and pay attention to the tempo, rhythm, or mood that he was trying to convey. Then the whole class had a short discussion on his work. Eli also stored a copy of his unfinished piece on his iPod, listened to it regularly, shared it with his friends during his spare time, and then modified it in subsequent classes. Later we encouraged Eli to incorporate visual images into his audio podcast and to submit his work to a statewide contest called "4-H Digital Mayhem Challenge." This further step not only made him consider the connection between the visual and the audio in media production but also provided stimulation to shift his learning from self-expression to communication with others. Whereas Eli's audio piece expressed his interest in music, his audiovisual podcast added a purpose and audience orientation that pushed him to ponder ways to deliver effective messages.

Achievements and Challenges

As we observed how youth participation in inquiry-based learning intersected with their interest-driven issue exploration through digital media, we realized that students' achievement lay in the learning process more than the end product. Moreover, student achievement in this case is situated, depending on each student's background, attitude, prior knowledge, and motivation. Overall, the students had fun making their podcasts. They expressed enthusiasm for their chosen topics, felt in control of the production process, believed their work could benefit their target audience, and took pride in their hard work.

Even those students who dropped out or only stayed for a short period of time learned something from the project. Their incompletion was due to various reasons, such as other after-school commitments, disappointment about the content of the course, and mandatory participation in homework labs. All of them had started their topic research, on issues that included the presidential election, war in Iraq, hunger in Kenya, immigrant assimilation in middle school, fashion design, and eating disorders. Their work-in-progress was discontinued at the information gathering, script writing, or narrative recording stage. However, they expressed interest in contributing to the collective good and concern for social action through investigation of what they considered an important problem for their self-identified communities.

We sought opportunities for youth community engagement using YCI curriculum modules (see Section 4). Our respective expertise initially contributed to recruitment and curriculum design, and later merged through team-teaching in an attempt to empower youth through multimedia. The multimedia activities employed in this project have sparked interest and demand from within the 4-H Extension Network. At the same time, implementation of such activities also provided experience in practical logistics for scholars, educators, and leaders of community informatics to envision how curricula can be realized, adapted, and expanded in a situated learning context.

The challenges we faced included student recruitment, attendance, and attitude, partly because of the nature of the after-school program. Coordinated by the school staff and led by park district staff and community partners, Urbana Middle School's SPLASH program offered a variety of free classes, including habit clubs, sports activities, and homework labs. The school coordinator supervised the SPLASH program, and the communication between the coordinator and community partners was limited to checking student attendance. As we observed, students' learning attitudes were more casual and playful while attending the after-school classes, compared to their regular schooling, and they tended to sample different SPLASH classes instead of committing to one. For example, three male students only attended the 4-H podcasting class once because of their disappointment with not being able to play online games and their resistance to the idea of "working during the after-school hours." As a result, we, outsiders who only came to the school once a week, found it difficult to control enrollment and attendance, which affected the learning progression we attempted to develop. Furthermore, we faced a dilemma in juggling the attendance with maintaining the educational focus; we welcomed and encouraged all students to participate in the process of making podcasts, but later we had to refuse students who only came to play video games.

For university-related project staff and community youth educators, a takeaway lesson is to find an onsite liaison, preferably one who knows the group of students well, right at the beginning of project planning. We lacked a school representative who shared our commitment and with whom we could communicate about project needs and issues. We realized that this is a significant component in community engagement projects involving youth, as the trust relationship that an onsite liaison has developed with youth over time contributes greatly to project attendance, involvement, and quality.

Implications for Community Engagement

Buckingham (2007, pp. 21-22) describes *personalization* as "a model in which individuals assess their own needs and become involved in managing the services they use, and in which service providers are required to be much more flexible and responsive to the delivery of their clients." Our project outcomes resonate with the finding that youth out-of-school technology learning experiences contribute to the delivery of personalization (Green et al., 2005). We encountered an instructional demand related to managing personalized learning style, content, and context while teaching with multimedia in an informal setting. As community sites offer a "third arena of learning, that which takes place beyond classroom and home" (Heath, 2001, p. 10), learners seek opportunities to fulfill an interest-driven need that they cannot achieve within home or school settings. In our case, the students signed up for the podcasting class for personal reasons, such as an interest in learning video production, a chance to get an early start on working with computers, and lack of access to equipment at home. Such learning motivations were associated with varying student backgrounds and prior knowledge related to literacy skills and technology. The learning content then focused heavily on one-on-one instruction that began with learners' existing experience and knowledge, rather than matching learners to predetermined learning materials and outcomes. On the one hand, this style of individual learning allows instructors to tailor feedback to suit the individual. It also encourages students to initiate their unique inquiries related to topics of interest. On the other hand, instructors are faced with the challenges of a small teacher-student ratio in the shift from mass delivery of instructional materials to facilitating learner-specific interactions. Indeed, we value the uniqueness of inquiry in relation to learning with technology drawn from community sites as a third arena of learning. To support this value, it is important to recognize the dynamics of instructional strategies, teacher-student interaction, and personalization of learning inhabited in informal learning contexts.

Curriculum modules tied to the notion of community inquiry can serve as *tools* for learners to examine their lived experience in relation to the world. Modules such as multimedia production and Internet safety—enacted through youth classes, workshops, and the YCI summer forum—are *forms* of inquiry. They represent ways that youth make sense of their experiences and themselves, solve problems constructively and creatively, and develop meaningful interactions and interconnections with their communities. Rather than being prescribed templates for community engagement related to technology, they are tools realized in and through situated learning contexts. Implementations highlight the process of meaning construction, rather than end products or fixed outcomes. That is, forms of inquiry are viewed as means within a larger end-in-view that enable learners to conceptualize their process of learning.

Importantly, this understanding of the modules can affect how youth community informatics projects are interpreted, facilitated, and evaluated. Emphasis on the process of learning allows learners to take time to explore and experiment, as well as to control what they want to learn. Likewise, it goes beyond the less pliable interventions seen in formal school experience, which often include strict project deadlines, top-down knowledge dissemination, and assessment criteria. Rather, the emphasis on process highlights the learners' ownership of the learning experience. In addition, it is worth noting that while we think it is important to celebrate youths' creative endeavors by showcasing their media productions, we pay more attention to their experiences in inquiry learning, and how their experiences spark a sense of empowerment, of being able to express their interests, communicate their concerns, and take action for community needs.

Unlike other community pilot sites presented in this book, in which the notion of community mainly refers to where the project takes place, our 4-H podcasting project at Urbana Middle School's after-school program used an interpretation that carried beyond geographic locations. Even though the youth shared a learning space, their understanding of community associated with their multimedia productions tended to focus on their interest-driven human relationships. To identify a community group as their podcasting audience, the students began with a topic of their own interest, drawn from their existing cultural or social experience, believing they could share their opinions and take action in helping people to gain awareness or make changes. Community groups that the students identified with included the families of U.S. troops, Americans who have a Kenyan heritage, Latino/Latina immigrant youth at Urbana Middle School, youth who are interested in media production or video games, and youth in general. Their notions of community moved beyond the territorial coverage to embrace a network of people with similar lived experience. During our class sessions, the students were engaged in investigating their chosen topics drawn from the communities with which they identified, taking audience background and reaction into account throughout their work. Moreover, they were motivated to develop their will in terms of social action and to embrace a sense of community participation. To support this development, we feel the role of instructors is to guide students' participation through activities such as self-reflection, class dialogue, and the production process. While instructors act as facilitators, we can offer a trusting relationship for learning, provide exposure to expand learners' existing knowledge, encourage them to be productive and creative, and challenge them to take a critical stand on issues of interest.

Final Thoughts

Youth participating in this project had little prior exposure to using digital media as a learning tool. Many saw technology as entertainment rather than education. The project showed them the potential of technology to support human relationships more broadly. This led them t experience a sense of empowerment in which they could represent their concerns and control the direction of learning. Yet more can be done to foster the transition from the individual sense of empowerment to fuller community participation. We need to enhance not only *their* understanding and undertaking related to youth participatory citizenship, but *our own*. Beyond the relaxation, pleasure, and personal growth, we need to develop an awareness that youths' use of digital media can contribute to the development of healthy and sustainable communities.

3. New Media Technology: Tools of Expression/Repression in Communities

Alex Jean-Charles

The media have always been a contributing factor of discrimination against blacks. For instance, ans who immigrated to the United States are often labeled as "boat people," "voodoo practitioners," and "carriers of the AIDS virus," and recently they are portrayed as "drug dealers" in movies and video games.

In Edwidge Danticat's famous novel, *Breath, Eyes, Memory* (1994), the narrator (Sophie) discusses her experiences being a child born as a result of a rape, growing up in Haiti and later moving to the United States, and her clashing relationship with her mother, who holds certain traditional beliefs and exhibits parental power over her. In *Breath, Eyes, Memory*, Sophie recounts the perception that others, particularly other young people, have toward Haitians. She explains, "Outside of school, we were 'the frenchies,' cringing in our mock-Catholic school uniforms as the students from the public school across the street called us 'boat people' and 'stinking Haitians'" (p. 51). Sophie continues to explain: "Many of the American kids even accused Haitians of having AIDS because they had heard on television that only the 'Four Hs' got AIDS—Heroin addicts, Hemophiliacs, Homosexuals, and Haitians" (p. 66).

Like the narrator, Danticat was confronted with the numerous stereotypes that exist about Haitian immigrants. In an interview with Alexander Laurence (2000), Danticat discusses her experience as a high school student in Crown Heights, New York, and how writing an article for a newspaper publication for New York Public Schools about her life as a young Haitian immigrant was the trajectory that led to her use of writing as a form of expression.

In the 1990s there was a dispute between the Haitian Diaspora and the U.S. Food and Drug Administration over the racist claim that Haitian people were one of the causes of the AIDS virus. On March 19, 1990, approximately 50,000 Haitians walked across the Brooklyn Bridge to demand justice, protesting the decision not to allow Haitians to donate blood. According to Paul Farmer (2006), this protest was recorded as the second largest demonstration in U.S. history since the Martin Luther King march on Washington. At the demonstration, I remember being happy and inspired to see so many young Haitian American youth in attendance and engaged in a rally to stop discrimination against Haitians in the United States.

Similarly, one of the participants in the project I describe here, Lucien, had an experience that shaped him and led him to understand the importance of engaging in his community in the Midwest. This experience occurred when he was 10 years old: "It was announced on the television and radio that a hurricane was approaching Haiti. On the sixth night while everyone was sleeping, the rain got stronger and the canals were full with water and blocked with garbage." As a result, the water had nowhere to go but to rise up rapidly. In the middle of the night, Lucien remembers hearing screaming, "The furniture was floating on the dirty water. There was a power failure due to the violent winds, all the electrical devices were malfunctioning, cars were useless, and the only way someone could move around was by canoe," which his family did not have. He recalled how he felt that day: "I was terrified, worried; I was shaking as my mother tried to calm us down."

The families had to work in groups to survive. They placed their belongings in the way of the flood to prevent more water from coming through. Lucien remembers sitting on the rooftop with the other children because the water was rising so high. Many of the families took to the roads to get some help. According to Lucien, "People who usually did not get along were cooperating and helping one another." In the community where he lived everyone tried to help even though they were all in the same desperate state, "In Haiti the person next door to you is a friend."

The narratives above depict epiphanies or turning points in which identity and power were explored and critically reflected through social justice, writing, and community engagement. Our project is situated in Gloria Ladson-Billings and Jamel Donnor's (2005) concept of the calls. The call is that moment at which, regardless of one's stature and/or accomplishments, race (and other categories of otherness) is recruited to remind one that he or she still remains locked in the racial construction. It is mobilized to maintain the power dynamics and hierarchical racial structures of society. The framework also draws from Michel Foucault's work on mechanisms of power (video surveillance technology as a metaphor of something that watches over, observes, or monitors something else) that are placed on young black males, particularly Afro-Franco Caribbean males. The findings show: (1) the participants have a sense of community; (2) they experienced anger with the one-sided perspective shown in mainstream media; and (3) the participants each experienced ridicule or shame in these spaces (schools and community).

From Community Engagement to Community Inquiry

The project was undertaken for my dissertation. I was also involved with the YCI group in two capacities. The first was that I informally joined the group, attended meetings, shared my experiences, and discussed issues related to participatory research with young people. The second was with a coalition of group members whose task was to go out into the community and assist with repair of various technologies in nonprofit settings. In this group I assisted with the servicing of computers that were in desperate need of repair at a community center in East St. Louis. During my visit, I met with several of the youth and throughout the day they worked alongside us as we demonstrated to them how to maintain the computers that had previously not been working.

It was an enjoyable day for the YCI group members and an enlightening day for the youth since they could once again have access to functioning computers at the community center.

In the summer of 2007, I facilitated a project-based learning participatory video project through the use of new media (video technology), to address issues of identity, power-control, love, and forgiveness in the Rogers Park neighborhood of Chicago and in Evanston, Illinois. Reflexive narratives, in the form of "video writings," were collected of five young black Caribbean males' views on the issues mentioned above. These issues were identified from a parent community forum that occurred a few weeks prior to the roundtable discussion with the five young men. The participants watched the video of the parent meeting and responded via video to the concerns the parents raised in the meeting. Some of the concerns the parents raised were around youth, media, and the local authorities in the community. The participants gathered this information, discussed it, and created questions to interview youth in the community for their video diary and response to the community forum.

During the pre-production stage of the video project, the participants met to brainstorm issues such as identity, power-control, and surveillance technology, which they had gleaned from the parent video. From these topics, they constructed questions around power-control, love, and forgiveness. Throughout the project, the participants were engaged in high-level social and cultural discussions of their experiences with new information and media technologies in the environment. The discussions were used to employ the participants in a critical and self-reflective thinking process. Through these processes, the participants not only learned about themselves, but they also gained knowledge about their community while simultaneously their community gained knowledge about them.

Throughout the project, the participants worked with state-of-the-art video production equipment and current digital audiovisual hardware. They were provided access and training in the use of Mac operating systems and editing software such as iMovie and Final Cut Pro. I contacted the Apple store to arrange a workshop for the program participants. On arrival, the participants were introduced to various video editing hardware and software. Thereafter, we were led to a conference training room where they were introduced to iMovie and Final Cut Pro.

The training occurred over the course of two days at the Michigan Avenue Apple store in Chicago. The first day was dedicated to learning the basics of iMovie, and the second day they were trained on Final Cut Pro. At the Haitian American Community Association center, the participants engaged in three major modules to produce their videos. The first module addressed the hardware needed to capture video and sound. In this particular module, the participants learned about various parts of the video camera and sound recording devices. In the second module, the participants learned the basic skills of the Mac operating system and various video formats. They learned about the differences between analog and digital video recording, storage media and sizes, and basic computer functions such as saving and retrieving a file. In the final module, the participants learned the video, sound, and composite software applications that would enable them to edit the raw materials. In this module, they learned how to render and transfer their final product onto a DVD media device.

At the end of the summer, the participants created a final video to share with their peers, parents, and the community. The video project opened the door for them to network with their community on various issues, including the use of closed-circuit television cameras in the community; and the collaborative efforts made to produce the final product may encourage the participants to take part in future social justice activities. In addition, the results of the project add to the current literature on young black Caribbean males' experiences and identity as they relate to power control, love/self-care, and respect.

Purpose

The purpose of the study was to provide an environment and new media technology that Afro-Franco Caribbean males could use to engage and discuss their views on issues such as power control, love, and forgiveness and to ultimately develop a video to share with the community. Moreover, the study sought to examine an epistemological approach (Creolization) that young black males, particularly Afro-Franco Caribbean males, might use to communicate, document, and share their everyday experiences in the Diaspora.

Technology is paradoxical. The same technology that is used to control and cause pain can also be used to liberate and cause happiness, but how? How can young black men enter into dialogue with oppressive signs of power control in urban communities since policies such as the No Child Left Behind Act do not provide the schools and the teachers with the flexibility to do so (S. Dillon, 2006)? The project sought to argue for alternative schooling where students can dialogue on issues that matter to them and their community, such as power control and surveillance technology. In this project, I sought to creolize both power control and video surveillance technology through project-based learning (PBL) rooted in the community inquiry of John Dewey (2005), the processes of learning-by-doing/making/producing.

Creolization as a method is an experimentation out of necessity. The experimentation is not to be different from the master or the slave, rather to belong, which in turn erases the binaries. Creolization is an approach toward interpretation that deviates from the hermeneutic (Greek [Western] god Hermes of interpretation) approach to include approaches as Esu-neutic (Esu, West African god of interpretation). In this method, we should be able to re-create new tools from what we learn in school and on the street. In the case of young black males, they will be able to reenact the conformity of the street life to construct a new set of identities.

In *Reinventing Project-Based Learning*, Suzie Boss and Jane Krauss (2008) interviewed teachers about using technologies in their classroom. In one of the narratives, a teacher explained how she would layer and implement technology in her daily lesson plans, but found herself coming up short when it came to engaging and connecting the students in the teaching and learning process. In other words, the way she implemented the technology in the classroom alienated the students in the teaching process. Through PBL, she found a way to get students more active and engaged in the classroom as "directors and critics instead of as passive learners" (p. 3). Instead of lecturing while students took notes, the students were also critically engaged in projects that went beyond the classroom while solving various problems the project might bring.

In PBL, learners (participants) usually engage in tasks that are meaningful to them. These tasks and issues are usually found in their everyday experiences in the environment and the community. In this project, the participants produced a video performance of their experiences dealing with issues of violence, video surveillance, and power as it relates to new media, the government, and the community.

Literacy is the ability to write. It is also the ability to identify, understand, interpret, create, network, and critically process "written" materials. In terms of technology, we do not think critically about technology the same way we think about the written signs we read and view in the media. We need to be able to understand/reflect/evaluate the nature and the use of technology around us to be technologically literate. The project sought to provide young black Caribbean males with technologies that they could use to re-create (creolize) materials to express themselves and deconstruct issues in their communities. Participants in the project were provided with an opportunity to use various underutilized methods of reflection, such as oral (audio) and visual (video), rather than the sole use of hermeneutics (written text). Also, the young men were encouraged to share their experiences when provided with the space, which they typically do not have, to express themselves and to discuss community issues in various creative formats. Ultimately, the goal of the project was for the youth to develop a way of expressing their views on critical issues in their community. Their stories were drawn from electronic written and oral diaries. They were encouraged to examine the power mechanisms (video surveillance technology or CCTV as a metaphor of something watching over, observing, or monitoring something) that surround young black men, particularly Haitians in the Diaspora. Near the end of project, the participants reconvened and were involved in a follow-up roundtable discussion on their experiences. The young men had an opportunity to discuss how they envisioned combining their individual data into one final collaborative video project. This video project was a collaborative, self-reflexive performance. They were able to draw on any type of artistic talents they had for the final product.

Theoretical Framework

Participants were positioned as researchers: The research process was one of "reconstructing the intellect, moving from research to activism, and the search for a revolutionary habitus" (Ladson-Billings and Donnor, 2005, p. 6) in these young men's experiences. In urban communities, the means (process or technology) of controlling citizens and the population have created the emergence of new security devices and computer technologies (panopticons) that bureaucrats placed inside and outside the community space to monitor the "practice of everyday life" (de Certeau, 1984). In addition to simply monitoring, the role of this technology in the community is

> to make the spread of power efficient; to make possible the exercise of power with limited manpower at the least cost; to discipline individuals with the least exertion of overt force by operating on their souls; to increase to a maximum the visibility of those subjected; to involve in its functioning all those who come in contact with the apparatus. . . . The final connection component in Panopticism is the connection between bodies, space, power, and knowledge. (Dreyfus & Rabinow, 1983, p. 192)

In his 1982 essay in *Critical Inquiry*, Foucault notes that "the exercise of power is not simply a relationship between partners, individual or collective; it is a way in which certain actions modify others" (cited in Dreyfus & Rabinow, 1983, p. 219). Power, in general, and specifically disciplinary power are strategic games. Foucault uses the pedagogical institution to express the strategic game of power as the game of truth (Foucault, Gutman, Hutton, & Martin, 1988, p. 18). He explains, "Power is not a function of consent. In itself it is not a renunciation of freedom, a transference of rights, the power of each and all delegated to a few" (Foucault et al., p. 220). In other words, power doesn't need resistance to be manifest. Power is "a mode of action which does not act directly and immediately on others. Instead it acts upon [others'] actions: an action upon an action" (p. 220). Therefore, "a power relationship can only be articulated on the basis of two elements which are each indispensable if it is really to be a power relationship: that 'the other' (the one over whom power is exercised) be thoroughly recognized and maintained to the very end as a person who acts; and that, faced with a relationship of power, a whole field of responses, reactions, results, and possible inventions may open up" (p. 220). One consequence of what Foucault says here is that power does not require an operator to exert it. An internalized sense of power, rather than outside forces, can be the way in which our actions are modified.

Foucault (Foucault & Gordon, 1980) notes, "The individual, with his identity and characteristics, is the product of a relation of power exercised over bodies, multiplicities, movements, desires, forces" (p. 74). Therefore, there is no "true" identity but a mere reflection of the self through others (Lacan & Fink, 2006). Surveillance then singles out individuals and regulates behavior, identity, and activities. Foucault (1984) notes that individuals should reflect upon the imaginary identity and create an illusion of conscious control of the self through their history and the history of others (p. 21). He sees the function and purpose of surveillance as the power to watch and gaze. As such, video security technologies do more than just reduce violence in both communal settings; they function as another means of facilitating power.

Findings

Participants in the project experienced (a) a lack of community involvement in the urban space in which they currently reside; (b) frustration with the perspective of their home country, Haiti, that is commonly shown in mainstream media; and (c) ridicule, shame, and violence in the spaces (school and community) that should be safe. Below are excerpts from data of various street and park interviews of the video produced at the summer program. This section also contains participants' responses from the round-table discussion that focused on the issues of power and forgiveness.

Street Interviews

In summer 2007, the program participants began a series of street interviews to understand the concept of power and CCTV installed every few blocks in the neighborhood of Rogers Park, Chicago. On a hot Saturday afternoon, we met at the Haitian American Community Association center to brainstorm a list of questions to ask any young person they might meet on the street. We packed the equipment and split into two groups. For adult supervision, my wife paired up with one group and I paired up with the other. As we were walking down the street with the cameras, boom microphones, and headphones, we seemed to draw some attention to ourselves. Young people whom the participants knew from school stopped them to find out what they were doing. Perhaps being on the other side of the lens means that they can express themselves and give an opinion on certain issues, something many youth have not been given the opportunity to do. Whatever the reason, they and many other young people the participants encountered decided that they would answer a few questions about power and surveillance technology in the community.

The participants encountered a group of Hispanic young men who were riding their bikes. Several of them seemed to already know Jacques, one of the participants, and agreed to answer a few questions. Jacques asked the initial question, "The first question I want to ask you is 'what does power mean to you?'" One of the boys responded that to him, "Power means to have control

over others, like I do to these guys (gesturing to the other boys on bikes) right
here. I control all of them and that's what power is to me."

The interview continued onto the basketball court at the park with a few
African American males. Jacques asks, "Who do you think exerts power?" One
of the young men responds, "Honestly, I think the government does most of
all. I think they keep a tight grip on everybody else." Jacques interjected and
asked, "Do you think they abuse it?" The young man replies, "Sometimes they
do, especially towards minorities. I can tell you that from experience." He then
proceeded to recall a situation when a police officer pulled him over. He felt
maybe he was in the wrong place at the wrong time, but again, he was right
here in his own neighborhood. During this particular incident, said the young
man, the police began asking him questions merely on the basis of what he
looked like.

Another youth on the basketball court was posed the same question about
power, and he responded, "Not only does the President of the United States
exert power, but also gangs in the community." That same afternoon, the
participants met a Haitian young lady sitting on the swings, and the question
about power was once again asked. She stated, "I believe God has power over
every man." She also mentioned that power could be exerted through physical
strength or a powerful mind, but in her high school weapons equal power.

The next day, we returned to the center to debrief on the street interviews.
At the roundtable discussion, we posed the question: "What does it mean to
have power?" Jacques responded, "Power means having responsibility." He
cited the superhero Spider-Man as an example of someone who wields power
responsibly. Jacques believed that if he were to have power that he would
probably abuse it because he is human. Lucien interjected and stated that
abuse of power is the case for many in the Haitian government, officials who,
he believed, do not use power properly or responsibly. In Haiti, he has
witnessed government officials using their power for wrongdoing as well as
using their power against people who resist them. He compared this to the
gangs in Haiti who use their power to kidnap people for money. Jacques
agreed but went on to say, "we all would likely do the same as those Haitian
leaders who abuse their power, if we were in their position." When they posed
this question to the youth in their community, they found that many of them
believe that power is a type of control that is primarily fueled by money. For
example, when a young Haitian American boy on the street was asked, "What
does power mean to you?" He replied that it means having access to money.
He recounted a situation when one of his friends did not have enough money
to buy something that he wanted. He made the friend do favors and tasks for
him before giving him the money. Another Haitian boy on the basketball
court also pointed out, "Power, it means like someone who got money and can
take over and stuff. Someone with money can take over the city or whatever
place." Thus, money was a recurring theme when the issue of power was
discussed.

Participants' Personal Reflections on Interviews About Power

During the video editing process, Jacques had an opportunity to reflect on what he discovered when he interviewed the youth in his community about power. While he agreed that a lot of rich people happen to be the ones exerting power over others, he does not feel that money is the true meaning of power. He believed that the media shapes the idea that money equals power. He continued and responded, "The first thing that popped up from their mind was money. Where do they get that? They get that from the media. The media wants us to believe money can get us everywhere." As an example, he cited many of the rap videos that depict people with money and power. He also mentioned a show on MTV titled *My Super Sweet 16* that depicts families spending a great deal of money on their child's birthday celebration. Jacques reflected that we should not be at all surprised when youth feel that money is everything when that is what they are shown every day.

David came to a different conclusion from Jacques's belief about power and money, based on his reflection on the responses of the people he interviewed. He discovered that power does not necessarily mean to have money, but rather the ability to make someone do something without the person receiving anything from you. He also felt that with power comes responsibility. He recalled an experience in Haiti, when he had a friend who would repeatedly throw garbage in the street. One day he decided to tell her not to put her garbage on the street because of what it does to the environment. He said that while she was not happy with being told what to do, she learned her lesson and decided to not throw the garbage on the streets ever again. David did not have to use money to get her not to put her garbage on the street; rather, he manipulated her into understanding that it was wrong.

When the discussion turned to the issue of "who exerts power?" the overwhelming response from the program participants was "parents or anyone older than us." The participants mentioned that they believed that as long as someone is older than you, then they would always use their power over you. When asked how they oppose the concept of power, they stated that protesting is one way they resist the power their parents have imposed on them. However, "this is not always effective, because protesting does not mean they will listen," says Jacques. Even though the participants acknowledged that they are not listened to, they all agreed that protesting is a way of gaining power. In Lucien's view, "When you revolt, you are on top of the world!" Jacques, the realist of the group, responded that while they may feel that they are "on top on the world," they really are not. Lucien, the optimist of the group, quickly responded, "well, at least you feel some type of change."

Lucien believed that those in positions of authority hold much of the power and those with connections hold much of the power. He mentioned that in Haiti, the president can "take all the money" but he did not believe that this type of corruption could take place in the United States because there are laws to prevent this from happening. He theorized that this is because in the United States, unlike Haiti, there are penalties and consequences for these actions. David mentioned that in Haiti every government office is filled with so much bureaucracy that something as simple as getting a license can take several days. He mentioned that one way to make the process faster is by giving money to a Raketè (middle man) to facilitate the process.

Face-to-Face with Surveillance Technology

Jacques mentioned that prior to the project, he thought that having surveillance cameras in the community was a good thing, but after reading George Orwell's *1984* (2008), he now has concerns about violation of people's privacy. He believes that too much surveillance could lead to manipulation and corruption. David still believed that surveillance cameras could be used for both good and bad purposes. He said that sometimes those behind the surveillance cameras will "do nothin' but let those black people fight . . . and if it [surveillance] was so good, then why do we have people dying at the crime scene? They [those behind the cameras] would stop it, not take pictures after it happens." Charles agreed and stated that whenever there is a fight in the street, all the cameras do is record the fight, and after things finally calm down, that is when the authorities use the film to question people. Charles mentioned that he frequently sees news reports of fights that occur in or near the Chicago schools or on the trains. He felt that if these fights were not caught on camera, no one would speak out and report it because they do not want to be called a "snitch."

All the participants observed that surveillance cameras are predominately found in poor, black neighborhoods. David reflected on one of the street interviews he conducted, in which a young girl gave the impression that she believes that "the cameras are there for everyone's protection and to help control us." David thought that she made this statement because she still has "the slave mentality" in terms of thinking that we need to be watched to protect ourselves from our own destruction. David rebuffed her argument and stated that his religious beliefs and the fact that he has God to protect him is all that he needs. When I asked if he felt there was a connection between surveillance and poor neighborhoods, he said, "Well, when people are poor and starving they can think of twenty ways to make money and 19 out of the 20 are going to be bad." Jacques agreed and stated that desperation and powerlessness lead to crime and violence. However,

> When you educate people and share power with people and have people on your side, they are not working against you, and they are not outlaws. It is when they are not sharing power, that is when you need the surveillance cameras.

Both Lucien and Charles, who are still in high school, retold their experiences of being stopped by police in the neighborhood. Over the summer, Lucien was on his way to school to participate in the Freshmen Connection program, which partners upperclassmen with high school freshmen. He was wearing "a dress shirt and nice shoes" when the police officer stopped him and asked if he was carrying a knife. The officer told Lucien that someone had reported a black youth coming off the train with a knife. Interestingly enough, Lucien had just disembarked from a bus, and he believed that the police officer had seen him come from the bus. He said that he was searched on the street in front of everyone, and when no knife was found he was allowed to go to school. Charles recounted a police encounter that occurred at a time when his brother was riding his bike, and the police stopped and searched him. He said that the cop eventually let his brother go, but not before telling him that he needed to wear a helmet if he was going to ride his bike at night.

Working the System: Coping with Surveillance Technology

When asked how they deal with issues of power, authority, and surveillance, Jacques responded, "As long as my rights are not being violated, surveillance is fine with me." He said that he tried to follow the rules and work with the system. He believed that working with the system, whether he agreed with it or not, would lead him to achieving his goal of obtaining a college degree. To some extent, all of the participants mentioned that not "getting into trouble" or doing anything "bad" was how they dealt with the issues mentioned above, so that those in authority have no reason to approach them.

To Charles, surveillance technology was not something he could do anything about right now. As long as it was not outrageous and violating his rights, surveillance was okay. In school, for instance, Charles explained,

> I am dealing with power and authority all the time. I try to work with it by following the rules, do what they ask me to. Even though they [those in power] are probably watching and have their ways to keep people under control, I have to stay focused.

He continued, "The way that I deal with it is that I know how to work with the system." He believed he had been trained to work with the system, through his schooling, parents, etc. That is why, he believed, he was dealing with it in a positive way.

Compromising is the way most of the young men seem to be coping with signs of authority in the neighborhood. To most of the group, "respect" is the most important way they can deal with authority. As David explained, there are two types of people out there, good people and bad people. The difference between them is that one type is respectful and the other one is disrespectful. David further explained, "Those who are respectful tend to play their way around the system, even if it means to compromise." Charles, on the other hand, said, "For the sake of my education, graduating high school, and obtaining a career, I need to stay focused." He did not have any advice for those unwilling to deal with or compromise with the system; "It's not as if I can give them a guide and tell them to follow it." Instead he had advice for those individuals with power, that they modify the system so that everyone could benefit from it.

Presenting the Project to the Community

After several weeks in the post-production stage, organizing all the information gathered through interviews, meetings, and video clips on iMovie and Final Cut Pro, it was time to present the final product to the community. The video consists of 10 scenes. In the opening scene, the participants chose to highlight the diversity of the neighborhood through photos and video clips they obtained from their cameras and on the web. The next scene highlights footage of the Haitian parent meeting at the center where the topic of discussion was the youth (particularly Haitian American youth) in the community. In the subsequent scene, Etienne responds to the footage of the parent meeting. Selected clips from the neighborhood interviews then immediately follow this. Both David and Jacques reflect on the first set of interviews, and Lucien reflects on the next set. Toward the end of the video, a segment on Nazi Germany and Holocaust survivors depicts footage on the concept of forgiveness. Eva Mozes-Kor, a Holocaust survivor, tells about the horrors of her time in the deadly genetic experiments camp in Auschwitz led by Dr. Josef Mengele, also known as The Angel of Death. Eva, now president of the Children of Auschwitz and Camp Lab Experiments Survivors (CANDLES), remembers,

> A set of Gypsy twins was brought back from Mengele's lab after they were sewn back to back. Mengele had attempted to create a Siamese twin by connecting blood vessels and organs. The twins screamed day and night until gangrene set in, and after three days, they died. (cited in Tarantola & Mann, 1993)

In July 2007, the Public Broadcasting System aired a segment of her story on forgiveness in *Religion and Ethics Newsweekly*. In the segment, Eva explains that "Forgiveness is nothing more and nothing less but an act of self-healing—an act of self-empowerment" (July 13, 2007). David reflected on this segment, which shows holocaust survivor Eva Kor discussing how she lost her family at the hands of Mengele, yet she still found a way to forgive to overcome her anger. David concluded that there is a need for people to forgive one another. He also mentioned the need for expression: "When you have someone who is a dictator like Hitler there is no room for a dialogue like we are having now. A dictator takes things by force. He tells you to do something and if you don't want to do it he pulls his gun and kills you." David mentioned that there are repercussions in choosing not to forgive and that choosing to only think of revenge can have long-term consequences:

There is a need for us to forgive one another. It is like they say in the Bible. You burn all of them [Bibles], what would it resolve? You can burn all the Bibles but at least one Christian will still have their Bible. So if you start taking revenge, there will be at least one left. That one left will become your worst nightmare. If it doesn't turn to a nightmare today, it will be tomorrow or even years down the road. That is why I think the best possible solution is forgiveness.

Overall, those in the community who attended the project presentation appeared to enjoy it. They were impressed with the thinking process in the footage, the songs that were selected, and the video effects the participants had created. After presenting the project to the community, the participants met to discuss the overall process of the project. Although the participants could not remember all of the steps (pre-production, production, and post-production) in the creation of the video, they enjoyed the fact that they had something tangible to present to the community. There was consensus that it is important for young people to be involved in some type of project-based activity in their community. It gives young people a sense of "civic responsibility to respect the law," Charles said. But some people in the group disagreed. They believed that the issue is not that people don't have a sense of responsibility, but rather, "They force them [to not be responsible], they don't have much of a choice" to do wrong sometimes.

Although the project was presented to the community, there was still much more to be discussed. Much of the discussions are presented in the overall project of my dissertation (Jean-Charles, 2010). Using PBL has helped the participants be involved and engaged in a dialogue with surveillance technology in the community.

Final Thought

The study provided the community (both local and scholarly) with an opportunity to hear the voices and concerns of youth in an urban space. In addition, it suggests a need for schools to create a curriculum grounded in critical pedagogy, in which power can be democratically shared.

Technology supports all basic human needs and that is why we cannot detach from it. Asking people in power to surrender their need for control of others, at least for the sake of survival and harmony, is as painful as being shot with a gun. However, the least we can do is to communicate through education to those who use these technologies as a tool to control others, to share their stories, open their hearts, and understand the pain these technologies can sometimes cause them and the community.

Young black men are living at a time when they have to deal with certain technologies that dehumanize, monitor, and scrutinize their bodies and souls in our schools and communities. One of the technologies that society uses to turn the soul for the greater good is education. However, the education that we provide today is not only designed to help cultivate or think for the self, but also for the state that mostly concerns itself with power. In *Society Must Be Defended* (2003), Foucault makes the argument that power is essential to serve the economy. Thus, the state's purpose in schooling is not to cultivate for the self, but rather to perpetuate economic power through educational capital. Jacques Ellul (1964) reminds us that "Education no longer has a humanist end or any value in itself; it has only one goal, to create technicians" (p. 248). The aim is to sell or force "good" knowledge on students in a way that will benefit an elite power structure. Examples ranging from my own experiences of oppression to the experience of the narrator in *Invisible Man* (Ellison, 1995) demonstrate that we are all victims of an oppressive system.

In *Invisible Man* (1995), the modern institutional and social systems have diverged so far from the original goal of serving all of its citizens that it limits or oppresses many to continue the elite power structure. Through the use of technology, society has alienated black people for so long that it has made them feel that the alienation experienced in Shakespeare's Caliban is normal. Black people did not choose to be, nor were born as, a Caliban (Henry, 2000). The new modern science and technological mode of production, which Karl Marx (1986) refers to as the capitalist mode of production, has transformed both the master and those the master oppresses. Marx notes, "Production does not simply produce man as a commodity, the human commodity, man in the role of commodity; it produces him in keeping with this role as a mentally and physically dehumanized being" (p. 121). If a young black man is to help himself, he needs to realize the alienation that has been placed on him. He needs to realize that this alienation is the root of his anger toward himself and society. Martin Heidegger (1977) believes it is through fine art or poetic revealing that the true self can be found. He notes, "The poetical brings the true into the splendor of what Plato in the Phaedrus calls the *ekphanestaton*, that which shines forth most purely. The poetical thoroughly pervades every art, every revealing of coming to presence into the beautiful" (p. 34). That is exactly what Foucault (1988) refers to as the "technologies of the self." You do not make the "self" happy or safe if you are treating it like a system or observing, collecting data, and giving treatment based on feedback per se. Rather, you must respect and love the body the same way you would love and respect the mind. You do not attempt to change or control the body; rather, you give the body the fundamentals to make it happy. There should be communication between the body and the mind and the oppressor (security surveillance technology, aka technology of control).

Ultimately, the goal was for the youth to develop a way of expressing their views on critical issues in their community. As Foucault notes, this form of communication can be diary writing, videotaping, oral expression, etc. As Paulo Freire (2000) explains in *Pedagogy of the Oppressed*:

> Love is at the same time the foundation of dialogue and dialogue itself. It is thus necessarily the task of responsible Subjects and cannot exist in a relation of

domination. Domination reveals the pathology of love: sadism in the dominator and masochism in the dominated. Because love is an act of courage, not of fear, love is commitment to others. No matter where the oppressed are found, the act of love is commitment to their cause—the cause of liberation. And this commitment, because it is loving, is dialogical. As an act of bravery, love cannot be sentimental; as an act of freedom it must not serve as a pretext for manipulation. It must generate other acts of freedom; otherwise it is not love. Only by abolishing the situation of oppression is it possible to restore the love, which that situation made impossible. If I do not love the world—if I do not love life—if I do not love people—I cannot enter into dialogue. (pp. 89-90)

Therefore, there was a need for young black Caribbean males to enter into a dialogue with security surveillance technology in schools and the community. Moreover, there was a need for alternative community-based schools that could help citizens critique the concept of power that has been implicitly and explicitly embedded in virtually every social and cultural institution in urban communities.

4. Beyond Human Sensors: The Learning Instincts of Youth Using Geospatial Media

Nama R. Budhathoki
Bertram C. Bruce
Jill Murphy
Kimberly Rahn

Young people constantly interact with their environment, as they play, walk around the neighborhood, or look outside the window of a bus on the way to school. They use their senses—sight, hearing, touch, taste, and smell—as a basic means to learn about and make sense of objects and their spatial relationships on the earth's surface. Since the time of hunter-gatherers, humans have used their five senses as primary devices in navigation and making sense of the world (Morville, 2005).

The advent of technologies such as global positioning systems (GPS) and digital cameras has enhanced the ability of youth to interact with the space in which they live. With the combination of human senses and these new devices, youth can acquire, process, and share information in ways impossible with the human senses alone. Alongside their biological senses, youth can now use a GPS device to measure properties of earth's surface, a camera to collect evidence, and computers to create digital products such as Google Maps. They can also share their products with others using the Internet. Thus, youth can serve as a source of information about natural phenomena, as well as a means to share that information with others in the world around them.

In the context of geographic information, Michael Goodchild (2007) first articulated such a potential: "the six billion humans constantly moving about the planet collectively possess an incredibly rich store of knowledge about the surface of the Earth and its properties" (p. 26). Indeed, use of digital technology and social media is pervasive among contemporary youth (boyd, 2007) and gaining recognition as a new social form called "participatory culture" (Jenkins, 2009). There is ample evidence that youth are willing to engage in the production and provision of a variety of information formats, such as articles in Wikipedia, pictures in Flickr, videos in YouTube, and locational information in web 2.0 geospatial tools such as Google Maps and OpenStreetMap (Budhathoki, Nedovic-Budic, & Bruce, 2010).

However, most studies consider youth engagement in digital media as an information phenomenon and employ an "informatics-centered" explanation. For example, in the domain of geographic information science, researchers' attention has largely been drawn to the organization, access, credibility, and potential use of youth-created maps and geospatial data. Little attention is paid to why youth create and share these information products, or to the impact of this engagement on the youth themselves. In this chapter, we focus on youth as the agents of this creative activity and attempt to show that the use of new geospatial media help youth to realize their natural instincts for communication, construction, investigation, and expression. We argue that the full understanding of youth engagement in new media requires a human-centered approach.

Human Instincts and Youth

Instead of focusing on the technologies or the characteristics of the information produced and used, we want to emphasize here the young person as learner. We draw from a learner-based taxonomy of technology uses (Bruce & Levin, 1997, 2003; Levin & Bruce, 2003). Their taxonomy in turn is based on the natural impulses of a child proposed by John Dewey (1900): communication, construction, investigation, and expression. In the Bruce and Levin taxonomy, the diversity of technologies for learning is captured by these four impulses or instincts of the learner. We see their taxonomy as a useful lens for analyzing youth engagement with new media, generally, and for understanding the processes and products generated in our YCI mapping project with rural youth.

Media for Communication

> If we roughly classify the impulses which are available in the school, we may group those under four heads. There is the social instinct of the children as shown in conversation, personal intercourse, and communication. . . . The language instinct is the simplest form of the social expression of the child. Hence it is a great, perhaps the greatest of all educational resources. (Dewey, 1900, p. 29)

Bruce and Levin (2003) note that digital media in school environments often focus on communication with peers or with those outside the educational system, especially in the language arts. Many innovative uses of technologies for learning have been means for augmenting communication. Most of the course package web systems (e.g., OpenCourseWare, Blackboard) explicitly present a communicative model. There are conferences, homework drop-boxes, announcement sections, test sections, lectures and lecture notes—all forms of communication.

Media for Construction

> Then there is the instinct of making—the constructive impulse. The child's impulse to do finds expression first in play, in movement, gesture, and make-believe, becomes more definite, and seeks outlet in shaping materials into tangible forms and permanent embodiment. (Dewey, 1900, p. 29)

Technologies can be used as media for learning through construction. Current constructivist approaches emphasize knowledge building. In fact, the recent constructionist approach explicitly focuses on the creation of external artifacts as important for learning. Several uses of technologies for learning have taken a construction set presentation mode (Kafai & Resnick, 1996). Even for older problem-based learning and project-based learning approaches, construction (either individually or jointly) plays a major role in learning.

Media for Investigation

> The instinct of investigation seems to grow out of the combination of the constructive impulse with the conversational. There is no distinction between experimental science for little children and the work done in the carpenter shop. . . . Children simply like to do things, and watch to see what will happen. (Dewey, 1900, p. 29)

Bruce and Levin (1997) established the primacy of using technologies for school-based learning through investigation in science, math, and engineering. The best examples of these science inquiry environments are the workbench websites, for example, the Molecular Science Student Workbench at http://mycyberbench.ncsa.illinois.edu, which has been set up explicitly to facilitate investigative processes, including the search of multiple databases and the analysis of retrieved datasets.

Media for Expression

> And so the expressive impulse of the children, the art instinct, grows also out of the communicating and constructive instincts. It is their refinement and full manifestation. Make the construction adequate, make it full, free, and flexible, give it a social motive, something to tell, and you have a work of art. (Dewey, 1900, pp. 29–30)

Supporting learning through expression is a fairly frequent use of new technologies in the language arts (Bruce & Levin, 2003). Much of the focus of theories of writing and other creative arts deals with the development of voice (Graves, 1983), a form of self-expression. One of the first tools developed for modern graphic interfaces was a series of painting and drawing programs (PaintPot from Xerox PARC; MacPaint from Apple). Computer-based photo editing, music editing, and video editing applications are other common examples of new technologies oriented toward expression.

Youth Mapping Around Illinois

We describe here one youth mapping project—cemetery mapping by middle school youth in Onarga, Illinois—to illustrate how new geospatial media help youth realize Dewey's instincts for learning. Others discussed in the book include youth community mapping in a rural setting (Chapter 8) and urban asset mapping (Chapter 10).

Cemetery Mapping in Onarga

A group of eight youth from Iroquois West middle school met weekly to carry out a community atlas project in spring 2008. They created about a dozen static maps that depicted different aspects of the community, including the location of their county in Illinois, the location of their town in the county, the location of their school in the county, along with the school district, local roads, and railroads. They used ESRI desktop ArcView GIS software and U.S. Census data. The group named themselves IWMapmasters (IW standing for Iroquois West) and organized a GIS day to demonstrate the outcome of the project to parents, teachers, and students. After the end of the community atlas project, six out of the eight youth in the group decided to continue their work and formed an after-school 4-H club. They created additional maps and exhibited them at the Iroquois County Fair in July of the same year. ESRI desktop software is suitable for GIS professionals or students at higher levels of education. By using such tools and creating a series of maps, this group of youth challenged the conception of what young people are capable of learning and doing.

Bolstered by the community atlas project, a group of sixth- and seventh-grade youth encouraged a teacher and a University of Illinois 4-H extension staff member to conceptualize a follow-up GIS project. They began to meet every Wednesday for about an hour after school. After a few meetings, the students considered three choices for mapping: historic sites, fire hydrants, or the cemetery. One young person said:

> We chose the cemetery mapping project as it is more interesting than the other two options given to us. We decided to map the cemetery when someone from the historic society of Onarga gave a talk on the differences among the cemetery symbols. We thought we would learn about the history of our town.

Youth then spent some time learning more about cemetery symbolism and visited the field to see the symbols in the real world. Youth spent the winter researching one or two individuals from the nineteenth century who are buried in the cemetery. They collected information about them using books and the Internet. Using Audacity, they also created audio podcasts to tell the story of each individual.

With the beginning of the next spring, youth visited the cemetery at least three times. They recorded the locations of the gravestones and the boundary of the cemetery using a handheld GPS device. Additionally, they captured other information about the gravestones: they created pictures and videos using a Flip camera and captured other details using a pen and paper. Thus, they were prepared to tell rich stories about the individuals they studied using multiple sources of information: audio podcast, geographic location of the gravestone, pictures and video depicting the symbols on the stone, and discussion of the meaning of the symbols with narrative text. What remained to be done was to map the locations of the gravestones and present the information using a spatial framework.

After their fieldwork, the youth met in the computer lab at their school each week for an hour. They created a map using Google Maps and integrated GPS tracks and waypoints, pictures, and videos as shown in Figure 4.1. The Google map-making was a collaborative process as they all mapped the locations of the gravestones in the same map. Prior to integrating information in Google Maps, the youth uploaded podcasts, pictures, and videos to the online site of their school; they used the URLs from the online site and hyperlinked those from their map. Youth also created a blog where they shared what they had learned and reflected on the project. When a push-pin in the map is clicked, it leads to a window similar to Figure 4.2 so that one can listen to the podcast, watch the video, read the narrative description, and get driving directions to the gravestone.

Humans have a natural desire to learn through communication, investigation, creation, and expression (Dewey, 1900). These basic human instincts drive us to observe our surroundings critically, ask questions, figure out answers, and share what we've uncovered with others. The inherently visual character of maps makes the pattern of the world readily visible and helps youth to critically observe and question the world in which they live:

> I noticed on google maps that the cemetary was not in the correct place. I changed it on the map. I also on google maps noticed there was a road I cannot find. I think there is not a road.

Discussion

The visual representation of the cemetery and roads in the community unsettles this sixth grader's knowledge about the location of those spatial features. It is possible that the locations of some of those features were incorrectly positioned in Google Maps. It is also possible that the youth's taken-for-granted understanding of the locations of those features is incorrect. In either case, it requires the youth to conduct field investigation to resolve this uncertainty. Thus, the visual power of the map functions as a trigger in activating the youth's investigative impulse.

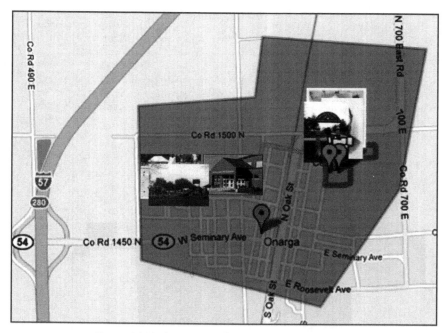

Figure 4.1: Online cemetery map using Google MyMap

Humans are imaginative and creative living beings who immensely enjoy the "pleasure of creation" (Benkler, 2006). The ease of use of emerging web 2.0 geospatial tools is enabling laypeople to create and share maps. Millions of people are taking part in this new mode of cartography and map-makings (Miller, 2006), providing them with the means to realize their creative instincts. While one of the authors was helping youth to create maps in the computer lab, another youth shared the map electronically with her mother within seconds after she created it. She was visibly proud of her creation. During our interviews with them, young people consistently mentioned what they had produced. As one 12-year-old girl said:

> We created a podcast, blog, map, video, and pictures, and connected them on the map. We showcased our creation to parents, teachers, others students, and community members.

Further, the human desire for creation grows when they know that their creation will be used by others. We found this to be the case with the youth involved in the Onarga cemetery mapping project, as the following remarks from two of the participants demonstrate:

Different people might benefit from the map we created. For example, Virginia High School is now doing a similar project. The historical society of Onarga was supposed to link our maps on their website. Other students from our school might be interested on some of the things we created.

Last week we discussed Google maps. It was interesting learning about how to use it and how much you can create using it. I sent my map that I created learning about it to my family and they enjoyed seeing it too. Google maps is a fun and easy way to share information with other people quickly!

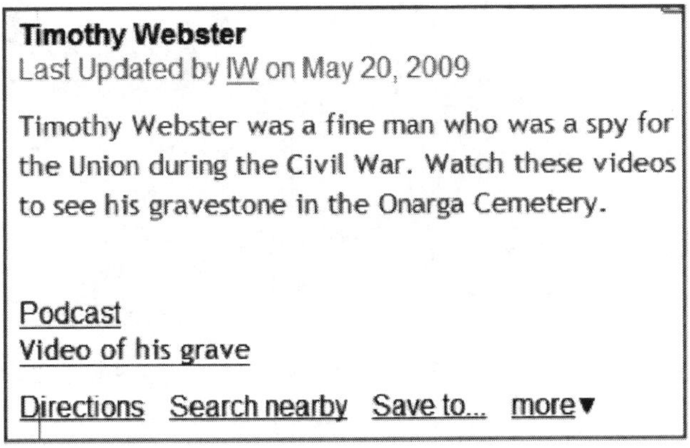

Timothy Webster
Last Updated by IW on May 20, 2009

Timothy Webster was a fine man who was a spy for the Union during the Civil War. Watch these videos to see his gravestone in the Onarga Cemetery.

Podcast
Video of his grave

Directions   Search nearby   Save to...   more ▼

Figure 4.2: Window that pops up when push-pin is clicked in Figure 4.1

Humans are social beings with the desire to meet other people, share ideas and experiences, and collaborate. Social networking sites such as Facebook address this communicative impulse. It is noteworthy that such sites sometimes strive to address our creation, expression, and investigation impulses as well; for example, you can create your own Farmville environment. Maps and place also play an important role in cyber-communities. Further, inequality and injustice often have spatial patterns. Maps and geovisualization, therefore, are especially well-suited to help youth interrogate social disparities, building their capacity for civic engagement and action to improve society.

While every individual has the instinct of investigation, creation, socialization, and expression, they cannot always fully realize these instincts. New geospatial media can help, and thus become natural resources in any society. John Dewey identified instincts for learning that help us understand the activities of the youth in these projects. But beyond that, he also saw the significance of geography for the curriculum, asserting that "the unity of all sciences is found in geography" (Dewey, 1900, p. 26). For Dewey, geography brought together the physical and social sciences. It was through a study of geography that we could best understand human activities, including how people meet their basic needs of food, shelter, and clothing. New media can be used to enable or activate human instincts for investigation, learning, discussion, collaboration, cooperation, play, and production. The youth mapping projects around Illinois demonstrate that geospatial media provide new opportunities in that direction.

Conclusion

The cemetery mapping project suggests that we can learn history through mapping. Use of new geospatial tools in the project allowed youth to engage in investigation, construction, and sharing. Youth engagement and learning with new media is evident in the following text that one youth participant posted on a project-related blog:

> Cemetery symbolism comes in many shapes and forms, much like the actual gravestones. In its simplest form you can tell how prominent a citizen is (or was) by the size of the gravestone. Also, engravings like broken chains symbolize a life cut short. Web sites like http://www.graveaddiction.com/symbol.html are great places to visit if you are interested by cemetery symbolism. One interesting tombstone that we found at the Onarga Cemetery was in the shape of a tree trunk. The name of the person buried there was Emory Gish. According to our research on symbolism the tree trunk showed a life cut short. The number of broken branches might symbolize the number of deceased family members buried nearby.

Although social networking sites respond to the impulse of communication, that is, the social impulse, new media often give short shrift to the other human impulses Dewey identified. Similarly, geospatial media have sometimes been used in a way that fulfills only the investigative impulse by prompting large numbers of people to act as "human sensors" in the collection of data. Adequately designed new media might provide an important opportunity to explore and cultivate all our natural instincts, and generate uses that benefit humanity.

5. "Now I Am College Material": Engaging Students Through Living Reflections of Self-Identity as a Form of Pedagogy

William Patterson

Shameem Rakha

The Youth Media Workshop (YMW) is a project developed by William Patterson in 2000. It was an extension of the Children's Television Workshop, the innovative entertainment-based education program created in 1967 to promote the intellectual and cultural development of preschoolers, particularly those from marginalized communities. But in contrast to the Children's Television Workshop, it uses indigenous knowledge, media, and popular culture as a form of pedagogy to enrich the education and social development of marginalized African American students in public schools. Youth in the project participate in an academic year, after-school program, which involves media production based on the oral histories of African American community members.

Patterson's theory of African American youth discovering "living reflections of self-identity" suggests that the skilled and conscious use of media tools has the ability to change both the educational experience and the culture of young people's disbelief in educational excellence and social responsibility (Patterson & Kranich, 2007). It is based on similar premises of Martin (2000), Aber (1993), Gonzales, Cauce, Friedman, and Mason (1996), and Brooks-Gunn, Duncan, Klebanov, and Sealand (1993), who do research on the social contexts of poverty, unemployment, and crime, and how the multiple domains of self, family, school, and community influence identify formation as it relates to academic achievement.

The theory is also grounded in the role that media play in African American youths' identity formation. Too often, African American young people emulate beliefs regarding success based on images and ideas produced through commercial media. These same young people must learn how to use media tools to tell their own stories and those of their community. Since its inception, the project has had an impact on the lives of the participants, both adults and students, the organizations involved, and on the community.

Social Capital and the Youth Media Workshop

Coleman (1988) defines social capital as "a variety of different entities, with two elements in common: they all consist of some aspect of social structures, and they facilitate certain actions of actors—whether persons or corporate actors—within the structure" (p. 16). He also highlights the importance of resources, which are reproduced and made available to individuals in social networks (Coleman, 1990). Hanifan (1916) used the term *social capital* in relationship to schools when he suggested that community involvement was needed to improve the state of West Virginia's schools. Members of the community, in this case, had resources available to them that the schools, in and of themselves, did not. As community members became involved in schools, the networks of information and resources available to schools would expand exponentially. According to Holland, Reynolds, and Weller (2007), youth are often seen as passive beneficiaries or recipients of social capital.

In the case of the Youth Media Workshop, instead of social capital being solely in the hands of the dominant group, this symbolic power is actively gained by African American youth through research and media production about areas of their own interest. They then can use this power to help them mediate their own school experiences. Much in line with the work of Tara Yosso (2005), Youth Media Workshop takes advantage of the capital that is inherent in communities of color, shunning the deficit perspective of many programs for African American youth. Here, youth capitalize on the wisdom of their elders and their lived experiences to help them see themselves within a broader, rich historical context.

Project History

From its inception, the project involved African American youth in media production. Before partnering with Public Broadcasting Service (PBS) affiliate WILL (now Illinois Public Media), Patterson's consulting firm, Innovative Ed Consulting, had created media-related initiatives for organizations that served potentially at-risk African American students. All Girlz Radio, B-Boy Radio, Rhyme Clinic, and Studio 109 were part of an educational media curriculum titled B.E.A.T.S. (Bridging Education, Arts, Technology, Scholastically). Through these initiatives, Patterson discovered that these "at-risk" students were inspired and engaged in learning about their own histories, the role of school, and social pressure, and how those elements affected their lives. It was during this period that Patterson began recognizing the scholarship emerging from his approach and found the theory that supports the mission of the Children's Television Workshop, which could be modified to help address the academic achievement of young people today.

In 2002, Patterson established a partnership with the University of Illinois PBS affiliate, Illinois Public Media, to expand the scope of the project into public schools to provide teachers with an innovative approach to educate potentially at-risk African American youth. More than 30 African American students from the local schools have participated in this project over the past seven years. The Youth Media Workshop has gone through many changes since then, due to attempts to make it more replicable to a greater number of schools, including those without access to the resources of a nearby university.

Originally, teachers in a local middle school were recruited to work on a biweekly basis with students in an after-school setting. The goal of the meetings was to introduce students to the issue being studied (originally, local school desegregation and busing) and to give them skills that would enable them to create a broadcast-quality one-hour radio documentary on the chosen subject. Students were taught research skills such as how to use the local library's archives. They were brought to the local newspaper archives to seek out information on desegregation and busing in their school district. Students were taught, with aid of collaborators from Illinois Public Media and Patterson, to ask meaningful questions and to conduct, record, and edit interviews. They practiced these skills with each other and with family members. Students were also trained to run recording equipment in the field as well as in the professional recording studio provided by the public radio station partner. In addition, students were taught how to tell a story using a storyboard and to overlay music into their documentary. This intensive year-long, after-school project also led to several field trips into the community, such as into local homes of older African American interviewees, the public archives, and the local newspaper. The students also had many opportunities to spend time on the university's campus, which lay at their back door.

In the third year of the project, the students were taught an interviewing method called "immersion journalism." Pulitzer Prize–winning journalist Leon Dash, a professor of journalism at the university, taught the students a method where they would sit down for two hours at a time with a local community member (in this case, local African American women) and ask about their lived experiences. Several times throughout the year, the students met with their interviewee (either in their home or place of work) and asked questions about the women's childhood, adolescence, and adulthood from the perspective of family, church, school, and community. Pieces from the interviews have been produced as short stories for the local public radio station.

In year four of the project, the students learned to use video equipment to tell a story. The culmination of their yearlong project was a half-hour documentary about a drum corps that once existed in a now often-neglected park in a predominantly African American part of town. The students did extensive research into the history of the park, its importance to the community, and into the drum corps itself. They did this, as in other years, with the aid of interviews, archive searches, Internet searches, and field trips to the local newspaper archives. The culmination of this project was the creation of a video documentary titled, *And the Beat Goes On: The Spirit in the Legacy of the Douglass Center Drum Corps.* These projects have taught students many skills, such as journalism and broadcasting, but also introduced students to many of the resources available in their community, including the multitudes of human resources that are available.

The project has evolved from the creation of extensive documentaries to students individually creating short (2–3 minute) historical videos on subjects of interest to them within the community. Students continue to research topics relevant to their lives. Patterson has used his own cultural and social capital to create what is called "The Well," a list of African American community members who are interested in connecting with youth and talking to them about their lived experiences. In The Well there are people who picketed the local JC Penney store due to their hiring practices, a person who was a part of the Negro Baseball League, people who desegregated local schools, and teachers who work with youths who drop out of school, to name just a few. One student attended a march against the killing of a local teen by police. He interviewed people about this tragic incident, and documented it using his camera.

Project Impact

An important component of this project is connecting students to older African Americans who can share their history. Students not only invited people to the local public radio studio to conduct interviews but also went to their places of work and into their homes to hold interviews. Students got to learn from those who had gone before, many sharing stories the students had never imagined. One interviewee, a retired African American woman, talked about traveling, explaining that she does not like to travel to local small towns and, indeed, won't ever do so at night. The students doing the interview were confused and so, being naturally curious, asked why this was the case. The interviewee went on to explain that in many of the towns surrounding Champaign, there had been laws that required African Americans to be out of town by sundown. The students had never heard of such a thing. This led to further research on sundown towns. The interest was so great that the participating teacher purchased *Sundown Towns* by James W. Loewen for her classroom and intertwined this history into a unit on the Civil Rights Movement.

Research Using Indigenous Knowledge

Students were taught research skills such as interviewing, Internet and archive searching, and reading for information in a practical manner within a natural context. They learned, quite quickly, that there was a wealth of indigenous knowledge (knowledge that a community accumulates over generations) within their community. They were taught how to gather oral histories and how to use the wealth of information that can be found throughout the community to learn more about themselves. The students learned, in a real way, that one does not need to do "traditional" research to find out about the past. Traditionally, classroom research on historical topics tends to place great value on encyclopedic knowledge—history as told by others. Students are taught to seek out information from "professionals" and historians. In the Youth Media Workshop, students learned that in addition to traditional approaches to research, they could gain historical knowledge from the people around them who were historians in and of themselves.

Often, this included knowledge of local oppression and discrimination, topics left out of their classroom textbooks. Indeed, they often found that information on African American history in the community was hard to find, except where it existed in the memories of their neighbors. This is an example of social capital in that students have been empowered to tell their own stories based on their new knowledge of this wealth of information held by those in the community. One example is that of the archives. Students visited our local history archivist, Anke Voss, who also teaches a class in community archiving. There, youth learned to do archive searches, book searches, and other methods available for finding out about an event or person in local history. Students spent time looking for information that interested them, such as about past relatives. They also learned how to do research using archived articles from the local newspaper. This was all done within a meaningful context of learning their own history.

Acquisition and Use of Social Capital

In another activity, participants were taken to see Melva Beal, one of the Little Rock Nine, when she spoke on the university's campus. During the question-and-answer period, one of the students rose to ask a question. Within the university venue, it was astounding that this eighth grader felt empowered enough to rise up in front of a packed room of primarily white adults to ask a question she had thought of during the lecture. At the end of the lecture, this same student purchased one of Ms. Beal's books and had it signed by the author. It was after this moving experience of hearing this one woman's struggle to integrate her school that this student was motivated to start the "Books before Boys" book club. She wanted to do something to help her friends be as moved as she was by this experience. As a result of the experience and the connection with Shameem Rakha, the teacher involved in the project (whom the student did not know prior to the project), this student led a group of 10 eighth-grade girls to read such books as *Like Sisters on the Homefront* (Williams-Garcia, 1995) and *The House on Mango Street* (Cisneros, 2009) and to discuss such issues as female subjugation, teen pregnancy, family, and empowerment. This can serve as an example of layers of social capital. Students were given access to the social capital of the university and its resources, and in turn, the student spoken of here, through her own agency, used her resources (both physical and social) to empower her friends to read, talk about, and create their own stories.

Participation in the project over repeated years led one student to decide she wanted to be a journalist. Though she had never had the desire to go to college, she was now, thanks to her newly found connections with the university, attending a few journalism lectures and speaking with students in the that department. This same student is now enrolled at the university. As this student said in a recent interview, "No reason to throw all those skills I learned away." Here is an example of social capital in a real sense. Champaign-Urbana is a small urban area where there is a clear "town and gown" division, and where people of the community, particularly people of color within the community, feel alienated from and by the university. Despite this fact, this student had access, unknown previously, to university resources. She also had the knowledge of how to present herself and ask questions, which in turn provided her access to a prestigious institution, which is a rarity within this marginalized community.

As a part of this year's project, students are being encouraged and given time to blog about their experience. You can see from the following blog entry the strong feelings evoked from participation in this project:

> My whole life I never thought I would be interviewing someone, but for now I think it's pretty cool because I like talking to people about their life and what it was like to be growing up in Champaign. The only thing I don't like is talking because I'm not a big talker. The reason I say that is because I don't really talk unless someone is talking to me.

It is a powerful testament to the project that a middle school student would feel empowered to interview an adult about her life. To be able to communicate with those who you feel are authorities in your life is an important form of social capital. Another example from the students' blog where one can see Patterson's notion of "living reflection of self-identity" is the following:

> Interviewing Ernie Westfield was interesting. I had a lot of fun. He explained his stories very well, so it was easy to understand and get interested in. I was excited to hear more of it. I think we have it easier now than he had it. In my experience there isn't as much racism as he lived with. He told stories about playing baseball in the Negro Leagues and not being allowed to play with whites. I play basketball and baseball on the park district teams and play along side blacks and whites or any races that want to join.

> Mr. Westfield had a good sense of humor. He used the stuff that he went through to tell interesting stories that got me thinking. He made me think about playing baseball again and trying different sports. He encouraged me to find my talent and really go for it! He didn't just talk about baseball, he also shared his poetry and talked about his kids and how he started a family here. From this experience I really learned that

he wants people to respect each other because the person you're mean to now, you might end up needing one day.

At the year-end celebration for the project, this student rose to tell the adult-filled room about his new-found love of poetry, which stemmed directly from his interviews with Mr. Westfield. The students not only learned practical information skills, but also learned how to speak in front of a large group of adults. When one can speak a story to those in power, according to Putnam (2000), one is exercising an important form of social capital—that of social engagement. After the first year of the project, the students attended a school board meeting to present what they had learned and to ask the district to help fund future projects. In the third year of the project they gave a workshop at the state's adult literacy conference to people working as literacy coaches for adults. They participated in a live television call-in show, where they answered questions from community members about what they had learned and how this affected how they feel about school.

Through this project, students learned how to "read" the media and its embedded messages. Media literacy gave the students the capital to decide what messages to accept, which to reject, and which to create and retell for themselves. They learned that they had power to create the story they wanted to tell rather than just believe the stories they are continually told. Through the life history of their elders, the students learned the importance of taking their own education seriously. They would often participate in discussions about the hardships their foremothers and forefathers faced. As many of the interviewees went to segregated schools, they were able to describe the joys and concerns of their schooling. Other interviewees attended integrated schools in the first tumultuous years of school busing. Their stories of hardships led one student to suggest that due to the struggles she learned about, she would never take her education for granted again. Indeed, it was this same student who came to admit whereas she had never thought this before, "Now, I am college material."

After the debut of the student-created documentary, *And the Beat Goes On: The Spirit in the Legacy of the Douglass Center Drum Corps*, the students were interviewed on local radio talk shows, promoting their film and sharing their experiences and the history they uncovered. Recently, some of these same students continued their film work to document the killing of an unarmed 15-year-old African American youth by the local police. These students have attended rallies, marches, and speak-outs on this issue. This is testament to the power of learning to tell your own narrative, even if it is counter to the dominant narrative. In addition, one of the Youth Media Workshop filmmakers sat on a panel with six other young filmmakers as part of the AFI-Discovery Channel SILVERDOCS Documentary Festival. He showed an edited version of the student-created documentary on the drum corps, and talked about how they made their films, what they learned, and how they got connected to media making. This was only the second time in seven years that the festival featured student-produced work.

Through the Youth Media Workshop, participating students made connections to community members and gained access to the university—so much so that they would give tours of the local PBS station as if they worked there. Not only was this community space one where the students felt empowered to tell their own stories, but for the first time this building, which was rarely significantly integrated, had students and community members of color sharing the space. Not only did the university help the community in this case, the community helped the University by adding its indigenous knowledge to the collective consciousness.

The project resulted in products that aired on local public and private radio and TV stations. These productions taught the public about local history that had been previously held tight in the memories of those marginalized within the community. The radio documentaries and movie were distributed to local libraries and museums, as well as on the web. When John Lee Johnson, a local activist, passed away, the local newspaper used the interviews done with him by the students to write part of their remembrance of him. Numerous stories have been told of teachers and university professors and students using the productions for their own classes and research.

Unforeseen Impacts

What follows is my (Shameem Rakha) reflection as a participating teacher who also served as a YCI graduate assistant. I participated actively in the Youth Media Workshop with middle school students for the first three years of the project. When first working with this group of young women, I remember feeling not up to the task. As an Asian American woman and teacher of 11 years at that time, though I thought I understood and respected the cultural capital my African American students brought into the program and into my classroom, working with the students in Youth Media Workshop helped me to realize that many of my assumptions, understandings, and teaching methods were inadequate. Spending time with these young women, two times (and often more) a week, learning with them about their history and lives, hearing their hopes (often dashed) and dreams (again, dashed) changed me. I learned of the wealth of the history of these students. I learned of the wealth of the history of our community, of the African American community, in particular. This not only led me to further understand my complicated racial identity but to determine to change my pedagogy to better reflect the gifts and meet the needs of my African American students.

I determined to teach in a way that would challenge the racial status quo, as much as I could. Though I had always taught a unit, for example, on the Harlem Renaissance, I decided to add more layered research projects into my English curriculum that would represent the lived experiences of African

Americans. Indeed, I went on to incorporate many of the interviews done by students in this project into the reading my students did in class. My relationships with my teaching and with my students were changed due to the tremendous capital this knowledge, these students, and this project gave me.

In reflecting on my decision to return to graduate school, I see now that much of that decision had to do with my work with the Youth Media Workshop. Learning of the joys and struggles of these students and members of our community helped me to decide to leave my profession to study and understand how we, as a society, and teachers in particular, need to change our perspectives about people and our way of understanding and being in the world if we are to make it a more equitable and hospitable place for all people.

This understanding, gained through my work with Youth Media Workshop students, and my understanding of "living reflections of self-identity," provided me with a changed perspective on teaching and learning, and this blended well into my work with the Youth Community Informatics (YCI) project, as I saw the intertwining of the goals of both projects. Much of my work with YCI centered around helping to create a community-based inquiry curriculum entitled "Community as Curriculum" (Chapter 15). This curriculum allows students to guide their own inquiries into issues in their community that are of interest and concern to the students themselves. It uses methods of inquiry much like those used in the Youth Media Workshop including document review, archival searches, Internet searches, and interviews, and much like the Youth Media Workshop, it includes an action, or creation component, so that students are not only informed on critical issues such as racism and food deserts but are given tools common to YCI, such as creation of websites, blogs, and documentaries, to empower them to be a part of the solution. In the process of participating in these inquiries, students using the Community as Curriculum lessons access social capital much the same way students did in the Youth Media Workshop.

In working with both of these projects I have learned a lot about teaching and learning, and one important lesson that will be with me throughout my days will be that young people are capable of learning complex concepts and issues, and of teaching others about these complex concepts and issues, if given the right tools and training on how to use them. The students now have opportunities, tools, and information they would not have had access to before. This is social capital that has led to change, and will continue to lead to change in our community and in the lives of our students.

Section 2

Learning to Act Responsibly in the World

All of the cases described in this book adopted a social justice youth development model. However, some can be viewed as focusing more on learning to act responsibly in the world. The issue here is not "behave responsibly" as that dictate is often applied to at-risk youth. Instead, it is about authorizing an agency that envisions individual growth as inseparable from that of the society. Responsibility implies legitimate participation, engagement, and shared ownership of societal resources and purposes.

Sally Carter, Shameem Rakha, and Chaebong Nam discuss this in Chapter 6, "TAPping In: Education, Leadership, and Outright Gumption." The Tap In Leadership Academy provides social and academic support to traditionally underserved youth with the goal of making university life more accessible. The project focuses on web research skills and digital photography. See http://new.tapinacademy.org/.

Within community-based participatory research, we are often confronted with establishing partnerships that span the boundaries of university and community, requiring us to navigate the intersections of sometimes awkward histories, unequal power dynamics, conflicting goals, strong prior beliefs, and the residual effects of past choices and assumptions. YCI sought to work with existing community organizations to foster inquiry-based programming. There were definite ideas about how established our partner organizations should be in their communities and what their programming might look like. But early on, our work with a struggling teen enrichment program challenged us to rethink those assumptions, to adjust our program focus, and to reframe and redefine the YCI project itself.

Teen Tech was identified as a community partner based on prior relationships with faculty and staff associated with the East Saint Louis Action Research Project (ESLARP, 2009). The YCI project was initially seen as a mechanism to continue work in this community with an existing teen-focused organization. But graduate students and staff working with Teen Tech found a group that was struggling. Teen Tech was not the established program we expected. We reached a point of needing to decide whether to continue the relationship. Realizing that past partnerships with Teen Tech had established a pattern of dependence on university partners, we continued working with Teen Tech in an attempt to establish a new pattern of local empowerment, autonomy, and sustainable partnerships. In Chapter 7, "Teen Tech, East St. Louis: Navigating New Community Partnerships," Chris Ritzo and Mike Adams discuss the successes and challenges of YCI's partnership with Teen

Tech, and how our interaction with them in the formation of a new partnership helped give our entire program new direction.

Jeff Bennett and Robin Fisher discuss similar work in Chapter 8, "The Learning Never Stops: Creating a Curriculum That Resonates Beyond the Classroom." When we seek to educate youth as a community of learners, to which community do they belong, and for which community are we preparing them? In the economically depressed farm town of Virginia, Illinois, high school educators are seeking ways to connect formal learning meaningfully to students' lived experiences. Via collaboration with the university, a new course in geographic information systems (GIS) and Global Positioning System (GPS) technologies was introduced during the 2009–2010 school year. The chapter coauthors are high school teachers who team teach this interdisciplinary class, which combines core agricultural science, technology, and math learning with a local history curriculum. They developed a GIS/GPS technologies course with projects including geocaching, a cemetery-mapping project, an oral history project, explorations of careers requiring GIS technology skills, and investigations of current community challenges through the analysis of publicly accessible GIS data, e.g., U.S. census data and local surveys (see also Chapter 4). Experiences and reflections regarding the course's inaugural year are explored in this chapter and considered through the lens of community inquiry.

6. TAPping In: Education, Leadership, and Outright Gumption

Sally K. Carter

Shameem Rakha

Chaebong Nam

The Youth Community Informatics (YCI) project worked with some community groups based on existing partnerships between the University and the community. An example is the work with Paseo Boricua, Chicago (see Chapter 9). Other projects were initiated within communities where no previous relationship existed (Chapters 2–4). This chapter introduces another model, one in which a community-university partnership was *driven* by a community member. In addition to describing young students' learning experiences with new digital technology, it discusses how the partnership was initiated, the difficulties this community member had to go through to bridge the "town-gown conflict," and implications for other community-university partnerships.

The chapter speaks with three voices: Sally K. Carter initiated the partnership with the university, involving most directly YCI research assistants Shameem Rakha and Chaebong Nam. Rakha interviewed Carter and translated her story into the main body of text for this chapter. Nam and Rakha convey their voices in the reflection at the end.

When Sally Carter earned her MBA from Kaplan University, she was aiming to find a "good" job. Instead, she found her passion. She became the founder and executive director of an organization for youth in Urbana-Champaign called Tap In Leadership Academy. Tap In is a nickname for Thinking In A New Perspective. In establishing the program's four core pillars—leadership, cultural awareness, literacy, and civic engagement—Carter realized that Tap In could not wait until college to prepare its scholars to be leaders. Action needed to take place immediately so that scholars could become civically active, productive citizens before their middle school years. Its inaugural six-week Summer Enrichment Program, prepared it for the subsequent Afterschool Enrichment Program, held in the fall of 2010. In addition to Tap In's core pillars, the after-school program inlcudes enriching mathematics, science, and foreign language skills.

Making Connections: The History of Tap In Leadership Academy

There is no telling the story of Tap In without talking about faith. Tap In started with one student named JC, Carter's son. While Carter served as an advocate and a voice for JC, not knowing exactly what to do for him, she prayed for guidance. From her prayers came two words that resonated with her, a lesson her uncle had given her years before: "Tap In." She knew that she needed to "Tap In" to herself. Her uncle had told her, "Your brain's job is to please you. When you tell your brain you want to jump, your brain tells your nerves, and you jump. When you don't have money, your brain tells you that you need to have money, and your brain begins to think of ways to make money." From these words, Carter realized that "Tap In" was already in her. She understood that people have all that they need within them, and have to Tap In to it. For Carter, everything we need to do involves tapping in—Tap In to learning, to education, to the community, to the university. As she puts it, "Tap In is a command—a way of life."

With three children, ages 9 to 14, and a supportive husband, Carter realized that despite their education and their focus as parents on their children's education, she felt the need to ask for help for her middle child— her gifted son. During his third-grade year in 2008, Carter wrote a letter to her son's teacher about her concerns. An excerpt is below:

> I sat there during the awards ceremony and watched the majority of your students receive academic merits while JC, your only African American male, received an award based on behavior...The question is: what needs to be done at school and at home to assure JC's academic success?

With her concerns, where could she turn? After a great deal of searching for programs locally, Carter was determined that she could create something different for the families of her community. She would start an after-school program that focused on cultural competence in addition to education and leadership, one that went beyond tutoring or after-school care. Originally, Carter had wanted to work in collaboration with the local schools; however, they needed money to help fund the extended hours and janitorial services that would be required by the program. Carter did not have funding for such services. Her focus would be on reaching families like her own, low- to middle-income families, and she doubted the program would have much money at all.

She asked herself, "What would I do if I *did* have money?" She decided that the first thing she would do was purchase food for the scholars. But where? The Eastern Illinois Food Bank was an idea, but they only allowed not-for-profit organizations to purchase food. Without any money, she could not pay to file for not-for-profit status—at least, not yet. So Carter found her first connection—her church. Stone Creek Church in Urbana offered to allow Carter to purchase food for her program through their account and to store the food at the church. She calculated how much bottled water the scholars would need for the six-week summer enrichment program and began collecting the water from the food bank three months in advance. This first success, however small in the eyes of those watching, gave Carter the confidence to continue planning, knowing that whatever it took, her program would start on time.

Without a confirmed location for the program, Carter set off to look for financial support for Tap In. On a trip to the mall, she was given her first bit of support. There she bumped into Angela Slates and Shameem Rakha. Slates and Rakha were YCI research assistants. Carter already knew Slates as a friend whose daughter had attended a prior summer program that Carter had coordinated. As a recent graduate herself, Carter knew that there were resources at the university. The question was how to gain access. "My experiences mirror the experiences of others in the community. I didn't know what GSLIS was." Carter thought, "I'm educated and clueless...There is a whole lot we as a community do not know about the university."

Later, Carter, Slates, and Rakha gathered to work on a grant application through the Champaign-Urbana Schools Foundation. To get this grant, Carter had to find university sponsorship, which she was unfortunately unable to do before the grant's due date. Another door seemed to have closed. Carter wondered why it was so hard to bring the university and its resources into the community, but within her wonder she had an idea. If the university would not come and help this program, she would do her best to bring the program to the university.

While visiting a sorority sister, who was the assistant program director of the university's African American Cultural Center, her friend offered to house the Summer Enrichment Program there. Carter was inspired by Nevada Street, the block of houses lined with cultural centers. Her mind reeled with ideas of how the students could go from cultural center to cultural center, learning about people and cultures of the world—learning that their world was so much larger than what they knew. With a confirmed commitment from the African American Cultural Center, and connections with the Native American House, Asian American Cultural Center, and La Casa Cultural Latina, Carter moved forward. She began to build a much-needed bridge between "town and gown" and began to develop her curriculum and program around the importance of cultural diversity and awareness.

In preparing for Tap In's Summer Enrichment Program, Carter became increasingly aware that people did not understand each other, nor did they take the time or energy to learn about each other. She further understood that this was a key cause of bullying. With this in mind, she enhanced the curriculum to center on various cultural groups, offering activities at a different cultural center each week, with the African American Cultural Center as the program's home base. "Nevada Street was going to be our campus," she remarked.

Carter walked the halls of the International Studies Building in search of volunteers to teach the students alongside the director of engagement for the campus performaing arts center, who was distributing flyers for a program there. As he introduced her to various contacts, Carter told each one about Tap In and collected business cards so that she could follow up with them via email the following day. Within days, Carter had a roster of university professors and faculty who would soon be responsible for teaching her scholars. One of the people was the senior program coordinator in the Office of Equal Opportunity and Access. She became instrumental in the development of Tap In Leadership Academy, offering her educational background, heart for children, and insight into university language. The connection between Carter and the director was instant, and she continues to play a large role in Tap In as a board member.

Through the connection to YCI, Carter learned about the Extension Service, which offered to provide curricula for the program. Now, with a confirmed location, instructors, curricula provided by the Extension Service, and food for the program, Carter knew she needed staff to help run it. She could not do this on her own. With the help of a grant, Carter was able to hire staff members for the summer program.

Just four days prior to the program's start, and two hours before the informational meeting with the parents of participating students, the floor fell out beneath Carter's feet. Unbeknown to her, the contact who had agreed to house the program in the African American Cultural Center failed to receive approval from the university administration. The university's legal department rejected the program: "Having young children on campus on a daily basis and not being connected to any university program would create a legal liability." The cultural centers did not have the needed insurance policies in place, nor did they have the needed building code compliances to house a program for youth.

Carter was crushed; months of work were lost. It was as though a major campus-community connection had been severed. Parents and students alike had been disappointed. Carter felt angry, betrayed, and remembers thinking, "the university doesn't give a damn about our kids." She had been repeatedly asked by university contacts about her affiliation to a grant or department, to which she answered, "No, I'm just a community member." At that moment, the "just" became very large. She no longer felt that she belonged on the university campus; Tap In was "just" for community members. Carter's spirit sank as she faced this challenging time.

With the support of her contacts, Carter went to the Community United Church of Christ and asked for help. They agreed to provide a space for her program. However, she couldn't afford the $1,000 fee. They suggested that she contact the foundation located at McKinley Presbyterian Church, another nearby church. This was the turning point. The foundation was also on campus and happened to be directly across the street from GSLIS and the International Studies Building. Carter again mustered up courage and walked over to McKinley Foundation to ask about renting some space. She found the office manager and told her about the program. Carter shared, "I don't have any money, can you still help me?"

The office manager kindly responded, "Let me show you what I've got." Carter was shown a room in the basement, dirty and filled with debris. Carter said, "I'll take it." The office manager told Carter that she would allow the program to rent the space for a dollar and told her she did not have to pay immediately. With that, Carter went home, found some paint, some friends, and some old Indian saris. Tap In Leadership Academy found its home. The McKinley Foundation proved to be an excellent resource for the Tap In program. It has provided several rooms for classes, as well as recreation space, and even kept the students and staff fed for a nominal cost.

Summer Enrichment Program and Tap In–YCI Connection

In June 2010, Tap In Leadership Academy began its six-week Summer Enrichment Program. Though the goal was to have 10 fourth and fifth graders and five middle school students from low- to middle-income families participate, the program ended up with 11 elementary students, along with five high school students who served as mentors. The YCI project provided three paid teen mentors to help with the Summer Enrichment Program. The three teens–Raisha, Clorisa, and Christina–were "graduates" of the Empowering and Engaging Youth Project (see Chapter 10), who were looking for ways to continue their informatics work in the community. Through E2Y, they had created a digital asset map of the northern part of Champaign. The mentors participated in the afternoons, assisting teachers and scholars.

From 8 a.m. to 3 p.m., Monday through Friday, the scholars learned leadership skills, money management and budgeting (through a token economy and Tap In Store), cultural understanding, health and nutrition, web design, and digital photography. Each of the enrichment activities was taught in an interactive, culturally sensitive manner. Thanks to the connections with the university, the scholars had access to university laptops with which to do their web design, research, and photography work.

University faculty, staff, and students taught the scholars about different world cultures, and staff from Extension taught about food and nutrition. One of the staff members, Turance, instructed the scholars on creating their own websites. The research assistants of the YCI program taught the scholars the elements of photography, the use of digital cameras, and digital editing. The scholars used mass transit to go on numerous field studies. They also did a career study on areas of academic and practical interest.

The Summer Enrichment Program culminated with an open house that included a showcase of the scholars' work. They displayed their photography and posters about careers they were interested in. Tap In has grown and in less than three years, Tap In has been awarded several grants on local, state, and federal levels. Partnership with the university and local school district is strengthened. Tap In serves more than 300 scholars in two counties.

Accomplishments and Stories: The Photography Project

Angela Slates and Shameem Rakha first introduced Sally Carter and her new program, Tap In, to YCI in the spring of 2010. To support the youth program, YCI conducted a photography project for Tap In scholars, a fun and feasible activity that could be completed within the six-period class schedule. In the first class, Rakha and Chaebong Nam, another YCI research assistant (RA), visited Tap In's new home, located in the basement of the McKinley Foundation. The RAs showed the scholars the basics of digital camera operation and then the group went to the quad, an open area at the heart of campus. There, the scholars played with the cameras and became more familiar with the cameras' functions. Divided into smaller teams with junior staff leading each group, the scholars explored the quad with their cameras, took photographs, and hung out with the other scholars.

The YCI RAs—Slates, Rakha, and Nam—thought that having students examine exemplary photographs could help the scholars create quality work. In the second class, scholars were asked to choose three favorite photographs from several professional photograph books borrowed from the Art and Architecture Library and think about the reasons for selecting the photographs. Each scholar presented his or her favorite photographs, which included a variety of themes, such as falls, islands, chairs at a café, a path passing through the forest, sea at dusk, a big Viking ship, mountains, etc. This activity aimed to encourage the scholars to be aware of their own aesthetic perspectives and draw inspiration from the exemplary photographs, which possibly could be transferred to their photograph project.

In the third class, the scholars went out again to take the project photographs. Nam told scholars to choose one theme for their photograph work, such as signs, buildings, nature, or whatever they liked. This theme-based activity was designed to help the scholars better articulate the messages they wanted to deliver and stay focused on them. The scholars were given various types of digital cameras with different features and functions. Nam stressed that the tool was not as important as the ideas that the scholars really wished to express, to discourage the scholars from thinking that the quality of the camera would determine the quality of their photographs.

The scholars walked around the campus to find places that best represented their themes and took photographs with their teammates. In the following class, the scholars learned how to edit photographs and apply filters such as black and white, sepia, matte, vignette, and antique using iPhoto on MacBooks. This task involved learning new digital technology skills, including using photo editing software and word processing—for some scholars this was their first exposure to these tools.

In the final class, the scholars introduced their favorite work along with their photographic themes and thoughts before their peers, mentors, Tap In staff, and YCI staff. With themes such as "nature," "wind," "signs," and "trees," the scholars presented various interesting images: flowers, buildings, signs, flags, chains, hands, dogs, a garden with a yin-yang shape, a rusty hydrant, an old motorcycle. The scholars freely expressed their aesthetic views with no fear of critiques and judgment, and the audience listened carefully to them. Their photographs were matted so they could be sold at their program's showcase event as part of a fundraiser to support Tap In.

Figure 6.1. One of Ana's photos

A week later at the showcase held in McKinley Foundation's Westminster Hall, scholars, their family members, interns, community members, and YCI affiliates gathered to celebrate the scholars' achievements. A considerable number of photos were sold that day, raising money to continue the program. Plans are in place to continue working with the scholars throughout the school year to develop a book (created through a web service that provides self-publishing electronic production) to document the positive impact made through the Tap In Leadership Academy.

According to Carter, the scholars' participation in the photography project "showed the kids that what they see in the world is not as gloomy as they might think. Their world is beautiful." The Youth Community Informatics project's involvement helped the scholars discover abilities they did not know they had. Carter shares this story about Ana, who came into the program as a very angry young woman.

Had you asked the scholar where she was from, she would have said California, but the truth is that she is from Guatemala. She did not think there was anything pretty about her, and she was what many considered a bully. The young scholar had many circumstances against her according to society. But when she held the camera, she began to see differently. She saw beauty all around. Even more beautiful were the people around her telling her how beautiful her work was. I was so proud when on Showcase Day, everyone was choosing her photographs as their favorites. Before Tap

In, this scholar did not know what she wanted to do when she grew up, but now she knows she wants to be in the arts. YCI put a dream in a child's hands. It was an important element of the program.

Carter noted that the photography project—a combination of digital learning, art education, social-emotional learning, and community engagement—contributed to the positive changes among many other scholars. Younger scholars had high school scholars as role models and were able to see positive behaviors modeled by them. The scholars' worlds were opened up beyond home, church, or neighborhood. They learned about their own history and that of others.

The Future of Tap In Leadership Academy

Carter continues this work. The academic year after-school program highlights study areas that her minority students might not otherwise emphasize, including math, literacy, and foreign language development. One focus is on Social-Emotional Learning (SEL), which helps students develop the skills to control their emotions, to resolve social conflicts in a nonviolent manner, and to make responsible decisions (Cohen, 1999). The four pillars of the Tap In program—cultural awareness, leadership, literacy, and civic engagement—are situated in this context. Another focus is on students' welfare in a broader way, beyond "cutting slack." Carter understands that students cannot learn if they are hungry, nor thrive if there is no one at home to help when the student gets frustrated. She also understands that none of these situations suggests that parents do not want their children to be successful students. Regardless of the situation, parents want their children to be successful in school and in life, even if it may not "look" that way to the establishment of formalized schooling. The program will continue to focus on the needs of the child, understanding that some families need assistance and need not to be judged. With this in mind, the Afterschool Enrichment Program provides dinner for the scholars on a daily basis and will run until 7:00 p.m., Monday through Friday. Carter notes:

> When it comes to the question of whether or not kids from low-income backgrounds should be cut slack in terms of education, my perspective is "no." I think kids from low-income families should be held to a higher standard than their privileged peers. Minority or poor scholars, when they graduate from high school and college, they don't have a strong support system, you know, at home, or a circle of friends that helps them get the next job or pushes them on. So, to me, the worst that you could do for them is to cut them slack. You're crippling them [students], because you are not preparing them for the real world. You're not preparing them to get out and fight harder than their counterparts. When it comes to Tap In scholars, I push them harder than they think that they even can go, because the real world won't have that empathy, if you will. People won't be sympathetic to the fact that, "oh, they come from a single family home, dad is in jail, mom is on welfare and probably doesn't

have time to devote to education, they don't have a computer at home." The world doesn't care. So we need to prepare them for that. So no, you don't cut slack.

The Tap In program continues to operate. College students offer homework help to both elementary students and high school mentors. Carter believes that this will be mutually beneficial, with the college students closer in age to the scholars, often speaking a more familiar language than teachers or parents. Each day will also afford opportunities for enrichment. For example, students receive hands-on science instruction at a campus laboratory once a week. At other times, scholars learn the Afro-Brazilian martial art form of *Capoeira*, which includes dance and music elements, a foreign language, or graphic design. There is an underlying focus on health, overall wellness, and recreation. Having the community come to the university allows the scholars to flourish in an environment of higher learning, rather than to fear it.

The intention is to build on Tap In Leadership Academy's four core pillars of cultural awareness, leadership, literacy, and civic engagement, and to nurture a generation of scholars who are aware, educated, and engaged in their community. Recognizing the strengths and challenges of all community members, and building upon them, the program extends beyond the community and defines the importance of civic engagement and global citizenry.

We found that the physical proximity of the McKinley Foundation to GSLIS was important. The Community Informatics Club became involved and provided volunteers to help teach Tap In. Martin Wolske, a YCI project staff member, decided to work with Tap In to help them build a public computing lab for the scholars, as well as other community members. He had been teaching a GSLIS class titled "Introduction to Network Information Systems" for 11 years. Students in Wolske's class learn about public computing spaces from a variety of perspectives (see Chapter 14). They learn about what makes a space one where people feel welcome, want to learn new technology, be creative, and collaborate, as well as about issues of technology, space, and adoptability. They then apply these skills by building computing spaces for community organizations. Wolske's class would make use of donated computers, adding peripheral equipment to fully equip a Tap-In lab. That process was a learning opportunity for both Tap In scholars and the university students.

Nam's Reflection

From my experience of teaching and working with youth for several years as a former social studies teacher, I can confidently confirm that Tap In has a great potential for holistic and critical learning. Tap In helped young students of color engage in a new social and cultural environment and learn various topics relevant to their lives through hands-on activities, as well as providing them with the skills and confidence to become young leaders. The photograph project Tap In conducted with YCI for the Summer Enrichment Program contributed to this by encouraging the scholars to freely express aesthetic talents and explore the new space using digital technology.

The most important lesson I learned from my work with Tap In, however, was from the unusual community-campus partnership, rather than the program per se. Tap In's cross-campus partnerships with several units of the university were ignited by "just a community member," Sally Carter. This was seen as quite different from typical community-campus partnerships driven by universities/colleges that secure grants with specific predetermined timelines. Originally YCI planned to only assist Tap In with their summer program. However, the program was extended into the school year and after the summer semester ended Rakha and I continued to regularly communicate with Carter.

This naturally led us to the next stage of the partnership. Since YCI is winding down in its last year, our focus was to find someone who would take over YCI's role with Tap In within GSLIS. Wolske willingly agreed to partner with Tap In for his class, Introduction to Network Information System, providing Tap In with a computer lab. GSLIS students in the Community Informatics Club also volunteered for teaching Tap In scholars digital media projects, including making stop-motion videos. In the meantime, Carter made efforts on her own to find other grant resources for Tap In, which made the program an independent and capable partner for the long-term sustainable partnership, rather than continuing to rely on university support. I watched Tap In gradually expand its connection to other units of the university and community organizations, eventually becoming one of the most influential programs for youth and families of color in Champaign. At the same time, "just a community member" was being transformed into an advocate of educational justice and welfare of those people in the community. Carter's transformation was surely inspirational to many people, as she proved that it is indeed possible that one can really make a difference with passion, courage, and resilience.

It cannot be denied that YCI's supportive climate toward community engagement was another important factor for Tap In's successful partnerships with the university. A cadre of engaged scholars in GSLIS, including Ann Bishop, Chip Bruce, and Martin Wolske, played a key role in tackling bureaucratic challenges, regulations, and lack of understanding and support on campus—they created an extraordinarily supportive environment for my work with Tap In.

Now that I am no longer a student and moving to the next stage of my career, I encounter even more directly the institutionalized atmosphere that too easily allows indifference to social justice and community engagement. My work with TAP In, as well as with other community partners, has shown me the profound significance of mutual respect, patience, and understanding for developing a working relationship between campus and community that will overcome that indifference. This is also the solid ground on which I navigate through obstacles and envision my professional responsibilities as an engaged educator and researcher.

Rakha's Concluding Remarks

Participating in this project, mostly from a planning perspective, has been eye-opening for me as a teacher in the community for 16 years. The holistic nature of the approach taken by Carter is insightful. How often did I, as a teacher, think about the whole child when teaching my students in their English classes? What difference would it have made had I done so? For me, Tap In is about looking at students as scholars. It is looking at them as having potential, rather than trying to fix what is wrong. It is about looking at families and family needs and ways these needs can be supported to help each child reach for their dreams. Tap In is about building internal capacity. I think the lessons learned by the approach taken within the Tap In project are worthy of study, not only for programs outside of traditional schools, but for those in more traditional learning environments. I look forward to learning more as I continue to work with this program within my role as a graduate research assistant for YCI, and as a volunteer.

Another important factor of this project was discussed at length by Nam, that of the ups and downs of community-university partnerships. As I began working with Carter a year ago when we first met at the local mall, I saw her struggle to gain recognition by the university. As a community member, and not as someone who was connected to the university, gaining entrée to the university was a battle. The ongoing questions of "What department are you affiliated with?" and "What grant are you affiliated with?" left Carter feeling like "just another community member." As someone who is both a long-time community member and a graduate student, I am concerned that there is such a disconnect between the two. The question for me becomes, "Why isn't there a place where community members can go to gain entrée? A place where community members can get help, or find out ways to get connected?" Perhaps there is. But as a teacher for many years within this community, and as a community activist, I have no idea where that would be. Carter's struggle to gain access to university resources to build a program that could ultimately help the university by improving community relations and by potentially pipelining local students into the student body has given me much insight as to the complex nature of university communities, and has also encouraged me to ask more questions about what can be done to improve community-university partnerships.

7. Teen Tech, East St. Louis: Navigating New Community Partnerships

Chris Ritzo

Mike Adams

As researchers working within struggling communities, we know that there are apparent power differentials and deficits that should be addressed in our partnerships and projects. University faculty and staff have access and resources that the "partnership" or "collaboration" brings to the table, but our partners often do not. The result can seem somewhat neo-colonial if not monitored and adjusted throughout the process. Even in the most successful project partnerships in the history of the East St. Louis Action Research Project (ESLARP), faculty needed to remain open to critical self-reflection and direct critique from the community (Reardon, 2005).

One of YCI's strengths was to remain flexible when forming new partnerships or renewing old ones. Our work in East St. Louis, Illinois, with Teen Tech illustrated the need for flexibility when forming partnerships with community organizations and had to adapt to their needs, even if that seemed to conflict with our initial intentions or project goals. The lasting importance of our work with Teen Tech was that we remained open to learn as much from our community partner as they may have gained from us (Linden, 2002; Meyer Reimer & Bruce, 1994).

About East St. Louis

East St. Louis, Illinois, is located directly east of St. Louis, Missouri. According to U.S. Census data at the time of the project, the population of the metro area surrounding East St. Louis, including the cities of Centreville, Madison, and Venice and the villages of Alorton, Brooklyn, Cahokia, and Washington Park, was 58,282. The population of East St. Louis itself had declined from nearly 82,000 in 1950 to 27,006 in 2010. Once a more demographically balanced community (~50% African American in 1950), 98% of residents were now African American.

Like many urban cities in the twentieth century, economic and infrastructure declines as well as environmental issues were prevalent in East St. Louis and have been well documented (Kozol, 1991; Theising, 2003). Median household income was $19,934 (compared to $56,576 for Illinois) and has been declining in both real and inflationary terms. Over one-third of the population is in poverty (compared to 13% for Illinois). Unemployment was at 18%, nearly twice that of the state of Illinois. About one quarter of the population over 25 does not have a high school diploma or equivalent, compared to 13.4% for Illinois. Neighboring cities and villages share similar devastation, some with nearly 60% poverty, median income as low as $17,348, and as much as 33% of the population without a high school education.

But despite the grim statistics, our partners in East St. Louis were working to reclaim their community and to counter the negative image of East St. Louis as seen from the outside. As one of Teen Tech's adult leaders explained, "They only tell the bad stories in the news. There are a lot of good folks in East St. Louis, doing good things." (Ms. Mary B., personal communication, September 2008). Stories like this expressed hope for the youth and families residing in East St. Louis and their work is focused on community activism and positive change. Since 1991, various neighborhood organizations and university departments have collaborated with the ESLARP on work with women's shelters, churches, and community centers (Reardon, 1999).

The partnership with East St. Louis is rooted in the community activism of local residents and a challenge to university administration to make good on its land grant mission. ESLARP began as a response to State Representative Wyvetter H. Younge (D-East St. Louis) who challenged the university "to demonstrate its commitment to the state's most distressed community by establishing an urban extension program in East St. Louis" (Reardon, 1999). The result was a university initiative to support grassroots community organizations and local government entities, and reverse the prevailing community skepticism at the time. Many were concerned about university faculty working in the community, finding grant funding to study conditions in their community, but not translating that research into direct community development efforts. The work of community activists, university students and volunteers, and faculty such as Ken Reardon provided an excellent example of locally driven university-community engagement. It led to the cleanup and renewal of the Emerson Park neighborhood and spawned hope, energy, and interest in expanding the success to other neighborhoods and initiatives.

The direct, participatory action-research work of initiatives like ESLARP and projects like YCI does not fit well to the standard model of disinterested, generalizable research most recognized by the academy. Instead it requires us to frame research questions collaboratively with nonacademic partners, dealing with unexpected constraints toward collaboratively identified goals. And while the public engagement mission of land-grant institutions provides a starting point to undertake community-based research, in practice it is only a beginning to the challenge and strain for both parties in finding common work that genuinely addresses individual difference and also works toward meaningful outcomes for both community and university partners. The challenges ESLARP has faced in comparison with that of other university-community partnerships has been documented well (Sorensen & Lawson, 2012).

About Teen Tech Team

Started in January 2005, Teen Tech Team is a youth program aimed at teaching youth computer hardware and software diagnostics, as well as business entrepreneurship skills. Teens learn to build a computer with donated parts. Along with technology expertise, teens also learn about business as they sell the used and refurbished computers to the community at affordable prices. Participating teens also have the opportunity to work with GSLIS students refurbishing computers for nonprofit organizations.

During the YCI project, the Teen Tech Team was staffed by Mike Adams, an employee of Computer Village (Computer Village, 2009) a nonprofit organization working in the St. Louis, Missouri, metro area to deliver technology training. Computer Village provides technology centers and computing skills instruction in the St. Louis metro area, but primarily in Missouri. As a resident of East St. Louis, Illinois, Adams, along with Don Holt, the executive director of Computer Village, began an effort with then Prairienet Director Paul Adams to build a computer refurbishing and entrepreneurial leadership program for teens in the metro east region.

The longstanding presence of ESLARP, Prairienet's established computer refurbishing program, and the resources of both Prairienet and Computer Village provided Teen Tech Team with the initial resources and contacts on the Illinois side to get started. GSLIS students worked with local staff and teen participants through projects in a service learning course. The initial Teen Tech curriculum was modeled on the work of Prairienet, a community free-net started in 1993 in Champaign, Illinois (Pea, 1995). Prairienet later became a unit within the university (Prairienet Community Network, 2012). Prairienet's community technology center programming included a refurbished computer to community members who had attended a training class. Computers refurbished by volunteers and students as part of service learning courses, have routinely been provided to community organizations in East St. Louis and other locations (GSLIS, 2010). This work continues through the Center for Digital Inclusion, which "strives to foster inclusive and sustainable societies through research, teaching, and public engagement about information and communication technologies" (CDI, 2012).

Based on this history, the YCI project looked to Teen Tech as a natural partner in the metro East St. Louis area. Initially Teen Tech operated in a space provided by a local church. Teens worked with graduate students and local volunteer staff to learn computer refurbishing and troubleshooting skills. But due to miscommunication regarding the use of the space and whether there would be rental fees paid to the church for that use, their initial partner location withdrew support for the space. After this setback, the all-volunteer program struggled to find a stable location, with the occasional assistance from university staff. They moved to a second location that also did not last, and then to the Washington Park library, a small facility that also houses a food pantry. Both of these interim spaces were negotiated primarily by university staff. This situation illustrates the disconnect among community partners coming from different backgrounds and experiences.

The YCI Project Model

The YCI project identified five pilot sites in which to work to engage youth in building technology skills. We envisioned a model where extended community engagement with youth and youth leaders at these sites would replace recruiting efforts that needed to be repeated with each new program. Our work at partner sites began in January 2008, and each semester was to involve intensive work with a new focal site. Based on site needs and the abundance of available partners, we adjusted to include ongoing work with all five focal sites, and connections with additional sites that were producing other youth programming.

A major portion of the curriculum was also adapted based on partner site needs. Our grant originally proposed a series of teaching "modules" adapted from the computer refurbishing efforts of Prairienet and a community engagement course offered by GSLIS. These lesson plans could be distributed to a community organization to improve students' technology skills and at the same time help them learn to build a community technology center, computer lab, network, or other technology project. As a research assistant, a large part of my (first author, Chris Ritzo) early work on the YCI project was to adapt content from the Introduction to Networked Systems course into lesson plans in *Inquiry Unit* format. Activities in these units followed a constructivist approach to teaching and attempted to use the philosophy of American pragmatism as articulated by progressive education pioneers such as Rousseau, Pestalozzi, John Dewey, Jane Addams, and Ella Flagg Young (Ritzo, Nam, & Bruce, 2009).

The units contained small chunks of content in various subject areas, meant to allow staff at partner sites to select content appropriate to their site. Taken together, the collection of inquiry units would allow staff and participants to construct a Community Technology Center that would meet the organization's technical needs. Content categories included Computer Basics, Planning and Organizing, Computer Security, Hardware, Software and Operating Systems, and Networking.

But as we began working with partner organizations, it quickly became clear that our curriculum plans and our approach to collaboration had to be shaped according to the needs of each community partner. We brought expertise in the technologies required for developing different curriculum modules and knowledge and experience with specific community sites, but we needed a fresh perspective. Based on our reflections on past Teen Tech/ university partnerships and inspired by the youth at Teen Tech in East St. Louis, we adapted our curriculum to focus more on the activity or outcomes made possible by technology, for example, oral history or community journalism, instead of simply on learning the specific technologies themselves. The content of new inquiry units shifted to focus on using technology to interpret, analyze, challenge, and communicate information. We emphasized using technology as a means to some end, rather than just teaching basic computer hardware and software skills.

The curriculum Prairienet used in many community technology centers in the 1990s and early 2000s was typical of efforts at that time to close the digital divide, focusing primarily on increasing access to computers and the Internet (see Chapter 14). Additionally, the aforementioned focus on basic job skills development, while valuable, did not challenge participants to question and address the root causes of the socioeconomic injustice affecting their community (Ginwright, Noguera, & Cammarota, 2006; Ledwith, 2005; Shor, 1992). This leads to the understandable dismissal of formal education and outreach projects as described by Llewellyn (1998) in *The Teenage Liberation Handbook: How to Quit School and Get a Real Life and Education*. YCI staff hoped to pursue a more integrated approach to skills development, by integrating technology use into activities such as Information Spaces in the Community, Community Oral History, Protest Songs and Wikis, and Community Journalism, while encouraging investigation, research, analysis, and interpretation of local surroundings and addressing issues affecting those communities.

New Partnerships, New Curriculum

When our project began, Teen Tech was identified as a potential community partner based on its past interactions with staff members of Prairienet, ESLARP, and GSLIS service learning classes. It was proposed that YCI could build on the past partnership with Computer Village and help bring a new energy and focus to Teen Tech in East St. Louis. Our partnership started during our summer 2008 YCI Youth Forum, when a group of teens, parents, and staff from Teen Tech Team were invited to Urbana for the two-day workshop. Participants from various partner sites participated in inquiry-based activities where they explored different "information spaces" on campus and used video, GPS, and other technologies to create media that reflected their perceptions and experiences. While planning this event we decided to prepare activities that could be accomplished in a short amount of time, leaving the previously mentioned computer hardware and software units for longer-term work at partner sites. A content review of the reflections of graduate students who planned and executed the 2008 Youth Forum indicated that staff and youth valued the flexible and creative use of technologies in the Information Spaces activity and the supportive environment it created for youth to prepare and share a presentation. Additionally, our reflections identified these values as central to the success of the forum:

- Youth-centered/driven activities
- Clear instructions, presentations, and explanation of activities by staff
- Flexibility for youth to interpret/reinterpret the activity and end result

At the end of the forum, all teens were asked about how they could carry what they did back to their home communities. What would they make videos about when they returned home? One young woman from East St. Louis said she would address violence in her community. What this teenager envisioned for her community and expressed to us marked a critical point in the YCI project. It was a pivotal moment when we began to shift our programming focus from simple skills-based training to goal-based activities in which participants learned and used technology for an expressed purpose. Technology skills were learned, but within a broader context and to achieve a specific outcome. Her subject choice in this case strongly suggested teens' need to voice their concerns about core issues affecting them and their communities.

Teen Tech's participation in the 2008 Youth Forum was a beginning point for our partnership. YCI staff began discussing how we could partner with Teen Tech to bring these ideas to their program. We agreed that a graduate student from YCI would begin working with teens and staff at Teen Tech, visiting East St. Louis approximately every two weeks and holding regular phone or Skype calls. The role for this graduate student would be to bring curriculum ideas, model teaching inquiry-based activities with the teens during periodic visits, and provide some technology support.

I was selected as the graduate student from YCI for this role and began visiting East St. Louis in September 2008. The immediate goal was to build on the success of the YCI Summer Forum, modeling the inquiry process with Teen Tech teens and staff. Using my background as an educator, I planned activities from a constructivist perspective, allowing participants to drive learning according to their own interests. We explored Cahokia Mounds State Historic Site using GPS units and talked about the difference between the name of the site and the community of Cahokia. This led to a discussion of the names of different neighborhoods in the area, why they were called by the names they knew, and what other names did their community have for them? I served as a facilitator to their exploration and we used technology as a means to that end and to express what they learned during the process. We brainstormed content for videos that would explore community histories and the oral histories of the people they knew, and social issues such as the root causes of violence in the community. We practiced interviewing and camera techniques and learned to do research and to use software and hardware as a part of the process of inquiry.

This was a big shift in the way that this group had worked in the past. Putting the focus on teens' critical thinking and research skills and providing opportunities for their exploration, discussion, group problem solving, and peer-mentored learning was somewhat challenging, as the teens were not used to doing this type of work in either this setting or at school. Teen Tech teens began researching social issues in their community, such as the causes and possible solutions to violence, but also had fun in the process with lighter topics such as community history. While I was hopeful that this process-driven inquiry learning would allow teens to engage with other people and groups in their community, the activities were still balanced by the perspective of staff who continued to see the program as a platform for teaching technology-centered job skills.

Navigating a New Path Toward Local Autonomy

YCI began with the idea of partnering with existing organizations serving teens as a way to leverage university resources in a sustainable way: infuse existing programs, not build new ones. While the goal was to engage youth with inquiry-based activities, getting to that point with Teen Tech took some time and required us to reevaluate our approach. When I began visiting East St. Louis in fall 2008, waning teen participation and infrastructure issues with their home at the Landsdowne Center in the Washington Park neighborhood kept us from doing sustained activities from week to week. It quickly became clear that Teen Tech needed a new start at a new location to build the program and teen participation. In the first few weeks of our partnership, Mr. Adams and Mr. Holt met with GSLIS Professor Martin Wolske and myself to talk about the YCI-Teen Tech partnership, negotiating roles and expectations.

From these meetings I gained a sense of the history of the past Prairienet/Teen Tech/Computer Village partnership, which informed my opinion that the initial partnership likely relied too heavily on the university partner for decision making and support, making the work of local volunteers more difficult when problems arose. For example, the Landsdowne Center was a facility operated by another social service organization, and Teen Tech's operation there had been partially negotiated by university staff. As such, Mr. Adams and other local volunteers had little leverage when dealing with infrastructure issues. A robbery had forced tightened security measures, and Mr. Adams was not given a key to the new security gates. The phone service outside the building had been stripped for its copper, effectively removing Internet access from the building. Repeated attempts to contact building staff to get the service restored were unsuccessful. Calls from Teen Tech staff were not returned. But when university staff leveraged a growing connection with the organization, Internet access was restored and the other issues began to be addressed. Despite being a community member with a key to the building, and running an established program for teens, Mr. Adams's requests were slipping through the cracks. That this changed at the request of university staff speaks to the continuing inequity between grassroots community organizations and established social service and educational institutions when it comes to social standing, social capital, and perceived authority.

I brought these concerns to the YCI group, and we made the decision to stick with Teen Tech Team despite the setbacks. The commitment became both to model new curriculum ideas with Teen Tech and to encourage the group to operate more autonomously.

An example of this focus on local capacity building was the process of choosing a new location for Teen Tech. Conditions at the Washington Park library had become insecure due to the break-in, and infrastructure issues such as the inability to contact building support, unstable Internet access, and a sewage backup all began to complicate using the facility for any productive work. Professor Wolske and I spent several initial visits with Mr. Adams and Mr. Holt from Computer Village in collectively identifying what we hoped would be a sustainable long-term facility for Teen Tech. At first, we were more active in the search for a new location (as past university staff had been), seeking connections on behalf of Teen Tech with other community organizations. Mr. Adams was included in all decisions, meetings, and negotiations, but none of the locations we initially considered came through. In the end, Mr. Adams found a pastor, Mr. Keith Mosby of Gethsemane Church, who was interested in allowing access and use of two rooms in their facility. Mr. Adams negotiated the new location himself. He had complete access with keys and alarm codes, and Pastor Mosby provided carpentry and other construction help to set up the new location for computer workstations. Additionally, Martin Wolske and I introduced Mike Adams to another community organization, Community Concepts/The Village Theater, in neighboring Centreville, Illinois. Community Concepts held workshops for youth in performance, audio and video editing, and produced a monthly variety performance night that was re-broadcast on local cable access. One of the young adults working at Community Concepts, and a former Teen Tech participant, began assisting Mr. Adams each Saturday, working with the teens in the program. From our perspective this had huge implications for local empowerment, given Teen Tech's beginnings.

Encouraging Mr. Adams's capacity to keep the Teen Tech program going and make more autonomous decisions ended up being a very positive outcome of YCI's partnership. Inquiry activities with Teen Tech began to blossom after they moved to the new location, and we continued to provide support but took care to allow Mr. Adams to make the decisions that affected the group's future. This negotiation of where the roles of YCI and Teen Tech begin and end, where they are connected, and how our shared goals are mediated is just as important as, if not more important than, the programming choices and interactions with teens. They returned to Urbana in summer 2009 for the second YCI Forum, eager to share their experiences and their work.

Analysis and Lessons Learned

YCI's core mission was to bring together resources and groups in local communities with the resources of the university to build more sustainable partnerships with existing teen-focused groups. We also wanted to bring new curriculum ideas to groups that were providing extracurricular or after-school programming. I visited East St. Louis approximately two Saturdays a month from September 2008 to May 2009, working with Mr. Adams to build new ideas, excitement and participation into the Teen Tech program, to model the teaching of inquiry-based activities with the teens during periodic visits, and to provide some technology support.

The YCI project challenged us to broaden accepted modes of learning, confront our assumptions about other people and other communities, form and communicate our own individual and community identities, and learn how to tell the stories of how we accomplish all this. At the focal site in East St. Louis, a group of teens used to meet every Saturday to work on computers, to learn about hardware and software and to sell them at a low cost. Teen Tech Team is now taking their activities in a new direction, exploring the creation of self-identity and community identity using biography, interviewing, and video production. This change in focus wasn't easy to accomplish. In addition to the infrastructure issues previously discussed, the idea of inquiry-based or process-focused learning was a bit foreign to the teens at first. Experiences like attending the annual Youth Forum helped teens contextualize the inquiry learning process, but many students have not had these experiences in the classroom.

The initial computer refurbishing curriculum used by Teen Tech had a practical, skills-based focus: learn to rebuild a computer and make a profit on the end result. The entrepreneurial, job skills focus was important, but as teens went through the program, there was a built-in limit on the learning they could accomplish. The process of going through an inquiry-based activity also leads to marketable job skills such as the ability to research, synthesize, and interpret information and to apply the results to decisions. But the more indirect nature of the inquiry process can make it seem oppositional to a more apparent, direct job skills training curriculum. As an example, while facilitating one session where teens were brainstorming possible people to interview for a video project, I recall Teen Tech staff providing a summary at the end connecting the discussion to how teens could use these skills to get jobs. As a graduate student who was really a guest at Teen Tech, I recognized that this was not my program to run, but that Teen Tech had its own end results in mind and it wasn't my place to try to change that. The teens completing inquiry-based activities were certainly learning valuable skills that would be useful in the workforce, but this was not the direct purpose of the activity. Rather, the focus was on teaching teens to think critically about the world around them: to investigate, create, discuss, and reflect; to move beyond basic skill building to a more goal-oriented, problem-solving mode of learning.

Shifting curriculum from skills-based training to more process-focused work has had its critics, particularly when students of color are misunderstood by white teachers (Delpit, 1995). But the prevailing sentiment among the graduate students on this project was that inquiry-based learning was initially foreign to many of the teens we worked with, regardless of cultural background. It was apparent that they were used to specific, task-based instruction in the classroom and in extracurricular programs. In our first few activities, teens were slow to contribute to group discussions, to make guesses in answer to questions, or to take a leadership role themselves in the activities. Part of their hesitance was surely getting used to a new, unfamiliar face. But slowly they began to see the adults from YCI and Teen Tech as facilitators in *their* learning and recognized the need to lead and direct their own learning in the inquiry process. One of the students who attended both YCI Forums (2008, 2009) began taking the lead in finding a way for all the students and leaders to communicate and share ideas beyond their weekly meetings. He suggested using a MySpace or Bebo page to connect students and offered to lead the effort among the group to decide, plan, and implement something. The need was clear: Although teens came to the same place each week, they were not in contact at all during the week.

What We Learned from Working with Teen Tech

Our experiences with the East St. Louis site have led to some significant findings. Being a community at some distance from Urbana-Champaign (a drive of three hours), we needed more active coordination and communication with Teen Tech and had to adjust our communication preferences (phone/email; in-person/virtual) to match the preferences of our community partner. Phone calls were more effective than email. Additionally, we focused on the need to clearly define YCI's level of involvement with a partnering program. As a result, we developed a method for initial assessment of partner programs when we were exploring future partnerships. A partner program may be functioning at various levels of autonomy themselves, and therefore would need the ability to interact with a university partner at different levels of commitment.

YCI's work in East St. Louis, in part, helped us define our model of "focal sites" with more clarity. We defined three categories of community partnerships, describing three levels of increasing connection, commitment, and collaboration with our partner organizations: *Network sites, Partner sites,* and *YCI sites* (see Chapter 12 for details).

Our work with Teen Tech may have begun at the Network or Partner site level, but it progressed in commitment to become a YCI site. In contrast to Paseo Boricua, where our graduate students were able to connect with an existing, sustainable program connected to a community charter school, the Teen Tech program in East St. Louis had developed from past partnerships with Prairienet leadership, and was initially more dependent on outside university assistance. Our difficulties getting started with Teen Tech as a Partner site may be partially attributable to this dependence. We're hopeful that the work YCI has done with Teen Tech over two years will help it become a sustainable program in its own right.

Challenges and Transformations

What does our community partner bring to the table? Is it solely the need for resources or access to technology? If the organization is to be sustainable, locally managed, and focused on its own needs, then the answer to these questions must be a resounding no. Communities in need have their own hopes, dreams, and goals, to which we can only be outside partners. We hope that our project emphasized that technology is only a means to achieving the goals and desired outcomes of nonprofits and community organizations. Simply closing a divide of access is not nearly enough. YCI's goal was to use technologies with a focus on how people can use them to inform, educate, create, and ultimately effect changes in their surroundings and situations.

The graduate assistants and staff involved within these communities faced challenges as well. We were compelled to engage in self-reflection and identity transformations as a part of the process. As researchers using participatory methodologies, we were both forming a new community of interest around the YCI project and finding where we fit personally into the field. In our work with partner communities, we were confronted with many issues and challenges: learning cross-cultural communication styles; acknowledging and addressing our positions within social and historical power relationships; the prevailing orthodoxy of educational practices in both schools and informal settings; the learned helplessness of disenfranchised communities; and the often incongruent goals of academic institutions and the communities in which we work. In many ways, the tensions in the history of progressive education mirror the issues we're experiencing in these community-based, informal education contexts.

Conclusion

Our work with Teen Tech in East St. Louis deeply informed our perspectives as community-based researchers. We were fortunate to be working on a project that was flexible enough to change focus when we found our community partner at a disadvantage. In effect, past partnerships that created Teen Tech contributed to the group's dependence on university staff, programming, and resources to exist. By shifting focus, we were able to mentor local decision-making and autonomy, and eventually return to our original goal to collaborate on new, inquiry-based programming. If we had not been flexible, we would not have learned this important lesson: that our ideas about what a community partner needs are less important than what they actually need. The amount of congruence between actual community needs and outside partner perceptions of those needs may be an indicator of the success of long-term university/community partnerships. We also endeavored not to be part of the problem. Our grant resources did provide an infusion to Teen Tech, bringing hardware, software, and training. To approach our work with community partners solely from a technology implementation perspective would have been unethical and could have led to unintended negative consequences. YCI could have easily repeated the pattern of previous university partners: negotiate a new location, donate resources for a new set of computers, and teach a new batch of teens to refurbish computers. Instead, we took the time to talk about our roles in the partnership, helping but not overstepping, and in doing so encouraged a more sustainable local organization.

Working with youth in underserved and underrepresented communities has necessarily prompted us to think about the implications and effects of historical oppression, including those based on race, ethnicity, class, and gender. Youth are attuned to the discrimination they may face and will hopefully find new and innovative ways to address these issues. Discrimination and bias are often present in the mainstream media that influence the communities in which they live. Common to all our sites is the youth's exploration of their personal identities, and of the identity and history of their communities through the use of digital tools. By providing youth with opportunities to produce their own media, youth are defining their own identities. How youth define themselves and their communities, as well as the processes they engage in while doing so, are transformational educational processes. These transformations are also of great interest to us as community-based researchers because they further our understanding of the tools and the processes involved in effective community-based education.

8. The Learning Never Stops: Creating a Curriculum That Resonates Beyond the Classoom

Jeff Bennett
Robin Fisher

Exploring GPS/GIS Technologies

Course Information: 1 year course, 2 periods, open to grades 11, 12

Prerequisite: 3.0 GPA

Description: This course will be centered on exploratory/project-based activities. These projects will be based on student-centered learning in the exciting world of GPS/GIS technology. The students will use GPS/GIS technology in their community and Cass County to map points of interest. Students will be networking through technology with students in other parts of Illinois and with experts in the field of GPS/GIS technology.
—from Course Offerings, Virginia High School, Virginia, Illinois

At Virginia High School, a new course concentrating on geographic information systems (GIS) and Global Positioning System (GPS) technologies was implemented during the 2009–2010 school year. Together, Robin Fisher, the agriculture teacher, and Jeff Bennett, the social studies teacher, "team teach" this interdisciplinary class, combining core agricultural science, technology, and math learning with a local history curriculum. Originally inspired by a GPS/GIS educational seminar Robin had attended in Chicago, a partnership with the Youth Community Informatics (YCI) group created the opportunity for an expanded vision of what she had initially conceived of as a supplemental science unit. Eight students—all boys—signed up for this untested experiment in inquiry-based, hands-on learning. Throughout this chapter, Robin and Jeff share what they experienced during the program's inaugural year.

VHS administrators had first learned about YCI's work through their participation in previous Dialogues in Methods of Education (DIME) meetings, hosted at the university. In fact, Principal Christine Brinkley and Superintendent Lynn Carter had been the ones to suggest that their school solicit professor Bertram (Chip) Bruce's involvement after Robin initially approached them about her interest in adding a GIS component to her curriculum.

The collaboration between YCI and VHS began in the spring of 2009, when several YCI team members traveled to Virginia to conduct two separate GPS workshops. The first introduced a group of Cass County educators and 4-H organizers to some of the community mapping activities that YCI had developed for other projects. For the second workshop, students from Virginia and neighboring Beardstown participated, along with community members of all ages, in a hands-on mapping activity. In the morning, workshop participants received an instructional overview of how to shoot video and use GPS receivers. Later, they split into several small groups, with each group deciding for itself a specific inquiry topic. They then headed out into the field to investigate their topics, recording their findings using both GPS and Flip video cameras. Before the end of the day, the groups had created videos and uploaded them to YouTube, created maps of their waypoints using Google Maps, and shared their discoveries with other workshop participants. The activity was designed to be a light-hearted, engaging introduction to the technology. Ideas raised in the workshops formed the foundation that Jeff and Robin used to further develop their new curriculum.

By October 2009, it was VHS's turn to return the favor by hosting the next DIME meeting. On a Saturday morning, four of the students from the newly launched GPS class shared what they were learning with the visiting DIME group. The historic sites around Cass County had not been mapped since the 1970s and students were busy locating and photographing the current condition of prior recorded sites, as well as identifying sites no longer standing and sites previously missed. Virginia students Nathan Ring, Jeff Wilhite, Jacob Jokisch, and Henry Christman then led DIME participants in a geocache activity that they had designed. In the discussion afterwards, Nathan Ring described in detail how the students were learning GPS, video production, science, math, history, and more. To those in attendance, his excitement was infectious. As Chip recalls, "Nathan became so absorbed in describing these activities that his words seemed to be rushing to keep up. At a certain point he had to pause, and then exclaimed, 'The learning never stops!' This is not the kind of account one often hears from high school students."

You're Always Welcome

A convenient, if loose, statistic seems to have become a shorthand definition for the City of Virginia: "It has a population of maybe 1,800 people" (City of Vriginia, n.d.). Local residents and others far afield rely on this modest figure to drive home what strangers should expect of the west central Illinois locale. But beyond its status as a "city" of negligible numbers, Virginia is also a remote farming community facing tough decisions about the future. The town's square, once the commercial center, has for the most part been left behind by box store progress. A strip of vacant buildings still contains the vestiges of more prosperous times; peek through now-dark storefront windows and you might catch a glimpse of another era—abandoned merchandise hangs hopefully on inaccessible racks.

Within the town are those determined to breathe new life into the local economy. On Virginia's website, city council members boldly announce to anyone paying attention that they're "open minded to all progress." "Come on over," says Mayor Steve Sudbrink, "you're always welcome." Community advocates like businesswoman Susan Young are striving to make this vision a reality. Young now owns three buildings on the square. Her Dr. Ugs Drugstore Café attracts all ages with free wi-fi and a creative menu—a giant step up from the standard dining-out options of subs versus pizza. Almost overnight, Dr. Ugs has become Virginia's local hotspot (indeed, its Facebook page boasts some 300 fans). But apart from creating a hearth around which the community can comfortably gather, Young and others have formed a grassroots group called Volunteer Virginia. This collective of "local volunteers and civic leaders working together on volunteer-oriented projects to improve the quality of life in Virginia" (Volunteer Virginia, n.d.) is actively engaged in assessing Virginia's possibilities. Involving the town's youth is a significant part of their plans for the future.

Ask: How Can We Make Formal Education More Relevant?

Just what, exactly, does this local situation mean for Virginia High School, "home of the Redbirds," which in 2009 recorded an average class size of only 10.9 students? Like many public schools, for years VHS has had to contend with improving its scores according to No Child Left Behind metrics. Cass County educators face the challenge of addressing bureaucratic expectations on a limited budget, while being true to a more authentic goal of making students' education relevant to their lived realities.

Can an education that concentrates on the three Rs prepare these sons and daughters of farmers—some of whom might want to revitalize their remote little community, some of whom might be prepared for flight—for the world beyond school walls? What does the "back to basics" approach teach them about agricultural practices or Virginia's future needs? And what do they teach this homogeneous, geographically isolated assembly of young people—99% of whom are white, 33% of whom are identified as low income—about engaging with the world beyond their doorstep? The challenge facing Virginia educators echoes the question posed by education researchers like Mark K. Smith, who asks, "Can we educate for community without being in community?" (Smith, 2001b).

Investigate: Motivations for Curriculum Development

Initiating this new course at VHS was not a simple undertaking. It involved numerous grant proposals, extensive planning, coordination with local and far-off collaborators, travel, and primarily a great deal of time and commitment. What was it that motivated these already well-occupied educators to take on such a novel, potentially risky, project?

Robin. With the way the world is going today, students need to have an opportunity to learn these new technologies. GPS is widely used in our area. It's used in agriculture—it's now an important part of farming. It's used to block out roads, the road signs are mapped with it, fire hydrants, 911 addresses, students have it on their phones—it's used everywhere. As the agriculture teacher here, I see a lot of value in this for students with an ag background, because they're going to go back to the farm and learn to use GPS in the tractors and in the field. A student here, Nathan Ring, is doing a summer internship with the Cass County Highway Department [using GPS to map and mark the condition of road signs in the area, many of which need to be updated]. Meanwhile his dad is using it in the field. A lot of these students, if they can learn it here, they can help their parents to learn about and update their technology. They can bring that technology to the older generation and help them to incorporate it and improve their quality of life. The sooner these kids can be introduced to it, the more they can learn about it, and maybe even be able to go into a profession using it.

Jeff. We know that these kids are going to go into fields that use these technologies. Kyle Nolan was a student in the class first semester; he now works for Cass Communications. He is using some of the technology in his job, and that's why he's not in the class the second semester. They basically gave him the opportunity to come work longer during the school day, and so we figured that was more hands-on training in a real-world application. I think the class really supported his ability and sparked this opportunity for him.

Kyle is very much a tech nut. He is a technology guru—one of those kids that's a problem solver. He can figure out a lot of things with technology, and Cass Communications is a place he had wanted to work in even before taking the class. But because of the things he was learning in the class, he became very useful to them. One of the things Cass Communications is doing is they're trying to deliver Internet access throughout the county. In the rural areas, they're broadcasting the signal through towers [known as rural high-speed wireless] so that people who live in the rural areas or farmland can get access to high-speed Internet instead of having to use the phone line. They're using GPS to map out where their signals are going to and where they're not going to, and Kyle is now a big part of that project.

Nathan has really seen it more from the farm perspective. He was so excited last fall when his dad and grandpa purchased their first GPS unit for their combine. They didn't get to use it last year because they purchased it at the end of the season, but since then they've bought another one for another tractor. That motivated him to start talking to the county engineer for Cass County Highway Department, and kind of drifting into that field through his summer internship this year.

Create: Growing a Curriculum

A key aspect of the GPS course is that the situation is always changing. The scope is dynamic, challenges regularly arise that require on-the-spot decisions and creative solutions, and they and the students are constantly evaluating the learning potential of the program as they work out what is effective and what isn't, and where they should go next. Sometimes the students themselves present suggestions for what should be covered, what might work, and what needs to be resolved. The constantly adapting, live-in-the-moment philosophy brings to mind John Dewey: "We always live at the time we live and not at some other time, and only by extracting at each present time the full meaning of each present experience are we prepared for doing the same in the future" (Dewey, 1938/1998, p. 51).

Together, teachers and students "engage in joint activities and discussions, help each other, and share information," and "build relationships that enable them to learn from each other." They are, in short, a group of people "who share a concern or a passion for something they do and learn how to do it better as they interact regularly" (Wenger, 2006). Essentially, they created their own community of practice.

Robin. We're kind of growing as we go through this. There was no existing Ag-Technology class, there was no GPS class; it's basically been created as a whole new course. Now we're into the second semester, and kids seem pretty excited about it. They have quite a few thoughts about whether they want to be in it next year and what they want to do.

Jeff. One of the things we had our students develop here just a few weeks ago was a new geocache. One day when it's nice this spring, we're going to split my American History class into groups, and we're going to have the kids who are in the GIS class lead them in an activity. We'll give those AH kids a geographic location, and they'll have to take the GPS unit and use the coordinates we provide to find the location, and then there are a series of questions about that location that they have to answer. So they have to use observation skills, critical thinking skills, problem-solving skills to figure out the answers to some of the questions.

Basically, we want to do that so that some of the younger kids see some of the fun activities that can be done with the GPS, so that next year we can feed them into the GPS course—make them aware of it. That was one of the problems this year, when we introduced this new course: some students were thinking, "Well, I don't know if I really want to take a new course," and so we had just eight boys that started out in the course. Right now we have six, we lost two to work opportunities. But those kids all liked the course and were pretty excited about it.

We had two boys who were seniors this year, so obviously they won't be back with us next year. But I think the four we have remaining are definitely going to take the course next year, so we'll develop a Year 2, which will then be unique. Because of our limited resources, we're going to be teaching Year 1 and Year 2 courses at the same time in the same room. We're going to rely on those second-year students to help us with the first-year students—to teach them some of the basics. And then they'll both have separate projects as well.

Robin. Just last week we were out doing one of our geocaches and the students came up with the idea of playing GPS hide and seek. We haven't quite figured out how to implement it but it was kind of a cool idea that the kids came up with.

Jeff. What they wanted to do was to use their cell phones and text their coordinates to someone else, and then have them try to come find them. The only reason we haven't been able to do that is that we have one or two—believe it or not—that don't have cell phones. I think we'll probably pair them up with someone who does have a cell phone.

Jeff. The main challenge has been the weather. Last fall was a terrible fall as far as the rain. That rain really hurt us as far as doing the oral history project. So finally, when the weather dried up and was nice, it was November—but November is very windy. We had the kids in front of a site recording video, explaining the history of the site, meanwhile the wind is just blowing all over the place. In the end, we took the videos of them standing in front of the sites, and then we had the students narrate over the video. So we're very flexible, and sometimes we have to change directions very quickly, but the kids seem to like that and they realize that's the way it works.

Robin. When we can't get outside, we're working with a series of GIS/GPS textbooks. The students are using some ESRI software, which involves teaching them how to work with GIS data on the computers. They're entering data, they're learning to read the maps, and learning about the program's interface and so on. This will continue into Year 2, where by the end, they'll hopefully be able to create their own maps from scratch. They'll have to accurately enter in the data and will be able to create original maps of our projects, rather than relying on [tools like] Google. That is a goal for next year.

Jeff. During the winter, one project the kids worked on was to research a career that uses GPS, and then they had to make a presentation. But one of the things that hopefully will come out of the 2010 Census is some really good information that can be used for mapping, that kids can learn how to use. They will get a lot of information about their community, clear down to block by block. Using that data will be a very real-world application of these skills that they are developing.

Discuss: Educating for Community

As we delve more deeply into this concept of "community," we must necessarily consider: To which community, exactly, do our youth belong? Whom do we (or should we) include in this community, and what are its boundaries? Should the boundaries be defined, as is often the case in today's schools, by school walls (i.e., "the Virginia High School community")? Is it enough to place these students within the local geographic context of Virginia itself? Or does this age of so-called global connectivity require that we entirely rethink our vision of community?

In the context of this chapter, it is worth noting that the origins of modern sociological definitions of community have been attributed to the work of Charles Galpin, who in the early 1900s launched the field of rural sociology through his work mapping the identifying characteristics of America's agricultural territories (Smith, 2001b, citing Harper & Dunham, 1959). Today, we might most usefully think about community in terms of how we identify ourselves, both collectively and individually. Social anthropologist Anthony P. Cohen (1985) argues that the most generalizable way to consider what we mean when we talk about community is to think in terms of a "community of meaning." We create communities through a symbolic shared identity of some kind. This identity is determined by a typifying characteristic that members of a community think they have in common with one another. In particular, however, this uniting feature must be something that others outside the group don't share—it is our collective otherness that draws us together as a "community" as much as our sameness. In effect, we define our community membership by what differentiates us from those who do not belong to it. But as Smith points out, "This leads us to the question of boundary—what marks the beginning and end of a community? . . . not all boundaries are so obvious: 'They may be thought of, rather, as existing in the minds of the beholders'" (Cohen, 1985, p. 12). As such they may be seen in very different ways, not only by people on either side, but also by people on the same side" (Smith, 2001b).

Jeff. Our goals are career-related and community-related for these kids. Both are important. We did an activity the first semester where our students picked historical locations in Virginia, and they marked them and recorded them on a map, and then they did a video oral history of that location and posted them on Google Maps. So the kids are starting to learn about the history of their community, and what the community used to have on the square. Right now the square is dying out. There is a movement in town to revitalize the square and to bring some businesses back. [In class we're exploring questions like] what kinds of activities and businesses were there, and what can we bring back to the community? So our students are starting to look at it from that aspect.

We're also about to start a cemetery project (see Chapter 4). Students are going to be learning about mapping the cemetery, with the idea of maintaining cemetery records. Cass County has 133 cemeteries, and a lot of them are not well taken care of. Some of them probably are in the middle of a cornfield. So we're going to try to show the students different cemeteries that are in tree lines—sites that you can't hardly see. We'll start by mapping a small cemetery and researching people that are buried there, with the idea that not only do the kids learn their own history but they also will start to connect with the idea that we need to take care of our local cemeteries because that is a strong part of our local history and our past.

One of my former students, his dad sits on the board that manages the cemetery, so when I asked him for permission to map the cemetery he was all excited about it. He mentioned our plans to the lady who does a lot of the mapping and maintenance of the cemetery, she was very excited about it and brought me old maps and new maps. She said to me, "Anything we can do to help you with this, just give us a call and we'd be glad to." So I think the local community support has been very good.

Community activities do tie in with our class, but it's something we'll be working on more in the future. Susan Young, who owns Dr. Ugs in town, she's very much wanting to revitalize the square. She has started this project, Volunteer Virginia, and has brought in students—Kyle is one who went to the meetings. Volunteer Virginia has committees of businesspeople, retired people—all age groups—and they are looking at working with the school. They came to a school board meeting, and they want to know, for example, how can the school improve its web page to draw people to come to school here? How can we draw people to live in this community? How can we grow this community? So I see us working with that group in the future.

One of the things Kyle is currently working on is trying to organize a career fair, where people will sit down and talk to kids about what kind of careers are available here in the county, to keep our students here in this area. How do we grow the City of Virginia? I think that ties in to some of the things that we're doing. It wasn't a direct result of this class, but it basically happened at the same time, this idea of community involvement with the school, and I do see us working together in the future.

The kids that we have are very interested in working more with the university, and one of the things we're really looking at for next year is how to maintain and grow the relationship we have with the U of I. Each student now has their laptop through the One to One program, and next year we're hoping to maybe set up a monthly video conference with grad students or professors, to allow the kids access to experts in the field.

I know that the two times that our students have had the opportunity—at the DIME meeting last October and at the iConference this spring—to interact with the U of I grad students and professors, that really made a big change in the kids, confidence-wise. What's really been neat is that two of the students are students with special needs. I've seen their confidence really grow this year, and I think a large part of that is through this contact with professors and grad students at the U of I. What's so neat is that the grad students are from countries all over the world. And so the kids, when we brought them over that day, they got a big kick out of meeting people like YCI Graduate Assistant Chaebong Nam [and other people from different backgrounds]. Basically it's an ongoing project and I just see it being that way for a long time.

Reflect: Educating in Community

The Virginia High School project differs from other partnerships described in the book by its collaboration with a "formal" education program. The GPS class concept germinated in the minds of Virginia educators as a means of providing their students with some important, current, technical skills. Through the process of developing the project, being receptive to possibilities, and being flexible to overcoming challenges, they opened the door for new community relationships.

In a number of respects, the GPS class seems to be building on benefits that we traditionally associate with "informal" (i.e., extracurricular) learning. The school's willingness to allow students to leave school walls during school hours to participate in apprenticeship-style opportunities is fairly unusual within our public school systems. It may be surprising to some that VHS educators recognize the advantages that come from integrating youth within professional communities of practice. It is perhaps no small point that thus far these opportunities have been initiated by the students themselves.

In Jeff's observation that the students have grown noticeably more confident through their connection with university partners, we see a telling example of what French society calls *la vie associative*—the benefits of association (Smith, 2001c). This type of social capital is, again, generally linked with non-formal learning opportunities, such as involvement in volunteer organizations that rely on highly participatory and collaborative democratic principles.

As we have seen, there is evidence of local support in Virginia for the work taking place in Jeff and Robin's class, as well as a general interest in the role that the school can play in buttressing community goals. There is a tangible sense that the community itself realizes that their collective future will depend on whether these kids stay or go—or if they go, what connections they maintain that may serve to bridge Virginia with a larger network of support and opportunity.

Extrapolating from Cohen's definition of a community of meaning, we might say that there are two sides to a community—a shared sense of identity, and a boundary that leads to the formation of an *Us* versus a *Them*. How, then, do we foster the warm, fuzzy components of community while suppressing the potential for exclusion or rejection of others? YCI attempts to resolve this problem through community inquiry. According to Bishop, Bruce, and Jeong

(2009), "[a] community-based orientation emphasizes support for collaborative activity and for creating knowledge, which is connected to people's values, history, and lived experiences. Inquiry points to support for open-ended, democratic, participatory engagement. Community inquiry is thus a learning process that brings theory and action together in an experimental and critical manner" (p. 22).

To some extent, in Virginia High School's GPS class we can see this definition coming to life. Clearly the course assignments involve collaborative activity among students and their teachers, and the creation of new knowledge that is connected to the students' values, history, and lived experiences. We also see the signs of participatory engagement in the active role of the students both in shaping the course itself and in their efforts to reach out beyond the classroom to find opportunities for themselves in the larger world. We see an open-ended inquiry in Robin and Jeff's commitment to "growing" their curriculum and embracing its dynamic evolution.

But how can we successfully avoid the limitations inherent in too narrow a community identity? Bishop et al. (2009) summarize community inquiry as "inquiry conducted of, for, and by communities as living social organisms" (p. 22)—a definition that parallels the idea expressed by Smith at the beginning of this chapter. The key here is in the phrase "living social organisms." The hope is that there is room within the concept of community inquiry to expand reciprocal relationships between self-identifying communities, and in the process transform the ways in which we can relate to others. The community inquiry approach seeks to bridge what may amount to differences in place, education, opportunity, economic circumstance, perhaps even ideology, to create new opportunities and new understandings. We create social ties—new partnerships—to open up possibilities. This does not mean that motivations are always altruistic or "enlightened." Indeed, motivations may often be self-serving. Ultimately, these ties change our collective situation; they may resolve old problems even as they create new ones.

Though only in the early stages, stronger ties with groups beyond VHS walls such as Cass County's commercial sector, Volunteer Virginia, and the university may lead these students and teachers to redefine community boundaries. Both educators and administrators have an important role to play in this community of learning. They are learning, too. And they recognize that by giving their students a passport to the world beyond school walls or even Virginia borders, there is a strong potential to transform the future. But as Nathan Ring succinctly told workshop participants, "the learning never stops"—not for the students, teachers, or any of us within the

YCI network. We learn from each other and from the new experiences that we create together. Even as we hope to expand the youths' awareness of other cultures and ways of life, we learn and grow through our relationship with them.

Section 3

Learning How to Transform the World

Some chapters speak explicitly to transforming the world. This section presents three such cases. In Paseo Boricua, YCI participated in the development of the multimedia curriculum of the Barrio Arts, Culture, and Communication Academy (BACCA). BACCA is an after-school program that cultivates theater, newspaper, radio, photography, and film/TV production skills through community-based civic engagement projects. The collaboration included an anti-underage drinking campaign, "This Is the Real Me," for which BACCA youth produced and disseminated culturally relevant community health information such as radio PSAs, photos, newspaper articles, and a published book (see: http://www.blurb.com/bookstore/detail/719537). The local alternative high school, Dr. Pedro Albizu Campos Puerto Rican High School, similarly uses multimodal writing projects that place the community at the center of the curriculum. Patrick W. Berry, Alexandra Cavallaro, Elaine Vázquez, Carlos R. DeJesús, and Naomi García discuss work there in Chapter 9, "(Re)voicing Teaching, Learning, and Possibility in Paseo Boricua."

Recognizing the barrier between the university and the local community, another project sought to provide an opportunity through which African American youth could cross the imaginary border. They could thus engage with the university for the purpose of investigating resources and assets available for them locally. It was also expected that this experience could empower the youth to see themselves and their community from a positive perspective, and to challenge the commonly held deficit view of African American youth. The project title, "Engaging and Empowering Youth (E2Y)," was based on these goals. African American teens from north Champaign canvassed their neighborhoods to identify job opportunities, summer activities, teen-friendly spaces, and informal and formal networks of support for teens. They interviewed business owners, community leaders, and others, then edited the digital video footage and created an interactive community asset map using Google Maps (see http://goo.gl/KsCmH). Chaebong Nam discusses this in Chapter 10, "Youth Asset Mapping: The Empowering and Engaging Youth Project (E2Y)."

Peer Ambassadors is a group of African American and Latino/Latina youth involved in mentoring and providing community services in Champaign-Urbana. They recognized a need for literacy and library services at the Champaign County Juvenile Detention Center. This led to Extending Library Services to Empower Youth (ELSEY), a collaboration to build and maintain a library that contains culturally relevant materials and programming reflective of the experiences and interests of youth in the juvenile detention center (ELSEY, n.d.). Jeanie Austin, Joe Coyle, and Rae-

Anne Montague discuss this in Chapter 11, "Creating Collaborative Library Services to Incarcerated Youth."

Chapter 9. (Re)voicing Teaching, Learning, and Possibility in Paseo Boricua

Patrick W. Berry

Alexandra Cavallaro

with

Elaine Vázquez

Carlos R. DeJesús

Naomi García

Three hours away, in a university classroom, two of us, Cavallaro and Berry, learned about the work that was taking place in Paseo Boricua, the mile-long stretch of Division Street near Humboldt Park in Chicago where stands the Pedro Albizu Campos High School (PACHS), a school striving to make its community the curriculum. With a pedagogical approach that fuses the best of John Dewey with Paulo Freire, PACHS inspires exploration of how learning and schooling could be more relevant, more consequential, and more connected to students' lives. Such a pedagogical approach would be an accomplishment in any school, but here it is especially poignant, for PACHS serves a community too often overshadowed by narratives of poverty and crime.

Like many other writing teachers, we have been encouraging students to voice their concerns—to "write back," so to speak—to their communities and to the larger public. Through the act of composing, we want students to confront issues of narration and reflection and to consider how their own accounts reify and challenge dominant narratives. Such concerns are central to our work in Paseo Boricua because the media has repeatedly reported accounts that critique the lives and potential of those who live in this community.

In this chapter—coauthored by an English teacher (Vázquez), an administrator (DeJesús), a student (García), and two university partners (Cavallaro and Berry)—we describe a multimodal writing project that negotiates the space between hope and critique and places the community at the center of the curriculum. We focus specifically on the narratives told and the tensions that can arise when different stakeholders recount disparate visions of this community. Our hope is that this research (see also Berry, Cavallaro, Vázquez, DeJesús, & García, in press) will illuminate how narrative renderings construct our understanding of reality and how this multimodal writing project demonstrates the need for a place where hopeful and critical stories can coexist.

Narrative Openings

Narrative means giving "the reader a door to open and walk through," write David Schaafsma and Ruth Vinz (2007, p. 277). It is the creating of worlds that can resonate with or challenge other narratives, other points of entry. For many who work at PACHS, that open door was conveyed through the school's rich history and the legacy of Pedro Albizu Campos (c. 1891–1956), a man known as "el Maestro" who was "convicted to eighty years imprisonment for what he said" (Villanueva, 2009, p. 632). Campos argued, and argued well, for the independence of Puerto Rico; the power of his words, of literacy, made some afraid and gave others hope. Campos's use of narrative was tied to his rhetorical skill. Victor Villanueva (2009) described Campos's crime as "being an effective speaker" (p. 632). Indeed, a central focus of PACHS has been on helping its students develop into effective speakers, and it looks to accomplish that goal by asking them to investigate and speak about their community.

Founded in 1972, PACHS has sought to address the erasure of Puerto Rican culture in the community and to address community problems, including a 70% student dropout rate (Lucas, 1971). Too often statistics like the dropout rate can stand in for the whole story, functioning almost as a proxy that limits our attention. Problematic narratives have been a recurring issue for more than three decades, as Flores-González and her colleagues (2006) noted:

> Since the 1970s, the young residents of Humboldt Park have been criminalized by the media as gang bangers, dropouts, and teenage mothers. The local high school has been called a "Teenage Cabrini Green," after the infamous Chicago public housing project, and its students have been labeled as "predators." (pp. 175–176)

Lost in such accounts are expressions of hope and visions for change. Like other educators (e.g., Bruce, 2008a; Bruce & Bishop, 2008; Flores-González, et al., 2006), we wanted to see how a study of narrative might prove helpful, particularly to those who work on literacy initiatives and who seek to attend to the multiple spaces and ways in which students and teachers learn. Following the work of Bertram Bruce (2008a), we wanted to explore how "[i]n the midst of urban poverty and racism, Paseo Boricua has engaged in community-building through processes of participatory democracy and active transformation of its lived environment" (p. 182). Thus we began our own efforts to collect diverse narratives about PACHS and relied on video cameras—used by students and teachers as well as by us—to refocus our attention from those stories that too often dominate media accounts.

Our turn to digital media, particularly video, to collect stories arose from an interest in how modalities other than the written word might help students, teachers, and researchers reflect on their work—and ultimately on their lives. As scholars such as Glynda Hull and Mira-Lisa Katz (2006) have shown, digital storytelling can provide students with an alternative means of voicing their concerns. When such expressions are placed in online forums, they tangibly illustrate what Dewey (1902, 1934) and a diverse group of other educators (e.g., Freire & Macedo, 1987; Horton & Freire, 1990; Jenkins, 2006) have long argued: that effective learning cannot be contained within the walls of a school.

Whether learning is recognized in Café Teatro Batey Urbano, a community space for youth in Humboldt Park that encourages public expression, or in the classroom at PACHS, we want to suggest that it is most fully expressed when it is integrated—when it resists the rigid compartmentalization that often informs classroom practice. Narrative inquiry with video can demonstrate the multiplicities of experience by giving voice to that which is sometimes unspoken, which can sometimes be left out of written accounts. In what follows, we recount our experiences working on this project and consider a few stories about community and change.

From Urbana to Paseo: Some Background

Cavallaro and Berry learned about PACHS through words and stories presented in a university classroom quite a distance from life in Paseo Boricua, which made them mindful of their own subject positions. Often white, middle-class college students and teachers make their way to schools such as PACHS, treading in the footsteps of others who have come before them. Linda Flower (2008) reminds us of the danger of this following, how it "may lead into roles and relationships that we cannot or do not want to assume" (p. 101). It can lead to representations that are shaped by stories accumulated before arrival instead of understanding that is developed by attending to life in the community.

When Cavallaro and Berry picked up video cameras, they wanted to celebrate PACHS. Their colleagues had told them about the remarkable work that was happening there, and they wanted to find a way to capture it on video. Mindful of their position as outsiders, they wanted to offer participants the opportunity to partake in the production of their own stories so as to avoid the imposition of external views on the lives and experiences of participants.

Cavallaro and Berry had originally conceived of a project in which students, teachers, and administrators would capture through video their own narratives about literacy and learning; however, the idea of producing their own stories on video was daunting for some of the teachers. Although they were extremely generous with their time, many of the teachers did not to want to make their own movies, which would have involved not only choosing the moments in their lives that would exemplify literacy and learning, but also deciding how best to represent these moments on video. The task, in other words, left much room for interpretation and also required a great deal of skill.

To accommodate different attitudes toward using digital media, Cavallaro and Berry interwove a series of interviews with teachers and administrators with a series of performative texts by students from Elaine Vázquez's English class, students who were eager (with Vázquez's support) to compose their own stories. Vázquez, as will be explored later, believed deeply in the need to connect her students with the larger world and was mindful of how digital media might support those connections. During one meeting, for example, she invited an author to join students via Skype to talk about her work. Vázquez also collected video footage and helped students remediate a poetry assignment that they had created for her class, an assignment about place titled "Where I'm From," a popular assignment among teachers with various inspirations including George Ella Lyon's poem (1999) by the same name: Rather than asking students to create a documentary that celebrated their school and community, Vázquez asked them to reflect on what this place meant to them, and the results were not always celebratory. In the end, Cavallaro and Berry were left with student video essays, footage recorded in class, interviews with administrators and teachers, and a great deal of uncertainty about how to organize this narrative.

The result of these efforts is expressed in a short documentary (Berry, Cavallaro, and Vázquez, 2009) titled *(Re)voicing Teaching and Learning in Paseo Boricua*. Highlighting the voices of both teachers and students at the Pedro Albizu Campos High School, it is publicly available at http://www.pedroalbizucamposhs.org/revoicing-teaching-and-learning-in-paseo-boricua-video/.

Figure 9.1. Community Is a Place for Everyone: Images from PACHS

Replaying the Movie of Paseo Boricua

In reflecting on the documentary, we were struck by the breadth of the stories that are told within it. The movie begins with the voice of José López, executive director of the Puerto Rican Cultural Center and a former teacher, questioning what teachers really know about their students, their students' parents, and their communities—and suggesting that the answer is "not much." English teacher Elaine Vázquez stresses the power of students' language—the recognition of which, she notes, that is finding favor even in the academy. We encounter stories by Carlos DeJesús, assistant director of PACHS, who was the first Puerto Rican from Chicago to go to Yale, along with stories by other educators who continue to believe in the possibility that schooling might serve their community better. Alongside such stories are those of students struggling amid poverty and abuse, providing a reminder that this community, like all communities, is not a static entity, but one constantly remaking itself in many ways, including through its stories.

When José López spoke about this community, he did so with a fierce determination that reflected a revoicing of a past that could all too easily be erased. Similarly, in the words of Juan Rodríguez and Elaine Vázquez, as expressed in the video, we see the enduring commitment that these educators have to their students. Their stories are anchored by an awareness of history, a narration of the past, and a reenvisioning of the future. When viewed in combination with the stories told by the students, which are often stories of struggle, we become aware of the complicated ways in which histories are narrated, the challenges of telling a story of what we might call a success, and the complicated role of literate practices in this representation of community narratives.

One might reasonably ask, *If we see our histories as containing moments of success, then why not share them?* Stories of transformation are, in fact, a part of how the history of PACHS is narrated on its website (Pedro Albizu, n.d.). The site features the words "Education Breaks Chains," an idea that informs much of the work of the school. Some 30 years ago, out of a belief that the "complex realities of Puerto Rican youth" were not being effectively dealt with in the Chicago public schools, a community group organized to petition and seek changes to the curriculum of what is now Roberto Clemente High School, including the addition of Puerto Rican history to the curriculum. When the school board refused, a group of community members, including parents, activists, students, and teachers, decided to establish an independent school to address these needs (PACHS Day Program, n.d.).

PACHS can take pride in a long history of community engagement. The school collaborates with community programs such as the Vida/SIDA health initiative and boasts many successful programs of its own, including a family learning center, an after-school enrichment programs, a cultural center, and a curriculum that remains dedicated to critical pedagogy and the fostering of change in the community. Students have the opportunity to take courses in Puerto Rican history, Spanish, and Latino/Latina literature along with the more traditional subjects of math, English, and science. However, there is nothing "traditional" about even the latter courses. The curriculum (PACHS, Our School History, n.d.) places an emphasis on "developing higher order thinking skills of inquiry and analysis, primarily through problem-based learning" that enables students to "engage in critical thinking and social transformation," providing the "educational experience needed to empower students." Learning, in this environment, is never disconnected from the idea of "social ecology," which "stresses the interconnectedness of people to one another [and] their community and world" (PACHS Day Program, n.d.).

Throughout the school are signs of Puerto Rican nationalism (as the montage opening this section suggests) as well as expressions of the school's commitment to community building. But the school's history—represented in words and images on the walls of the school, on the website, and in publication—is always subject to alternative readings. Several years ago, René Antrop-González (2003) described how gentrification in Paseo Boricua led to the presence of young, upper-class professionals who viewed these images in a negative light:

> According to school supporters, the school is now considered by many of these new residents to be an "eyesore" because the exterior of the school building is covered with a series of painted murals depicting the faces of former and current Puerto Rican political prisoners. Also painted on the high school's walls are Puerto Rican nationalist slogans, such as "Down with capitalism!," "Long live a free Puerto Rico!," and "No to colonialism!" (p. 239)

During their visit, Cavallaro and Berry encountered signs not only of political hopes but also of the school's commitment to community building and caring, such as "Community Is a Place for Everyone" (as seen in the opening montage) and "To Live and Help to Live," words that José López poignantly mentions in the video. It is the latter sentiment that is captured in López's narrative and that is imparted to those who work with López, including one of his former students, PACHS Assistant Director and coauthor Carlos DeJesús. We focus on DeJesús's account because his story provides a counterpoint to those told by the students. It is a story of possibility—granted, his is an exceptional case, but it is the type of experience that undergirds so much of the work that goes on at PACHS. Additionally, DeJesús's distinctive narrative provides an institutional ecology that reinforces a notion of the possible.

To Yale and Back: Carlos DeJesús, Literacy, and Education

"I realized that my passion was not necessarily education," Carlos DeJesús told Cavallaro and Berry as they sat in the Vida/SIDA in the spring of 2009, "but ways of benefitting the community." On the wall behind DeJesús was a painting that included the words of Otto Rene Castillo, calling it "beautiful to love the world with eyes that have not yet been born." As we view the video, we are reminded of how education at PACHS is neither "business as usual" nor neutral. As assistant director of PACHS, DeJesús has a long history of community activism in the Humboldt Park area, including work as the executive director of an organization focused on public housing and the Latino community. While he strongly believes in the transformative power of education, he is still very much aware of the material realities of students: "How does a student go home to do their homework when there are fifteen people living in a four-room apartment? Where do they study? How do they study?" In questioning where and how students compose, DeJesús's remarks underscore the necessity of attending to the lives and conditions under which students learn and how their writing, their literate practice, is tied to material conditions.

Figure 9.2. Carlos DeJesús, Assistant Director of PACHS, met with us at Vida/SIDA

DeJesús's education history was shaped by broader social concerns and supported by the guidance of caring educators. "I keep getting drawn to education," DeJesús explained, "because of my story, because I'm a high school dropout and I have a certain affinity [with] students who have dropped out." Despite his excellent academic record, DeJesús dropped out because school felt so disconnected from the rest of his life. When he spoke with a guidance counselor, he explained that he wanted to get his GED so that he could fix engines, his projected career path at the time. During that meeting, the counselor asked him if he had ever considered *designing* engines rather than *repairing* them. For DeJesús, this question opened a door, allowing him to imagine how education might help him reconstruct his life. As he continued to share his story, we learned that DeJesús's career path had been anything but predetermined, as he explored a variety of careers in auto mechanics, engineering, and medicine before ultimately working in education and community service.

Literacy researchers have been cautioned to look critically at stories of upward mobility that is credited to literacy gained by way of formal education. Such stories can appear overly idealistic or even mythic, as literacy historian Harvey Graff has warned (Graff, 1979; Graff & Duffy, 2009). Still, educators tend to be drawn to stories of remarkable success. After all, isn't that the reason why many of us become teachers: to effect positive change in the lives of our students? We know how readily such stories are consumed in the media and in popular culture.

But with DeJesús, we saw something more than an oversimplified tale of upward mobility. We saw a story of an extraordinary change in perspective that went much further than just some abstract notion of how school could pay off. We saw an individual who might have made the educational ascent popularized in the movies, but who nevertheless told his story with the depth of someone who had recognized the harsh social and economic conditions affecting the lives of those around him and who ultimately returned to the community to help others. DeJesús followed numerous career trajectories before returning home to Paseo Boricua. His story is perhaps more about the power of imagining new stories, new ways of seeing the world, than it is about literacy. It is this imaginative element that John Dewey (1934) wrote about in *A Common Faith*. Inspired by George Santayana, Dewey explained the need for an imaginative extension:

> The limited world of our observation and reflection becomes the Universe only through imaginative extension. It cannot be apprehended in knowledge nor realized in reflection. Neither observation, thought, nor practical activity can attain that complete unification of the self which is called a whole. The *whole* self is an ideal, an imaginative projection. (pp. 18-19)

As we listened to DeJesús's story and heard how others admired him, we too recognized that extraordinary things can indeed happen in everyday lives and saw the power of ideals, tempered by a recognition of social constraints, in dealing with community struggle and imagining alternative ways of thinking about education and the role of school.

Diverse Critical Pedagogy: Elaine Vázquez's English Class

Figure 9.3. Elaine Vázquez and scenes from her students' movies

During their time at PACHS, Cavallaro and Berry also worked closely with Elaine Vázquez, a dedicated English teacher who, in designing her curriculum, combined feminism and the work of radical political educators with her own experiences with diversity. Originally confronted with issues of her own white privilege as an undergraduate, Vázquez began to immerse herself in theory about combating oppression through education. Like DeJesús, she maintained a hopefulness about what was possible, was cognizant of the historical successes of Paseo Boricua, and sought to address these accomplishments as juxtaposed against the everyday realities of her students. Vázquez's commitment to critical pedagogy (e.g., Freire & Macedo, 1987) and Augusto Boal's Theatre of the Oppressed (Boal, 1996) led her to explore storytelling through performance, to develop a curriculum that invited students' lives into the classroom through multiple media and modes of expression. Her work, having generated a broad spectrum of narratives, illustrates the ways in which hope coexists alongside local struggles and how digital media can support the joint articulation of seemingly competing narratives.

One example of how Vázquez created opportunities was the assignment she developed, mentioned earlier, called "Where I'm From." Each student was asked to write a poem about the place he or she had come from without actually naming that place. The poems the students wrote showed a community still struggling, wherein the ideals of education had not yet fulfilled their promises. The assignment allowed students to share images of their daily realities and gave them a platform for voicing the complexities of their lives and the numerous crises and problems that still confronted members of the Paseo Boricua community even in the midst of its many progressive and successful programs.

Through her English curriculum, Vázquez invited the lives and struggles of students into the classroom while simultaneously creating opportunities for the students to write back and to go public. She helped students capture their stories with video cameras and then share them on the class blog, thereby reaching a broader audience. The students' videos were, by and large, marked by moments and images of pain and struggle.

One piece that stands as a particularly striking example of a narrative of community life is the video featuring coauthor Naomi García, one of Vázquez's students. García's words bring many of the community concerns to the forefront as she uses her poem as a space to weave together conflicting versions of life in her community. Her poem expresses her pride in being a Puerto Rican and a resident of Paseo Boricua while also highlighting the prevalence of abuse, gang membership, machismo, and homophobia there. She repeats the phrase "I'm from a place" as a way of locating her position as a member of the community she describes in her writing. For instance, she says, "I'm from a place where *arroz con gandules* is a familiar taste," but she also adds, "I'm from a place where to men it was okay to beat your woman if she got outta line" and "where I as a young Latina feel scared to roam the streets I'm from/I'm from a place where two women can kiss, but don't let it be two men." As García blends the personal and the communal in her work, moving from her individual life to general observations, she gives the sense that she is talking about not a unique experience, but one that is familiar to many members of her community. Much of her poem focuses on the serious problems community members still face. For example, according to García (as well as other students), the issue of a homophobic double standard that allows for the acceptance of lesbian women but not gay men has not been adequately addressed. Even with the striking successes of Paseo Boricua, García's poem serves as a reminder that community goals are never fixed, but always evolving.

Moreover, as we were shaping this project and working with García, we began to see the great challenge that comes when students are allowed to critique and their critiques have the potential to extend beyond school. We see courage and discretion—and, indeed, we had to factor those issues into the shaping of the final film and this writing.

On the Edge of Success: Narratives of Community Building

The diverse range of stories presented here begins to show how community building is never simply either a story of success or a narrative of failure. As educators, we need to create spaces that capture the diverse range of experiences students and teachers face. Educators, we contend, should neither simply relate narratives of accomplishment nor focus solely on the obstacles to success. We need both perspectives. By maintaining a productive dialectic between the world we have and the world we want, we can know our history and promote needed reflection on the everyday ways in which individuals understand their lives. The stories of the students and teachers at PACHS do not exist in a vacuum, but are written against the background of other narratives about Paseo Boricua. Community stories like those told here provide individuals with an opportunity to write back to other members of the community and to a public that often does not understand them. As Flores-González and her colleagues (2006) describe it:

> Accelerated gentrification in the Puerto Rican community since the 1990s has propelled youth to join the struggle to preserve their community. Targeted by police, school officials, and the punitive "low-tolerance" measures that accompany gentrification, they resist and challenge unjust practices through hip-hop, dialogue, and civic participation. (p. 176)

In such expressions of self and identity, we find narratives of resistance and of hope.

There have been productive critiques of hope (e.g., Ehrenreich, 2007), especially when hope is conceived of as wishful thinking—when it appears to ignore the lived lives of individuals. We contend that hope is a vital component in literacy research and in community building, but that it must be situated with and against the experiences of its participants. The above brief accounts suggest the need for, and value of, maintaining a productive tension between diverse tellings that allows for multiple expressions of belief about what is and what is not possible.

In a sense, we are advancing a theory of critical hope that resonates with what Dewey (1934) described in A Common Faith: "[A] theoretical stance," writes Dewey, "can sometimes lead one to see new possibilities in the world. . . . The determining factor connected in the interpretation of the experience is the particular doctrinal apparatus into which a person has been inducted" (p. 13). Community stories like those told here remind us that community building is always a work in progress and that it requires attention to what Paulo Freire called "untested feasibility," or "the future which we have yet to create by transforming today" (Shor & Freire, 1987, p. 153).

The videos discussed here provided an opportunity to reflect on the many types of stories we could tell. We initially asked ourselves, would we tell a singular success story? No—we were certain we would not. But we were at first unsure of how much emphasis to place on present-day struggles. We have come to believe that we must sustain the complexities of community stories by seriously considering even those narratives that can sometimes make us uneasy. Community success depends on where one looks and the stories one obtains. We argue that sustaining community requires opening a space where triumphant stories can stand alongside those of struggle.

10. Youth Asset Mapping: The Empowering and Engaging Youth Project (E2Y)

Chaebong Nam

Champaign is well known for the landmark it shares with its twin city of Urbana: the University of Illinois campus. While surrounded by small farm communities, Champaign comprises college town, micro-urban areas, a research park, and residential areas. Northern Champaign has historically been populated by working-class African Americans, and, despite its proximity to the university, has remained socially and culturally separated from it. The dividing line is simply a street called University Avenue. Still, each side of the street possesses a visibly different social atmosphere, presenting a typical town –gown separation. Many people saw a great need for a group dedicated to working with the residents of public housing.

It was out of that need that the Champaign-Urbana Area Project (http://cuapweb.org) was born in 1988 with a strong focus on youth justice. Director Patricia Avery, who had worked with African American youth and families in the area for about 20 years, was concerned about the undesirable influence of the town-gown separation on local African American youth. She noted that many African American youth from lower income families in northern Champaign did not dare to cross certain geographic boundaries:

> Sometimes African American students, they don't go outside of their neighborhood boundaries. . . . Right in our community, we have the University of Illinois, which is a mark of our community. But many young people from urban communities, they don't go across University Avenue because they feel it doesn't belong to them. That university . . . feels gated to African American students who are from urban areas.

Recognizing this gap, in the fall of 2008, YCI formed a collaboration with three community organizations: Champaign-Urbana Area Project, Peer Ambassadors, and Illinois Public Media (WILL), a member-supported service at the university. The aim of this campus-community partnership was to provide youth who lived in the communities north of the university with an opportunity to cross the imaginary border and investigate resources and assets available for them locally, such as job opportunities for teens, youth programs, recreation centers, and more. Community asset mapping was chosen as the approach for carrying out this task, both for its explicit focus on resources and the capacity of the community (not on its problems or deficiencies) and for its potential for effective information sharing.

We expected that the new project would encourage youth to actively engage in the community and empower them to see the community from a positive perspective, in the face of many negative views of African American youth and communities. The project title, "Engaging and Empowering Youth (E2Y)," originated from this goal.

Participants were recruited through projects at WILL, including the Youth Media Workshop (see Chapter 7). The Champaign-Urbana Area Project managed the project, including organizing the schedule and staff, communicating, and writing reports to the funding agent. WILL donated Flip video cameras to be used for the project and taught the youth mappers important technological skills throughout the project. WILL also provided a space for E2Y's major events, such as the opening ceremony, a group discussion, and the closing ceremony, as well as hosting the E2Y project webpage on their website. YCI worked most closely with the youth mappers, which included preparing a curriculum for the project, leading the canvassing, providing lab sessions, and conducting public presentations with the youth.

I became involved in E2Y through my work with YCI as a graduate student. In this chapter, I share the excitement, achievements, challenges, and lessons that youth mappers and adult partners experienced during their participation in E2Y. I hope that this chapter offers guidance to readers imagining and conducting creative community asset mapping projects in their own contexts. Portions of the chapter are reprinted with permission from Nam (in press).

Participants

Five youth mappers completed E2Y, which lasted from the beginning of 2009 to the spring of 2010: Raisha, Clorisa, Christina, Dave, and Ian, all high school students. Raisha and Christina, both 16 years old, and Clorisa, Raisha's younger sister, had been close friends for a long time and had previously conducted a multimedia project with YCI. The two boys, Dave and Ian, were 15 years old and were new to YCI. The youth mappers who stayed until completion guessed that the other youth participants had left early because the training was too long (having been conducted over the course of almost two and a half months) or because of the delays in the overall project schedule. Adult partners from community organizations and the university worked with youth in various stages of the project. I put the primary focus of this chapter on the youth experience with the project, although the adult partners also played an important role.

Community Inquiry

Community inquiry is a social and educational practice that connects learning with lived experiences in various everyday social contexts (Bishop & Bruce, 2007). The term community inquiry is not exclusively associated with one particular field but widely used in many disciplines with varying traditions. The notion of community inquiry in this book has its origins in progressive education. Progressivists such as John Dewey and Jane Addams highlighted the connection between learning and lived experience. They maintained that students should be connected with real-life situations interwoven with community, work, social norms, culture, and other parts of everyday life. In this view, it is important that learners understand the world as a whole and learn to handle complexities, which can help them grow into engaged and critical citizens who participate in a collective effort to serve a public good (Bruce & Bishop, 2008, p. 705).

Dewey defines inquiry as "the controlled or directed transformation of an indeterminate situation." Indeterminate situations are those that expose the gap between current needs and realities, and are characterized as troubled, ambiguous, confused, full of conflicting tendencies, etc. Inquiry begins with a desire to resolve the issues of indeterminate situations, a desire that is a natural feature of human cognition (Dewey, 1938/1949).

Bishop and Bruce (2008) analyzed inquiry into these five steps: *Ask*, *Investigate*, *Create*, *Discuss*, and *Reflect*. In the *Ask* stage, people facing an indeterminate situation raise questions and identify problems. In the *Investigate* stage the inquirer engages in a variety of activities, searching out new factual conditions; this involves opportunities for people to learn diverse, authentic, and challenging materials and problems. The *Investigate* stage requires people to interact with other people and resources, to encounter new social environments, communicate, and negotiate. New material conditions or ideas obtained from investigation are then represented in concrete ways. In the *Create* stage, people produce specific observable and unobservable products. The *Discuss* stage is where participants listen to others' opinions, examine the new ideas, and articulate their understandings; in this way, personal learning experiences become a social enterprise. The *Reflect* stage involves a meaning-making process that includes judging whether or not the original indeterminate situation has really been transformed into "a determinate and unified whole." In this stage people look back at the initial question, the investigation path, and the products and conclusions, as a whole. This reflection process may initiate new questions, leading to continuing inquiry.

These steps of inquiry overlap with each other, do not have sharp boundaries, and do not necessarily occur in linear order. In real situations, inquiry entails multiple cycles without any definitive ends, and also involves embodied action to transform situations, beyond merely thinking and intellectual play (Bruce, 2009; Bruce & Bishop, 2002). Finally, it is important to recognize that inquiry-based learning is not a method or an option to consider for teaching and learning; instead, it is what actually happens when people *do* learn (Bruce & Bishop, 2008, p. 709).

Community inquiry (see Chapter 1) expands the agency of inquiry from an individual to groups of people, organizations, and the community at large. Everyone who has knowledge of the situation should, ideally, participate in the communal effort to solve the problem. People from diverse backgrounds must be able to express their thoughts and ideas without any fear of judgment or prejudice. Their perspectives should be equally respected, and fair communication and negotiation processes should be always encouraged. This participatory dimension supports a democratic approach to knowledge production (Bruce & Bloch, 2013).

Youth Activities in Mapping

Community asset mapping exemplifies community inquiry. This activity, which begins with discovering the existing resources and strengths of a community, rather than its deficits, is rooted in the "asset-based community development model" (ABCD; Kretzmann & McKnight, 1993, 1996). It aims at achieving sustainable community development from the inside out and is an effective strategy for the visualization and sharing of information with members of the community. The map creation process that encompasses active participation of community members in raising questions and collaborative investigation echoes the participatory knowledge production of community inquiry.

In what follows, I describe how the E2Y's asset-mapping project progressed in following the inquiry cycle introduced above: Ask, Investigate, Create, Discuss, and Reflect. As mentioned earlier, the boundaries between steps in the cycle are fuzzy, and so framing the project with these steps may oversimplify the actual activities.

Ask. E2Y grew out of a concern about the deficit view of the community and the local youth who lived in north Champaign. One assumption was that not enough information existed about resources available for youth in the area, including location, contact information, kinds of services, and more. E2Y intended to counteract the deficit view through actively addressing this indeterminate situation by creating an asset map. Among the main issues: "What resources are available to youth in our community?" "How do we effectively support youth community engagement and learning?" More broadly, "How can we contribute to a better understanding between African American youth and Champaign-Urbana residents?" These questions were initially shaped by adult partners who then guided the youth mappers to explore the next steps of inquiry.

Investigate. In the next stage, the youth mappers engaged in many different activities to discover the local assets, including door-to-door canvassing, interviews, and trainings. This stage included the most intensive fieldwork of the project. Prior to the fieldwork, the youth mappers underwent training where they acquired the knowledge and skills needed for fieldwork. For the basic learning module of the project, E2Y adapted Youthworks (Siegel & Kramer, 2007), which was a curriculum about youth mapping previously developed by the university's Illinois Rural Families program. E2Y brought

Youthworks into the digital era, as we customized its guidelines to fit our purposes and relied on computers, GPS, digital cameras, and the Internet in designing interviews, creating entry standards for each organization profiled, processing the data gathered, and disseminating what was learned.

During the summer of 2009, the project conducted preliminary canvassing in northern Champaign to cast a wide net for new information about local youth assets. The canvassing consisted of passing out flyers to inform people about E2Y and request information on local assets people knew of. In canvassing, the youth mappers and adult partners distributed a thousand flyers informing residents of the purpose of the project in northern Champaign. Incorporating inputs of the members of the neighborhoods, the project team created a new list of youth serving agencies. At this stage, the youth mappers' participation in decision-making was slight, but as the project went on, the youth mappers voiced their thoughts on the project and made good suggestions for improvement.

The youth mappers began interviewing the youth-serving agencies listed in the newly created directory at the end of August 2009 (see Figure 10.1). This was the part of the project that interested the youth mappers the most. Prior to the actual interviews, the youth mappers conducted mock interviews with adult partners, learning what is expected in a real interview and how they could effectively deliver their message. They practiced each component of the interview, including greetings and introductions, asking questions, writing down answers, and making videos. A professional staff member of WILL (one of the adult partners) helped the youth with operating the cameras and maintaining good camera angles. The adult partners provided constructive feedback on all aspects of the interview process; in the end, the youth mappers became comfortable with conducting their real interviews.

For the interviews, the adult partners prepared templates of an organizational profile and an interview questionnaire. Adapted from Youthworks, the templates were customized based on feedback from both the adult partners and the youth mappers. The organizational profile was a simple form displaying brief information about the agency, and the interview questionnaires included more in-depth questions. Through the interview, the youth mappers were able to apply the skills and knowledge they had acquired. Visiting different places and organizations in the community for the interviews helped the youth mappers learn much about their community and community programs.

Create. The Create stage focused on the questions "How do we share new information about local assets with others?" and "What are the effective ways to do so?" Digital technology was integral to the way E2Y gathered and presented the data. Keen interest in digital technology, apparent throughout the project, was the major motivation for youth participation, and the effort to support youth motivation naturally led E2Y to use youth-friendly media tools that would also be easily available for the general public. The E2Y team employed Google Maps as a tool for data visualization and information sharing, based on the YCI's prior experience using Google Maps in other media projects and workshops.

Figure 10.1. Youth setting up a camera for an interview.

The youth mappers gathered at Saturday lab sessions. During those, they edited their interview videos, uploaded them to YouTube, and typed their interview answers and organizational profiles in Google Documents. They then created the E2Y map via Google Maps and edited the info windows for the location markers of the youth-serving agencies where they had interviewed. These info windows resembled comic-book word balloons, which allowed the youth mappers to include hyperlinks to the interview questions and to the agencies' organizational profiles; videos of the interviews; and brief descriptions of the agencies, as seen in Figure 10.2. Although the youth mappers found editing the info windows to be challenging, they were proud of their final product. The complete E2Y map displayed metadata of the local assets, as it offered information on multiple aspects of the youth-serving agencies in the community. This map was accessible through both the official E2Y website (http://illinoisyouthmedia.org/e2y), hosted by WILL, and the YCI website.

Discuss and Reflect. In this project, Discuss and Reflect seemed inseparable. As they became engaged in the main part of the project, the youth mappers began to more actively express their thoughts about the project and experience. Closely working with the youth mappers, I had the opportunity to have conversations about the project on various occasions, and tried to turn these conversations into meaningful reflection. The topics covered in these conversations included what they learned, what challenged or interested them the most, what other effective ways to advertise the map would be, and so on. Moreover, youth mappers became outspoken about certain setbacks in the project (e.g., the delayed schedule) and made suggestions for improvement.

In mid-October, the whole E2Y team, including both the youth mappers and the adult partners, held a group reflection session to listen more carefully to the voices of the youth mappers. Both adult partners and youth mappers reflected on where they were, what the youth mappers had learned so far, and what improvements were needed. The three girls, Christina, Raisha, and Clorisa, made good suggestions for improving the project from their perspectives. These suggestions included having a concrete contract with the youth mappers about hours and responsibilities, additional staff recruitment, effective canvassing, training time reduction, youth-led fundraising, and more. These insightful comments from the youth mappers taught the adult partners important lessons about the project, which they otherwise would have missed.

Among the important reflective activities was a public presentation. On completion of the E2Y map, the youth mappers began presenting it. The first presentation took place at the closing ceremony for E2Y held at WILL in December 2009. Before their parents and the adult partners, youth mappers presented their favorite "balloons" (the info windows of the community agencies they interviewed) on the E2Y map. They talked about why they liked these specific places, what the agency was about, and what they had learned from the project. All participants in the room were impressed with the level of achievement and commitment of the youth mappers for the project over the past 10 months. This presentation experience prepared the youth mappers for subsequent public presentations.

On February 3, 2010, the youth mappers presented their work at the iConference, a nationwide conference that brings together scholars, professionals, and university students who are affiliated with the "iSchools," university departments devoted to the study of information and technology. At this conference, they presented the E2Y map, shared their experiences with the conference participants, and led a small lab session to teach others how to edit Google Maps. Afterwards, some of the youth mappers (Christina, Raisha, and Clorisa) were also invited to graduate courses of GSLIS and to several meetings to talk about their experiences with E2Y. As they gave more talks, the youth mappers became more eloquent and confident in their presentation. It appeared that many questions they were asked helped them reflect on their practice from multiple perspectives.

Figure 10.2. E2Y Google Map.

The reflection stage also prompted the participants (both youth mappers and adult partners) to think about how E2Y would make a difference in the community. Or, in Dewey's terminology, it raised the issue: How would the project contribute to transformation of the initial "indeterminate situation" (the lack of information of local resources available for teens) into the improved determinate situation? This led to reflections on the project from a broader perspective, not only centering on the final product and its potential impact but also reflections on the nature of the community inquiry practice as a whole. This process brought about new questions and suggestions for future projects, which could initiate new inquiry in turn.

Youth Learning Outcomes

Learning about the community. "We really didn't know that our community had such resources." The youth mappers said that E2Y helped them learn much about their community in multiple ways. Despite the physical challenge of canvassing, the youth mappers regarded it as worthwhile in improving their geographical knowledge of their neighborhoods, calling their attention to street names, signs, and the locations of community organizations. It was also through canvassing that they first gained attention from classmates in school.

Some classmates of the three girls recognized them on the E2Y flyer, bringing it to school to ask about the project and their roles in it. Clorisa talked about this experience in a project reflection interview:

> I learned about the different areas in the neighborhoods, know what streets I am on, pay attention to signs...I met people who have done good in the community and other youth will be interested in. Some of our friends saw us in the paper about [the project]. It was really cool.

Most importantly, the youth mappers were surprised at the rich resources their community offered for teens. For instance, Christina emphasized how much she enjoyed the two-and-a-half-hour interview with Mr. Cordell of the National Council of African American Men. Christina said that the actual interview was done within a half hour; Mr. Cordell talked about his personal history and the history of African Americans in Champaign for the rest of the time. An interview with a community organization for kids with Down syndrome was another favorite. She said that the interview made her aware of the syndrome and the social prejudices about it.

The interview experiences played a pivotal role in helping the youth get to know the community better and recognize its positive aspects. It is important to note that in addition to the interviews, a wide range of interactions with various groups of people in the local media center, community organizations, and the university contributed to the youth mappers' positive learning experiences about their community as well. For these youth mappers, this project was one of the few opportunities to interact with adults from different backgrounds who cared for the community, respected youth voices, and appreciated their dedication to this project.

Interviewing and social skills. The youth mappers gained interview and communication skills as well as social confidence. They learned how to interview people, how to avoid being shy, and how to be polite to people even when confronted with rudeness during the canvassing and interviews. The youth mappers said that they were nervous in their first interviews, but as they conducted more interviews, they became more relaxed and learned to enjoy them. For instance, in Christina's final interview, she made a smooth transition from one question to another (having memorized all the interview questions) and maintained healthy eye contact, as well as creating her own questions to probe further into issues. On the way home from that interview, Christina said, "I just wanted to know more about the program and its services. That was really important to other youth."

Raisha reported learning social skills: "I learned how to interview people, how to talk to people, how not to be scared when I hand out flyers." She added, "I learned how to be more respectful to people and even if they be rude to you, but just be respectful and say, 'Thanks.'" Ian added that he had improved both his ability to interact with others and his ability to explain a project to adults through this mapping project. Ian was usually quiet and shy during the project, but his presentation at the iConference was full of wit and humor, eliciting laughter. Ian also talked about his learning experience with E2Y in a confident tone at the conference. Further, the three girls connected their acquired interview skills to their future job interview preparations; Raisha said:

> I want to be a nurse in the future. When I get an interview, I know what to say, since I used to be an interviewer and I know how to interview. I know how to say something back positive. I know how to, like . . . [Clorisa whispered to Raisha, "Have a good conversation"] have a good conversation with a person.

Learning new media skills. New technology skills were a major learning outcome. Given their own Flip video cameras, the youth mappers were also passionate about playing with cameras and making videos throughout the whole project. They learned from WILL's professional staff members important basic film skills such as setting up tripods, getting good camera angles, and avoiding backlight, in addition to video editing skills.

Youth mappers also learned skills using video editing software and various online tools such as Google Maps, YouTube, Google Docs, Flickr, and more. They achieved different levels of mastery and interest in these technological skills according to individual differences in interest in and aptitude for technology. Dave had a particular interest in learning new technology skills, and Ian impressed the team with his consistent passion for learning new skills and sharing his experiences. Christina and Clorisa, who were relatively quick to grasp new skills, took the role of interns among the team and taught their peers to finish their tasks successfully. I respected the youth mappers' pace for learning and emphasized collaboration and mutual support during the lab sessions—getting the youth mappers to achieve the same standard was not the priority of the project. Ian talked about his achievement at the iConference: "I was too far away from the computer at first . . . but we actually posted something on the web. I learned to type better now and find stuff on Google. At first, it was very hard."

Taken together, E2Y was not just about mapping but about holistic community learning and action for change. Their work addressed a practical need of the community: producing information about local resources available for teens. The youth mappers crossed the invisible gate and participated in campus-community activities; they learned to work with other adult and youth partners, communicate with members of the community, and inquire into important local issues using various tools and methods. The interviews they conducted with youth-serving agencies and their work with adult partners and other support networks for E2Y helped the youth mappers to foster a positive view of their community (and vice versa) and themselves.

Discussion and Implications

E2Y developed from the participatory culture and longstanding commitment to social justice among the partner organizations of the project. WILL, a local public media center, has made many efforts to reach out to the community and invited local youth to their youth media workshops. CUAP, as introduced earlier, has strived to improve the welfare of families and youth in need of help and support in the area. Since 1993, GSLIS has worked with the surrounding region through Prairienet and its community networking projects to promote equity of access to digital resources and teach the skills necessary to access and use those resources. Against this backdrop, the partner organizations brought their own expertise and experience in community engagement into E2Y. Several other community organizations as well constituted the collaborative nexus for community inquiry in this project by providing interviews, curriculum resources and guidelines, personnel, and financial support, among other things. The collaborative effort to form a space for community inquiry (Ritzo, Nam, & Bruce, 2009) became a solid foundation for this project and should not be overlooked.

Toward the end of the project, however, new questions emerged about the potential impact of the project on the community, in particular regarding accessibility and availability of the map among community members. Those questions included: Can people who live in northern Champaign have access to this information? Where would they be able to get the information such as home, libraries, schools, community organizations, etc.? What are other effective ways to increase the availability of the map? What types of map, other than online-based maps, would be useful to the audience that does not have immediate access to the Internet? The decision to use online information distribution inadvertently prevented residents who did not have the relevant digital resources and skills from using the E2Y map.

This experience provides an important lesson in approaches to strengthening the participatory dimension of community inquiry—all who have knowledge of the situation should participate in knowledge production; people with different backgrounds bring diverse perspectives, engage in conversation and negotiation, and develop solutions that are more effective and equitable. Encouraging groups of community members to discuss what type of representation would best work for them is vital. Those dialogues will initiate further inquiries in how people use new information and find it useful or not, and so help the community both to identify new needs and to improve the map. These inquiries will eventually lead to a larger agenda of requesting equal access to information and encouraging concrete action toward that goal in the community. This continues the cycle of community inquiry, developing its scope and depth of issues and participation for social change.

Lastly, I want to draw attention to the issue of the *authenticity* of youth engagement. The youth mappers in E2Y were not fully included in its decision-making process, although toward the later stages of the project they developed a critical understanding, and offered good criticisms and suggestions that would improve project performance and contribute to youth ownership. The insufficient inclusion of youth mappers' voices in the project, even if unintentional, may have kept the project from reaching the goal of authentic youth engagement.

The definition and practice of "authenticity" in youth engagement varies according to context. It does not necessarily require the exclusion of adult partner guidance; rather, the adult partners can play a critical role in helping youth learn to share ownership and then gradually fade away from the power position. With a focus on youth-adult relationship dynamics, future projects need to pay more attention to developing models to improve youth ownership based on active and mutually interdependent relationships between youth and adults in their own contexts.

Conclusion

I would like to juxtapose E2Y with the Hull House mapping project completed almost one century ago. Hull House was a settlement house founded in 1889 in Chicago, becoming a place where ordinary people—mostly European immigrants—voluntarily engaged in community-building activities, created dialogue and mutual understanding across different cultural backgrounds, and collaborated with community institutions to meet their community needs. As a part of these efforts, in 1895, Hull House completed the mapping project *Hull House Maps and Papers*, about various social issues in their neighborhoods—mapping different nationalities, wages, sweatshops, and child labor. The map allowed people to better understand the real issues of the community and cope with them more effectively, thereby contributing to long-term community development. In spite of gaps in both time and technology between the E2Y map and the Hull House map, I can see commonalities between the two in the pursuit of community inquiry and the use of a map as its tool. This comparison also says that the essence of community engagement—how the voices of the community are fairly and actively conveyed in it—remains the same in the digital age.

Through their participation in this project, the youth mappers were able to cultivate positive perceptions of the community and develop social skills and digital literacy skills. In addition, the work addressed practical community needs and challenged the deficit view of the community—E2Y was thus not just about mapping, it was also holistic community learning and action, making the community a better place to live, work, and play. There were limitations, but these provided important lessons and ideas for improving future projects. The concept of community inquiry proved effective for understanding community engagement, and additional exploratory applications of this "lens" could improve the sophistication of the theory as well as its usefulness and range.

11. Creating Collaborative Library Services to Incarcerated Youth

Jeanie Austin

Joe Coyle

Rae-Anne Montague

I see this library giving youth a chance to build new beginnings that can help them in school, like when a teen is in front of a class they develop this anxiety that puts fear in wanting to read at all, like a doubt has crossed them. This can also give them a chance to build some sort of imagination that takes them away from this place for just a minute, then bring them to back to reality. There might be books that teach them a lesson or two on how to make certain decisions. This is how they can benefit from this library. —Veonia Gross

I can still remember the times that I was in the detention center and I know that we really never had too much to do when we were in our rooms. So I think having a library in the detention center is very important because some people like to have things to do to keep their minds off of the fact of actually being in the detention center. I myself felt like having books to read kept me occupied and it was like a getaway also because I didn't have to think about being in the detention center. —Jessica Morris

The quotes above are from members of the Peer Ambassadors (PAs), a group of African American youth in Champaign County that focused on restorative justice and peer education in the surrounding community, including the Champaign County Juvenile Detention Center. The statements illustrate the ways in which providing library services in the juvenile detention center positively affects the lives of incarcerated youth. These quotes emphasize the need for youth in the detention center to have access to materials that speak to their lived experience, allow them to build and exercise their literacy skills, and to feel that there is a concern in the community for their well-being. Extending Library Services to Empower Youth (ELSEY; http://elseyjdc.wordpress.com) was launched in 2009 as a collaborative project seeking to understand and meet these needs. Overlapping with the Youth Community Informatics project in productive ways, ELSEY involved youth, staff, and students from the university, other local information providers and the community. The group focused on increasing the life chances of incarcerated youth by providing library materials and services in the juvenile detention center, building youth investment in their communities, and linking youth to a variety of local resources.

Why Library Services in Juvenile Detention Centers?

Reading plays an important role in identity formation for youth. According to Rothbauer (2006), reading provides a means by which young people "can understand the world and their place in it." Summarizing a number of studies related to youth and reading, Rothbauer found that

1. Reading allows young people to envision and create potential futures.
2. Reading means gathering and organizing information about the wide world and how it works and how one fits into it.
3. Reading enables young people to mediate competing claims for truth in their lives.
4. Reading is an escape from the pressures of everyday life.
5. Reading transforms lives. (p. 116)

Access to relevant, useful, and representative reading materials facilitates understanding across many realms. Reading provides valuable tools for negotiating the world and is a safe means for testing out various character traits and life decisions. Access to materials is especially important for youth held in detention centers, many of whom may experience a lack of access to materials, and face intervening factors such as low literacy rates, high daily life stresses, and the need to balance a variety of emotional and educational challenges (Bodart, 2008; Venable, 2005).

In the United States, nearly 100,000 young people are held in a detention center on any given day (Office of Juvenile Justice and Delinquency Prevention, 2009). Nationally, the majority of these youth come from groups that are already underserved by traditional libraries (Wald & Losen, 2003). Approximately three-fourths of youth located in juvenile detention centers are African American, and youth from this population are predominantly male (Office of Juvenile Justice and Delinquency Prevention, 2008). Lack of relevant services in traditional libraries may lead youth to feel that they are not welcome in these spaces, further reducing the likelihood that youth will use libraries as a resource.

Incarcerated youth are largely distanced from resources such as books, magazines, and other media. In addition to being physically removed from library services, many youth in detention centers have encountered factors that mediate their likelihood of or ability to seek out information. Literacy levels may affect the likelihood that individuals will have access to materials that are intellectually stimulating and at the same time comprehensible to the youth. While the age range of youth in detention centers is typically 11 to 17 years old, one-third of these youth read at or below a fourth-grade level (Hayes, 2007). Popular assumptions about youth as nonreaders, coupled with the fact that many of the materials that youth choose to read may not be validated in an educational context (websites, magazines, etc.), negatively affect their perceptions of themselves as readers (Rothbauer, 2006).

Despite the factors that discourage reading, youth regularly express interest in reading and the value of accessing library materials while incarcerated. "Shannon," discussing the value of reading while in the juvenile detention center, states, "Truthfully, I don't know what I would've done without those books . . . it was like my little secret, a place I could go when everything else was wrong" (in Dittmann, 2001). Youth are more likely to engage with materials that reflect their lived experience and represent their interests. As stated above, this means finding materials that deal with complex life experiences that do not patronize the youth and do not include an excessive amount of vocabulary that is too difficult for the youth to comprehend.

While access to relevant library materials provides a means by which youth in a detention center can build their literacy skills, access alone does not guarantee that youth will seek out additional resources after they have left the center. Information about community resources can be linked to library programming. Library programming in a juvenile detention center should focus on linking youth to libraries and other information spaces and equipping them with the skills necessary to use dynamic community resources. Programming should focus on youth agency within information spaces. By increasing youth agency and connecting youth to community resources, juvenile detention center libraries can greatly influence the lives of incarcerated youth and the well-being of their communities.

One model to provide useful and informed programming at the juvenile detention center library is a library supported by a group of community collaborators that are invested in the success of the youth in the center. These community partners may include public and school librarians, community groups, youth that are concerned with improving their community, and any other interested contributors. This style of collaboration allows partners to use their strengths in supporting the youth, and can increase the youth's knowledge of resources located within their communities. This model also distributes the cost of providing services across several institutions.

Numerous programs and libraries provide information services to youth located in juvenile detention centers, yet standards for library services in juvenile detention centers have not been updated for more than a decade (Association of Specialized and Cooperative Library Agencies, 1999). ELSEY used available guidelines while integrating a collaborative approach to maintaining a juvenile detention center library. The project models effective practices in juvenile detention center libraries emphasizing youth information literacy, reduced recidivism, and connecting youth to community resources.

Partnering with Juvenile Detention Centers

Circumstances and detention center policies shape the types of library materials and programming that can be offered in the juvenile detention center. Partnering with staff and administration at the detention center to develop collection development policies and to discuss any restrictions regarding access to materials increases the likelihood that the center will be positively supported and sustainable. Restrictions to discuss include the format of materials, space for materials, the nature of content, and what type of access to technology youth will have (Will they be able to use a catalog? Are they allowed to listen to audio books?).

Additional considerations relate to the day-to-day functioning of the library. Groups hoping to establish library services in a juvenile detention center have to address whether and how the library will be staffed, and if so, by whom. If there is a formal policy for youth checking out books, guidelines will need to be established regarding how books will be checked out and checked in, and who will be responsible for these actions. If the library is located in a designated physical space, the organization of that space will need to be discussed. Issues to address include whether or not books should be kept in an organization scheme (such as Dewey Decimal), or if organization by subject is adequate for youth to locate the materials they seek. These decisions may be mediated by funding, staffing hours, or the availability of volunteers.

Collaborating to provide library services in juvenile detention centers involves maintaining a careful balance between the needs of all involved parties. Youth interests in materials must be balanced with the information access policies of the center. In addition to this, partners should not be asked to contribute beyond their means, should see that their contributions are worthwhile, and should have an ample voice in making decisions about the library and its programming. It is helpful for partners to have a working relationship and to meet fairly regularly to remain informed about the progress of the library. Designating a project manager to oversee scheduling and to check in with partners to ensure that needs are being met can be useful in ensuring a balanced collaboration between many busy partners.

If there are youth partners, partners with institutional power should make room for youth voice and contribution. In the case of the ELSEY project, this has been accomplished through three main actions, all suggested by the PAs. First, a youth partner chose to act as co-coordinator on the project and communicate regularly with the project manager. Second, meetings and projects were planned to accommodate the schedules of youth partners. Finally, youth took an active role in creating and implementing programming in the juvenile detention center. An added benefit of youth acting as peer mentors in the juvenile detention center library is that the youth held in the juvenile detention center are exposed to examples of youth efficacy in creating community change.

Beginning ELSEY

National data about youth in the juvenile justice system stands true for youth in the Champaign County Juvenile Detention Center. Demographically, the youth align with these statistics (75-77% of the annual population is African American, and 66% of that population is male). Additionally, the youth have complex information needs that involve not only language literacy skills but also an awareness of community resources and opportunities. In seeking to meet the information needs of the youth located in the center, it was important to the staff to provide diverse reading materials prior to ELSEY's launch. While staff expended considerable effort and personal resources in providing library materials to youth in the center, limited experience with library services and funding affected their ability to continuously support the library as a link to other community resources in the area. The center partnered with other community groups, such as the PAs, to provide this link to community resources through workshops for the youth. The PAs contributed this important function by conducting focus groups with residents to determine the scope of their information needs and desires and holding discussions with youth in the center to evaluate available services and materials. They also contributed information to shape policies related to the nature of the collection, including weeding and materials acquisition (collection development).

In focus group sessions with the PAs, youth in the center repeatedly expressed motivation to read, many for the first time in their lives. Popular requests for materials include entrepreneurship, parenting, narratives of individuals who experienced incarceration (and how they made it out), African American historical figures, career and college planning, sports, and strategies for navigating institutional structures such as welfare, juvenile justice, and public health. After doing a thorough "weeding" process of materials that were out of date or badly damaged, the PAs and ELSEY partners determined that the collection was in need of more fiction materials that represented the identities and lived experiences of the residents. Additionally, these materials needed to be provided at multiple reading levels to reflect the diverse reading abilities of the youth.

Like many JDC libraries, the one at the Champaign County Juvenile Detention Center does not have the resources to employ its own librarian. Due to staffing and funding constraints, a major facet of this project is to work collaboratively to ensure the daily maintenance of the library space. Working across organizations to agree on an organizational scheme for the library collection, establishing clear signage, and developing a system for shelving materials was foundational to this goal. The establishment of a sustainable practicum opportunity for students from GSLIS to practice juvenile corrections librarianship supports these needs and opens possibilities for growth. GSLIS students and faculty collaborate with the staff to develop successful practicum opportunities. Some initial practicum activities included further focus group sessions with the youth to determine the most appropriate organizational structure for the library's materials, the establishment of a computerized catalog, an initial collection development policy, and fundraising and grant writing to acquire more resources for future materials purchasing. The importance of this foundational work cannot be overlooked as a means to create the conditions through which incarcerated youth access materials and develop critical literacy skills to effect change at both the level of their individual life and the community level.

To support the youth in the process of developing these critical life skills, the PAs created library skills training workshops for the youth. Building on the physical collection, this work provided the resources for youth to develop an improved sense of community and library services and resources. Equipping the residents with knowledge and skills related to the local public library system ensured that youth would be more likely to seek out information related to their interests after their release from the detention center. Linking youth to libraries, community resources, and peer mentors will reduce the likelihood of recidivism and build healthier communities.

Fostering a Collaborative Approach

An agency seeking to adopt the strength-based positive youth development approach to juvenile justice must develop collaborative relationships not only with provider agencies (e.g., mental health centers, substance abuse treatment providers, etc.) but with a wide variety of community agencies, such as schools, parks and recreation departments, conventional youth development agencies (e.g., Boys & Girls Clubs), mentors (e.g., Big Brothers/Big Sisters; local colleges), community arts organizations, neighborhood organizations, and many others that may become apparent after considering specific youths' interests. Some of these may serve as community service sites; others may be engaged for skill building with particular youth. These kinds of collaborations bring benefits not only to the youths, but to the program generally by "opening up" the traditionally closed culture of juvenile justice to other perspectives and influences. (Barton & Butts, 2008)

The initial partners were committed to improving the lives of the youth in the detention center by providing library materials and information literacy programming, and linking the youth to resources available in the community. These partners sought to provide services to youth in the center to empower them to use community resources upon release. While the roles of these partners have been discussed in the above sections, it may be helpful to clearly describe the roles and functions of the various groups and individuals involved in ensuring a sustainable project long into the future. These collaborators include staff and administrators at the center, youth and staff from the PAs, individuals affiliated with GSLIS, volunteers at the local Books2Prisoners program, and local school and public librarians.

It is the stated mission of the center "to further justice by providing a safe, caring environment that guides children in our care toward productive lawful lives, and enhances community safety and well-being." Staff have an investment in the success of the youth housed there and in reducing recidivism among them. To this extent, they have worked to establish programs that connect the youth to community groups.

The center's desire to reduce recidivism and increase the life chances of youth upon release led to collaboration with the PAs. This group of African-American and Latino/Latina youth (ages 13 to 24) located in Champaign, Illinois, provide peer to peer counseling, peer education, and leadership in the surrounding community. The PAs use their own experience to connect to their peers and to identify and address social justice issues. As part of the partnership with the center, these youth led workshops and discussions with teens and guided the overall collaboration process in ELSEY.

The PAs identified the revitalization of the juvenile detention center library as a means of improving the lives of youth in the center. They partnered with GSLIS with the goal of increasing their own information literacy, extending each agency's awareness of community resources, and physically maintaining the library. GSLIS in turn seeks to be involved in projects involving the variety of ways that information is used in society. Its mission statement reflects this emphasis:

> People use information for analysis, inquiry, collaboration, and play and in so doing, change the world. The Graduate School of Library and Information Science is dedicated to shaping the future of information through research, education, and engagement, both public and professional. Our mission is to lead a revolution in the understanding and use of information in science, culture, society, commerce, and the diverse activities of our daily lives. (GSLIS, 2009)

Students and faculty from YCI became involved with the library project in August 2009. One of the initial sparks was a visit from the PAs to GSLIS as part of their early collaboration on the E2Y project (see Chapter 10). During this visit, they also discussed the needs and aspirations of local youth with the GSLIS dean and YCI team members. Members of the GSLIS community have supported the project by providing input on organization, materials selection, fundraising, and project promotion, work originally conducted by GSLIS students in their role as YCI research assistants.

Individuals at GSLIS had previous collaborative relationships with Books2Prisoners and the Urbana Free Library, both located in Urbana, Illinois. Books2Prisoners is a community-based group of volunteers that collect donation materials to mail to prison inmates in Illinois. They also stock two jail libraries in Champaign County. As part of the library project, Books2Prisoners shares donated materials and advice regarding collecting books for the library. Urbana Free Library is a top-ranked public library that serves 1,000 users a day (Urbana Free Library, 2009). Several librarians serve as faculty at the GSLIS, and students have been involved in providing community programming on-site or in collaboration with the library. For example, YCI graduate assistants participated in conducting a project where youth made videos set in the library. The youth services librarian has been especially instrumental in creating a partnership with the ELSEY Project.

Other community organizations and individuals contribute to the project in a number of ways. School librarians in the area have suggested titles for materials that will be relevant to the youth's lived experiences while matching the literacy levels of the youth, as well as provided insight into engaging youth through programing. The Center for Children's Books, located in GSLIS, has contributed materials to the project.

Linking diverse groups together in revitalizing and maintaining the library adds strength to the project's ability to increase the quality of life of incarcerated youth while in the center and upon their release. Linking youth to community resources helps to ensure that they will be aware of services that can meaningfully affect their lives. The connection of the youth to community spaces and groups is one means of creating a support network for previously incarcerated youth. Youth's familiarity with community resources, and their own feelings of efficacy within those institutions, builds their sense of inclusion and investment within their own communities. Building relationships among youth and providing them with programming to enhance their information literacy skills equips them to negotiate various institutions they encounter.

The desire to improve the lives of incarcerated youth and to support youth in using the public library and understanding their own ability to request services and materials drove the collaboration among the members of the ELSEY project. Considering this, it is especially important that connections be established between the youth and the public library. Low literacy rates, limited exposure to the library, and, in some cases, limited support from previously encountered institutions (such as schools) may be barriers to the youth's willingness to utilize the public library. This project addressed these barriers by providing materials and programming valuing the lived experience of the incarcerated youth while equipping them with the means to navigate the protocols of the public library.

Linking Incarcerated Youth to Library Services

The ways that individuals come to understand the world, to negotiate cultural institutions, and to position their own identities within cultural contexts is directly related to language and information (Freire, 1970/2000; Shor, 1999). Literacy and access to information influences a person's ability to negotiate the world in which they exist. Limited access to information and exposure to negative messages about individual ways of knowing and lived experiences reduces the likelihood that individuals will be able to negotiate institutions such as school and libraries. This occurs through outright messages regarding ability, and through the hidden curriculum in the classroom, in which the voices and experiences of dominant groups (white, male, heterosexual, middle and upper class) are valued over the voices and experiences of other groups (people of color, women, alternative sexualities) (McLaren, 1989).

For incarcerated youth, the effects of negative messages about their ability to learn or change the world and institutionalized messages about individual efficacy are evidenced in the low likelihood that the youth will return to formal school settings after leaving the detention center (Vacca, 2008). These factors may compound with low literacy rates to further reduce the prospect that incarcerated youth will have the skills or desire to use the public library upon release. One third of juvenile offenders read below the fourth-grade reading level (Hayes, 2007).

The initial years of the Champaign County Juvenile Detention Center library project emphasized increasing youth's familiarity with library services while exposing them to myriad literature that spoke to their lived experiences in line with their wide range of literacy skills. As youth used the materials in the library, they gained practice in reading, increased their literacy skills, and acquired stronger vocabularies and knowledge about the world and themselves. This is a life-changing experience for youth. Amy Cheney, a librarian at Alameda County Juvenile Justice Center's library, states:

> The most important thing is to get the kids excited about reading and writing, and to use that to help them connect with the world at large. They're disenfranchised. They may not have been introduced to standard concepts basic to our society. . . . Many of the youth incarcerated here don't understand the concept of their opinions having merit, or their lives having value. Sometimes when people get locked up, it's the first time they've had a chance to stop and take a look at what's going on in their lives. When they are here, they have clothes to wear, a place to live, food—that's not always true "on the outs." There, they are spending so much time taking care of necessities and staying alive, they don't have a chance to take a look at the big picture. When their basic needs are met, then they can begin to look at themselves and their lives— how they got here, and how they can get to a better place. (in Bodart, 2008)

Providing the youth with opportunities to reflect on their lived experience through texts, as described by Cheney, is one of the means by which maintaining a library in the juvenile detention center can reduce recidivism. Fostering literacy development through access to materials, the opportunity to discuss materials, the time to read, and free choice of reading materials is another (McKechnie, 2006). Increased literacy leads to a heightened ability to engage with institutions such as schools and libraries, and heightens feelings of efficacy and power when dealing with these institutions. It also increases the individual's investment in the community, thereby reducing the chances that the youth will reoffend (Jones, 2001).

Critical thinking, reflection, and an understanding of the context in which information is generated are important aspects of linking incarcerated youth to library services. Encouraging youth to develop and refine critical thinking (rather than rote retention of information) is necessary if youth are going to begin to understand the actions that led to their involvement with the juvenile justice system and the social and cultural factors that influenced those actions (Austin, 2012). Critical literacy and critical information literacy programming involve the youth in working toward a more socially just world. The ability to evaluate sources of information, especially in regard to the intentions of the author; the ways that class, race, and sexuality are valued; and an understanding of how social norms and standards come into play in the text positions the youth to evaluate whether, why, and how the materials that they encounter reflect their own experiences, voices, needs, and desires for information. These critical literacy skills can be employed by the youth to evaluate their place in the world and to improve traditional library services.

Critical Literacy Programming

Teaching for critical consciousness, or critical pedagogy, is marked by the admittance of power structures in the classroom and the desire to restructure power distribution in a way that facilitates learning but does not diminish individual experience. Adults can not only provide information but also use their power of influence (a power that many teens are not given) to support the efforts and contributions of teens toward a more socially just world (Shor, 1999).

To enact information literacy skills in the public library, incarcerated youth need to be equipped with knowledge about the library. Use of the public library requires an understanding of how it is organized, how to search for and find materials, how to request materials, and how to do more in-depth investigation about types of materials available. For the youth to be able to use the public library to their highest advantage, they must also have knowledge of other types of services available, such as community programming and forums, and the opportunity to use public computers, the Internet, and library databases.

The detention center library is organized like the local Urbana Free Library while including input from the youth located in the center. Fiction materials are located in one room of the center. These books are organized by reading level into picture books, chapter books, series fiction, young adult fiction, science fiction and fantasy, mystery, and graphic novels. Books in these sections are then alphabetized by author's last name. Genre stickers make it easier for youth to locate their own materials. Nonfiction books are located in a classroom adjacent to the fiction room. They are grouped by subject area, with prominent signage so that youth are able to easily locate the materials they seek.

In an effort to connect youth with the local public libraries, PAs collaborated with local librarians and other information professions in the community to develop videos related to library services. The PAs partnered with GSLIS to discuss the types of information to be included in these videos, and how to provide library-centered programming. In fitting with YCI's emphasis on creating communities of inquiry, this style of implementing programming included space for all parties to learn—graduate students gain experience providing programming to youth, the PAs learn about library services and increase their experience leading and facilitating workshops, and youth in the detention center gain knowledge about library services while learning from peer-mentors. This restructuring of authority in the learning environment provided the PAs with the power to create and modify programming as they saw fit while still incorporating adult support, guidance, and knowledge.

The PAs led a discussion with youth in the detention center regarding library organization, using questions such as:

- Do you think books should be organized by their reading levels, so books that use big words are in one section and books that are easier to understand are in another section?
- Can you find what you want in the library here? What do you think would make the books easier to find?
- What nonfiction sections are most important to you? (Explain nonfiction.) For example, sports, history, biography, science, health, advice and self-help, cookbooks.

Organizing the library in a way that is similar to the organization at the city library, while incorporating youth input in section areas for nonfiction books, increases the likelihood that youth will find materials in the detention center library and will gain familiarity with how materials are arranged in a public library. The library also includes a computer catalog of materials. Due to security issues, to date, the catalog is not available to youth in the center. If this changes, we expect exposure to using a computerized catalog system and familiarity with searching for materials will diminish the level of intimidation youth may feel when using computerized catalogs and looking for books in other libraries in the future. Featuring librarians from the community in the programming videos familiarizes the youth with information professionals in the area. This may reduce the intimidation that some youth may feel in approaching librarians.

Additional programming at the library has included information on various aspects of library services such as subject headings, reference sources, how to locate materials that are not available on the shelves (using catalogs, WorldCat, and interlibrary loan), as well as requesting materials for library purchase. In addition to a materials focus, workshops address the ways in which local libraries can be utilized to further residents' educational and employment goals. There is emphasis on discussion and the ways in which youth position themselves in relation to the public library as an institution in their communities. More recently, in addition to collection development and sessions aimed at increasing information navigation skills, library collaborators have included reading groups, a writing program, and author visits as part of a multiyear grant (Mix IT Up!, n.d.).

The writing program offered through Mix IT Up! provides youth an opportunity to express themselves through various forms of writing including poetry, autobiography, critical essays, and fiction. The authors publish their work biweekly in *The Beat Within*, a magazine based out of San Francisco that features the voices of youth in detention. Each week, youth gather in a circle in one of the classrooms and participate in a variety of writing workshop activities. The writing program is tailored to support each youth's creative goals. Youth in this program have participated in national poetry contests, developed artwork that has been published in print and digital media outlets, and produced self-published autobiographies and books of poetry. By tailoring the writing program to support individual creative projects, youth are able to develop writing skills in the forms of writing in which they are most interested.

Before participating in the writing program, some of the youth do not identify as writers. These youth may initially perceive themselves to be "bad" writers or as lacking the basic skills to produce good writing. This messaging comes from a variety of institutional sources and negatively affects the ability of youth to become self-advocates. To address this, the writing program enlists the help of a large group of volunteers who provide feedback to the writers. After each workshop, the writers' work is digitized and sent out to a large email discussion list of volunteers. The volunteers represent a wide array of backgrounds, careers, and relationships to writing. Each week, they provide a dynamic set of supportive comments for the youth. The relationships formed through this communication benefit both the youth and the volunteers. The youth learn how to incorporate feedback and revise work, while the volunteers are given the opportunity to read great writing and become educated in the social conditions of the youths' lives.

For some of the volunteers, this is the first time they have engaged with incarcerated youth. These volunteers often express how the youth have educated them on myriad social issues confronting youth and significantly affected the ways they understand the social world. Other volunteers are incarcerated in prisons and jails or have previous involvement with the justice, mental health, and family services systems and have a deeper understanding of institutions the youth are navigating. These individuals are often able to speak to many of the lived experiences detailed in the youth's creative production. The incarcerated adults who provide feedback are eager to support youth in imagining alternatives so they can develop new ways of living in the world that do not lead to future incarceration.

Facilitating these kinds of connections between the inside and the outside of the justice system is important to improving self-efficacy and imagining a more livable world for youth. Youth write each week understanding that their audience is broad and represents many different lived realities. The varied backgrounds of the volunteers is important to the writing program's success as well as the ability of youth to improve their self-efficacy. Often, youth who initially identified as non-writers become the writing program's most prolific writers and published authors.

The writing program and other ongoing critical information literacy programming is designed to support youth in increasing and using their own power within their community settings. This is one aspect of creating more socially just and inclusive library services for the youth and their communities. As Swanson (2010) notes, libraries as institutions have historically favored majority ways of knowing and perspectives. It is likely that youth in detention centers will be underserved by libraries or that their interests will be overlooked when building library collections. Youth engaging in critical information literacy programming will gain an understanding of the library that enables them to advocate for the inclusion of their own voices and ways of knowing by locating and requesting the purchase of materials that match their needs and interests.

Conclusion

Youth in juvenile detention face many challenges. Access to information relevant to their experience through library services offers an opportunity to forge connections and move past hurdles. Linking resources with youth's questions and concerns provides examples of new possibilities and facilitates a reduction of alienation. Involving collaborators and mentors—especially peers—in developing and delivering services enables a strong model of collaboration. Peers are agents of positive change.

Through this collaborative initiative, participants demonstrated their commitment to understanding the needs of incarcerated youth in Champaign County and working collectively to provide resources of value to them. As our interaction grows, we will continue to consider issues of importance to the youth and options to link them with resources from our community.

Section 4

Evaluating and Making Sense of Youth Activities

Many YCI projects could not be included in this book for reasons of space. For example, the town of Rantoul, Illinois, became economically depressed following the closing of the Chanute Air Force Base in the early 1990s. Working in Rantoul High School with a group of juniors called Youth Democracy, YCI provided Rantoul youth with the tools to investigate, document, and disseminate information about the impact of poverty on their community (see http://youtu.be/gzq01Qe_UPc and Bouillion-Diaz, Ritzo, & Ayad, 2009). In another case involving the Urbana Free Library, YCI university students worked with library staff and younger residents to learn motion picture techniques and produce a variety of movies about the library, the community, or fantasy worlds. In addition to the activities discussed in Chapter 7, the Teen Tech Team trained teens in computer and networking skills along with social entrepreneurship. Teens used GIS mapping and video production to tell stories about their community. The Mary E. Brown Center there has served as a community center supporting academic, sports, and technology activities since the 1960s. YCI engaged with the program staff to increase inquiry-based activities, such as citizen journalism, blogging, and video production. See http://www.metroeastdigital.org/youth/.

But rather than trying to include every example, we thought it more useful to offer some overview perspectives. We used tools such as field notes, study of the digital artifacts produced by youth, and surveys to assess learning by youth, youth leaders, community partners, parents, and university students and staff. We also analyzed the impacts on community partners, international connections, LIS education, and more. The results are discussed in detail in the final report on the project (Bruce & Bishop, 2011).

Chapter 12 represents one effort to make sense of the whole effort. In "A Needle in a Haystack: Evaluating YCI," Iván M. Jorrín-Abellán calls for a formal evaluation of the set of practices that constitute the innovation to better follow up its evolution. YCI staff are always balancing options, making decisions and choosing different paths to follow. Although these are relevant and valuable forms of informal evaluation, a step forward is needed to reflect formally upon the practices. He proposes a "play script" to illustrate the complexity of the evaluation, as well as the need for a responsive and multi-leveled evaluation.

Angela M. Slates and Ann Peterson Bishop talk about overarching themes in Chapter 13, "'It Takes a Community': Community Inquiry as Emancipatory Scholarship, Indigenous Agency, Performative Inquiry, and

Democracy Education." The chapter explores the praxis of community inquiry, juxtaposed against school-based prevention programs. It asks what can be done for youth in marginalized communities. Community inquiry is analyzed here as a tool for creating an educational system that resists the deficit model and, moreover, a tool for introducing university students to critical pedagogy.

Through this work, we have developed tools that represent both the means and the ends of the process, or *ends-in-view* (Dewey, 1939). These are what we used to carry out the projects, but also what we created as we wrestled with diverse situations and values. In Chapter 14, "Citizen Professional Toolkits: Empowering Communities Through Mass Amateurization," Martin Wolske, Eric Johnson, and Paul Adams discuss some of the digital technologies we used and developed. Public computing centers (PCCs) provide critical access to Information and Communications Technology (ICT) resources where inequities exist. These facilities become meeting places for citizen professionals to participate in communities of practice working toward common goals. The challenge remains how to empower more communities through access to, and training with, citizen professional ICT. Chapter 14 describes the use of customizable citizen professional toolkits to empower youth from economically disadvantaged communities to engage with their community as citizen professionals.

Chapter 15, "Youth Community Informatics Curriculum," by Lisa Bouillion Diaz, presents the curriculum with its *inquiry units* used to organize activities in the community. These units represent a summary of what we learned, as well as tools for further inquiry.

12. A Needle in a Haystack: Evaluating YCI

Iván M. Jorrín-Abellán

Setting

We live in an interconnected world where the deepest learning can happen anytime and anywhere. This new way of living and learning underscores the need for innovative educational experiences as catalysts for the many different learning options our society demands. In this globalized scenario, informal settings are called to be on the cutting edge of new learning practices to reinvigorate our out-of-date school systems. Standard-free environments constitute an ideal "test-bench" for innovations, much more adapted to the needs and challenges posed by twenty-first-century society. That is, in my opinion, one of the affordances of Youth Community Informatics (YCI).

As mentioned in previous chapters, YCI comprises a collective of graduate students, professors, youth leaders, and volunteers working within underserved communities located throughout Illinois. The project tries to actively engage youth in their communities to take on the issues that are affecting them. To do so, it promotes technology-enriched activities, allowing the communities to use them firsthand for their own benefit and sustainability. For instance, youth have been making documentary films and podcasts about community issues (poverty, crime, available assets, etc.), have participated in the archiving of local cultural documents and artifacts, and have created community asset maps using GPS/GIS technology. The YCI project does not focus solely on technology but on the educative experience of youth in the community.

Bertram (Chip) Bruce claimed that "There is no doubt that new forms of learning are already happening through social networking" (Bruce, 2008b, p. 27). I agree with him in a double sense. On the one hand, I believe that accessibility to information as well as to its multiple support formats has contributed to the appearance of these new learning models. On the other, he himself (in collaboration with a motivated and devoted group of people) is trying to recruit youth into library and information science (LIS) careers with a set of engaging, educational activities in after-school programs that deeply promote new learning opportunities. I have experienced it.

Hence, assuming that there are such new forms of learning, should we not think in new ways of making sense of them? Shall we not need new ways to understand what is going on with the new learning environments fostered by our society's needs?

My first contact with the YCI took place in 2005–2006. I soon realized that although the whole project was far away from any kind of large-scale and grandiose initiative, its implications with regard to my research field (educational evaluation) were vast. The initiatives promoted in the last years by YCI, as well as its intrisic nature, challenge traditional approaches to evaluation in a number of ways, promising broader fields of endeavor. The aim of this chapter is to reflect on these challenges to define a formal way to better make sense of YCI as a whole project. I propose here the basis and requirements of an evaluation approach that seeks to give answers to the emerging needs posed by YCI, that is, a path to find the evaluation needle in a haystack.

Cast of Characters

Implications of the characters in a play are crucial, just as they figure in understanding how things work in complex projects such as YCI. Many actors are involved within this initiative. Some of them are individuals. Others are groups with a set of assigned roles that function as particular entities. Others are not human beings. Although some of our readers may be surprised, we do believe that some of the supportive technologies integrated in the project function as invisible teammates (Jorrín-Abellán, et al., 2008), whose consideration would help to better comprehend YCI as a whole. The main characters in our play are the following:

Individuals

- YCI Staff: YCI leaders and Graduate Students (see more at http://www.cii. illinois.edu/ArchiveYCI/index_PageID298.html)
  Ann Bishop: Director/Integrator
  Bertram (Chip) Bruce: The oracle
  Lisa Boullion-Diaz: Extension specialist
  Martin Wolske: Community technology expert
  Chera Kowalski: Cross-site linkages developer
  Chris Ritzo: Librarian 2.0
  Moustafa Ayad: Social Journalist
  Nama Raj Budhathoki: Mapping expert
  Chaebong Nam: Curriculum developer
  Mojgan Momeni: NGO specialist
  Iván M. Jorrín: Evaluation scriptwriter
- Youth leaders: At least one in each of the 14 different places in which the YCI initiative is takes place.

Groups

The work of YCI in communities can be described at three levels of increasing connection and commitment (*Network sites, Partner sites,* and *YCI sites*). Each level can be seen as a character type with similar features. Understanding them as groups of actors could help to simplify the complexity of the YCI ground.

Network sites can be any group or individual with similar goals connecting to YCI through the Internet or other means. International sites such as those in China, Nepal, and Spain are good examples.

Partner sites constitute the second level. Local community organizations generally begin at this level of engagement, where we initiate connections with existing youth programs, or explore possibilities for collaboration with local staff. Examples include working with library staff to plan youth-focused workshops, or collaborating with youth in 4-H clubs in creating maps of community assets.

YCI sites are at the highest level of engagement. They have established a deeper connection with the YCI team to develop challenging programs dedicated to engaging youth with community issues. These sites have dedicated space and staff time to partner with YCI in longer-term projects. Some of them are Paseo Boricua in Chicago with its youth poetry project (Chapter 9); mapping and library projects in Champaign (Chapter 10); a computer rebuilding project in East St. Louis (Chapter 7); a mapping project in Iroquois County (Chapter 4); a youth democracy project in Rantoul; and a mapping project in Virginia, Illinois (Chapter 8).

Machines

In addition to the actors mentioned already, there are other "invisible teammates" that contribute to the functioning of YCI in a number of ways.

- YCI website: The Youth Community Informatics website is used for communication with project sites and larger public. It also serves as a repository of evidence related to the activities promoted by YCI.
- YCI wiki: The YCI wiki is intended to support internal discussions as well as the collaborative writing of documents.
- YCI discussion list: The email list supports asynchronous communication among YCI members.
- Mobile Citizen Professional Toolkit: This kit has been developed with the aim of providing youth with the common tools used by professionals such as journalists, planners, and scientists to facilitate their daily activities. The items in the kit provide the tools to do photography, audio and video recording, and mapping. Along with these components, the kit also includes an ultra-mobile laptop computer and video capture card to create multimedia productions (see Chapter 14).
- iLabs: This is a web-based suite of software tools that can be used to form an interactive website and create inquiry units. It is free of cost to all users. Users create an iLab website by filling out a simple web form that determines which tools and features they want to include on their own iLab website.

The Show: Backstage

There is an evident "stage fright" related to the complexity and implications of designing an evaluation plan for the YCI project. Anxieties for YCI graduate students since the evaluation could increase their workload. Anxieties for YCI leaders as an evaluation could bring out some structural issues affecting the whole project. Anxieties for the evaluation scriptwriter are due to the multiple facets, settings/scenarios, and actors that need to be taken into account to evaluate all the YCI activities.

Storyboard

The next two sections of the "play-script" will be devoted to illustrating a few of the activities promoted by YCI in 2009: the YCI 2009 Summer Academy and a mapping workshop conducted in Virginia, Cass County, in spring. Both experiences serve to deepen understanding of the evaluation challenges posed by YCI.

Scene 1: Reality Bites; Creating Unity

Today is Wednesday, July the first. It is 9:30 in the morning and we are in the third day of the 2009 YCI Summer Academy. We have spent the last two days working with almost 30 teenagers from all over the state. All of them have been working for the last year in YCI projects within their communities.

I don't exactly know the reason, but I cannot take out of my mind Sting's song "Englishman in New York": "I'm an alien, I'm a legal alien, . . . I'm an Englishman in New York." Maybe it is because I'm a foreigner in the Midwest, or because the title of the YCI Summer Academy ("Music can make you snap, it can make you bop, but does it have the power to make you act?") is making me reflect on the power some songs have. I am not an Englishman, and I am not in New York. I'm a Spaniard in Champaign-Urbana, a small metropolitan area in east central Illinois. Champaign-Urbana is also home to the University of Illinois, and *Newsweek* has named the town as one of the top 10 tech cities (outside of Silicon Valley) in the country.

After a brief introduction, Jessie Fuentes, a youth leader who works with the Puerto Rican Cultural Center in Chicago, takes the mic:

> I think it is only fair to say, since this workshop is more on a personal level than the ones you guys have been doing in the last couple of days . . . I'll talk a little bit about myself and the work I do back at home. Two years ago I was one of those teenagers selling drugs, gang banging and all that stuff . . . and the program I run now tries to help other youth get by. . . . They helped me through the process. . . . It is a space called Batey Urbano. It is a youth center for action and reflection for Puerto Rican youth. We have a studio, where we teach teenagers on how to use pro tools and how an online radio station functions . . . or how to do a play, how to write poetry, and many other ways of artistic expression. When I first walked in this place . . . well, I've always written poetry . . . I've always been a spoken word artist since I remember, but

walking in this space, I was never politically aware of what is wrong, I was never able to think critically on my decisions on a day-to-day basis. So when I walked in this space, they taught me things like from how our economy is going down, to things like discrimination and racism. After that I became more politically aware, so my poetry has stepped up to a better level than what I have ever written before. . . . When I started writing poetry, I started writing about reality based of the stuff I live at home, or about what I've seen in the streets or in people in the same circumstances I was in. So after about a year I became . . . I started at PACHS (Dr. Pedro Albizu Campos High School), an alternative school that provides the youth, with the same circumstances I had, turning their lives as drug dealers and gang bangers to professionals . . . right? . . . My whole life changed then. I started to get involved with the community, and now I run Batey Urbano. You can see now the dramatic change in my life. And it was the community and the people who have done that.

Figure 12.1. Storyboard

So now that I run this place, our main focus now, has been the youth who have been forgotten. Students who have been expelled from high school, drug dealers, or people who live in unstable homes. So our focus has been recruiting this group of people, bringing them in and kind of making them politically aware of their situation, making them reflect. We use spoken word to let them take out all the stuff they've been through. . . .

I'm gonna share with you one poem. This is called "So-Called Lines." This poem was written because I sit at home a lot and like, think. You're like, writing on this paper and you feel like this paper is going to run out soon because you have so many things going on, right? So many thoughts and words and you're not sure if this paper is going to be enough to kind of explain through everything you've been through, so this poem explains that . . . .

I take the thoughts from my beautiful mind
and I lay them down on this so-called line
See I live a life of struggle,
with ambitious goals and a heart full of trouble
If I live for today cause I don't know what's coming tomorrow,
so I live like a rocket scientist, doctor, lawyer, 9 o'clock at night, and I sing in the shower,
So I try to live by the happier days cause when I get thinking,
I think about the darker days,
my pop's been fooling around, mom's got put into rehab,
and an inch of a mile, split of a second, I lost everything that I had,
man, I feel so worthless,
like this so called beautiful dream isn't worth it,
how am I supposed to live by something I don't completely believe in,
people tell me keep trying, I promise you'll make it, just believe in it,
then why the hell am I in the same spot hardly moved an inch?
man the street's overrated, and the government is crooked, two buildings the government took it
Feeding us lies through radio and television;
brainwash the little shorties don't let them have their own visions;
I remember when I was younger we used to play things like hide and go seek,
and now we have kids at the age of 10 just wanting to hit the streets,
getting exposed to gangs, guns, drugs and violence
and that killed my brother 2 years ago,
and made the whole crowd silent,
you see this here this is the shit I go through every day
but I try not to make excuses, I just try to find the better way,
but it's so goddamned hard when you feel like you're alone
and the only thing that keeps you company is the liberty to sing a song,
to think that I try to write my thoughts on this so-called line,
but the truth is this shit is too small for the shit on my mind.

This is an atypical activity, but one that resonated for all of the participants. The spoken word workshop took place the last day of the Summer Academy and was led by Jessie Fuentes. At the time of the workshop, she was a freshman at Northeastern University and was a well of information for others in her community. She became a role model by showing that graduating and attending postsecondary school is an attainable goal. After her initial presentation and a couple of rhymes, she invited youth to compose poetry by reflecting on their lives. The poems they produced were moving and illustrated both the depth of reflection and the challenging circumstances of all YCI youth, regardless of whether they lived in rural villages or big cities. It would have been impossible to conduct this workshop the first day of the Summer Academy, since a high level of mutual understanding and confidence was needed among participants to create such unity, such empathy and understanding when their poems were shared aloud.

As can be seen in Evidence 1, participating youth spent the previous two days investigating political and socially charged songs, such as Marvin Gaye's "Inner-City Blues" and Bob Marley's "War." By researching the issues within the songs, teens then created multiple forms of media, such as zines, videos, and slideshows, to share the information they found and to share their own thoughts on the issues within the songs.

Evidence 1: 2009 YCI Summer Academy Agenda

Monday, June 29th, 3 p.m.–6 p.m., RM 126
3:00-3:30—Introduction to YCI—Who we are and what we have been
    working on; Showcasing youth work
3:30-4:00—Icebreaker activities; Group formations
4:00-6:00—Intro to Projects video; Speakers: Michael Pollock: Protest Songs and Research, Arthur King: Local Music and Research. Song List and group discussion of song issue(s)/topic(s)

Tuesday, June 30th, 8 a.m.–6 p.m., GSLIS, RM 126
8:00 – 9:30—Mini-workshops: Intro to Various Technologies and Methods (GPS/GIS—Nama; Video and Audio—Chris; Print—Chera)
 9:30-11:30—Champaign Jazz Tour, Champaign Public Library, Douglas
    Branch
 11:30-12:00—Urbana Free Library—Discussion on the library as a place for
    research with Teen/Reference Librarian, Carol Inskeep
12:00-1:00—Lunch and Video Games @ UFL
1:00-2:00—Planning Projects and Research
2:00-6:00—Continue Planning/Research and Work on Projects

Wednesday, July 1st, 8 a.m.–12 Noon, GSLIS, RM 131
8:00-9:30—Wrapping up projects
9:30-10:30—Spoken Word Workshop—Jessie Fuentes
10:30-12:00—Showcase of Projects

Song List
• Bob Marley, "War"
• Bruce Springsteen, "Born in the USA"
• Marvin Gaye, "Inner City Blues (Make Me Wanna Holler)"
• James Brown, "I Don't Want Nobody to Give Nothing"
• Sleater Kinney, "Entertain"
• Bright Eyes, "When the President Talks to God"
• Dead Prez, "Animal in Man"

Scene 2: Mapping Around the School

It is early this Saturday morning. Moustafa drives the big Ford Excursion truck on our way to Cass County. Nama, Chaebong, Mojgan, Chera, and I have coffee after a quick stop at Dunkin Donuts drive-thru in Champaign. The radio is on, the road is empty. A straight line cuts the corn and soybean fields as far as I can see. It is a sunny day and I feel excited. We have a dense agenda (see Table 2) for today. We arrive in the town of Virginia at 9:15 a.m. after two hours on the road (see Figure 2).

Teachers and administrators at Virginia Community Unit School District 64 are designing a GIS/GPS course where students will be working in the community, designing projects to be used by the community (see details in Chapter 8). To be ready for the course, they want to learn how to use GPS and Flip cameras to better develop their course. That is the main reason for this workshop.

Virginia is an agricultural community and many of the jobs in this area use GIS/GPS technology. These include military jobs, agriculture, and the construction of roads and buildings. The course will offer students the opportunity to solve real-world problems within the Virginia community. The class includes 11th- and 12th-grade students who receive two credits for the course; one credit will be in Social Sciences and one credit in Agriculture.

Virginia has one school, a K–12 facility run by Virginia Community Unit School District 64. The facility is broken down into units: Virginia Elementary School, Virginia Junior High, and Virginia High School. The high school has recently been removed from the academic watch warning list. The school is located in a two-story brick building. It is currently not in its best condition. Some broken steps, leaks here and there, classes being held in the halls . . . "We have changed the roof this year . . . we had leaks all over the building," said Jeff Bennett, the Social Studies teacher.

The workshop takes place in two different rooms. The first is Jeff's classroom, where the walls are covered in the projects done by students. Twenty-one desks are cramped in the available space. The room also has two blackboards, a smartboard, several bookshelves, TV and video devices, and three Macs and two PCs. The rest of the workshop takes place at Lab 202. The school received a grant a year and a half ago to buy 30 iMacs, two laser printers, and a bunch of digital cameras. All of them are installed in the lab. They are also planning to get 110 Macbooks, one per student at the high school.

The workshop starts at 10:25 (see Evidence 2). The participants are seven youth (between third grade and high school), five adults (one parent, Jeff Bennet, one community social worker, and two others), and the six of us.

After the initial icebreaker, Moustafa does a brief introduction to inquiry-based learning and YCI by using a video clip created by youth at Rantoul (another YCI site). The beginning of the session is driven by the question, "What are the stories you want to tell?" The aim of the workshop is to learn how to tell stories from the community using GPS, Flip cameras, and interactive maps.

At 10:50 the group is split into thirds to try the use of Flip cameras by creating one-minute video interviews. After 20 minutes, Moustafa encourages youth to talk a little on the recorded interviews. At 11:30 Nama explains, by using one of the previously recorded interviews, what to do in the afternoon session to link maps and videos using YouTube and Google Maps. At 11:45, there is a brief demonstration of using GPS devices in the parking lot. Lunch time goes from 12:10 to 12:45. Burgers, vegetables, and homemade pie make us enjoy a relaxing time all together. The afternoon session begins at 1:20. The three groups start looking for stories until 3:00.

My group finds Jack. He makes and repairs old wooden toys in his own restored cabins. We record him while he kindly explains how people lived during the civil war. He shows us many old artifacts used to prepare butter, to go hunting, and even the clothes used by people in the past century. The group marks with the GPS device every single step of our route looking for our own story.

At 3:10 we go back to Lab 202 to meet the rest of the groups. We spend the next hour and a half processing the videos, managing location data, and creating a Google Map with all the information gathered. Each group does the same until 4:30 when the presentation and discussion of the work done starts. The workshop finishes at 5:15 and half an hour later we are in our way back home.

Evidence 2: Virginia High School Agenda

Saturday, May 2nd, 10 a.m.–5 p.m.
10:00–10:10 Introduction (YCI members)
10:10–10:20 Participants' introduction and speaking about purposes/interests
10:20–10:30 Introduction to inquiry in learning
10:30–10:50 (Discuss/brainstorming) "What are the stories you want to tell?"
10:50–11:05 Handing out Flip video cameras, Creating one-minute videos
11:05–11:20 Play back the videos and discuss "Where do we go for investigation?"
11:20–11:50 Get out of the room and play with GPS
11:50–12:30 Give a short tour of the overall process for connecting stories to places
Lunch 12:30–1:15
1:15–1:30 Moustafa's quick demonstration of video technologies
1:30–3:00 Field work (collecting location and other data)
3:00–4:30 Lab work (process videos, location data, and create maps)
4:30–5:00 Presentation and discussion/reflection

Intermission

The previous scenes describe two particular moments of the many produced by YCI in the last couple of years. Both of them took place in different settings, with different participants and different aims. They represent, in part, the diversity of the many sites across the state of Illinois. They also illustrate the variety of practices under the umbrella of YCI. The wide extent of these practices, in addition to their diversity and the number of participants involved, are probably the main practical challenges to evaluate YCI as a whole

(Nam, Ritzo, & Bruce, 2009). This particularity crystallizes in a number of aspects/threads that could be followed to better understand how the project works, its worth and merit.

Evidence 3 summarizes some of the issues and tensions that emerged from both scenes. Almost all of them could help to conduct an extensive evaluation of each site, and some of them could even drive the evaluation of YCI as a whole. But, taking all of them into account would be impossible. Many aspects can be evaluated, too many options, many ways of understanding evaluation. But, why is YCI evaluation so complicated? Is there a reasonable way to make it happen? It is not that easy, since YCI challenges traditional approaches to evaluation in many ways.

YCI challenges typical evaluation approaches because it relies on contexts of activity that vary from formal to informal sites. Moreover, its activities welcome collaborative inquiry that is challenging even to collaborative evaluation, since the contributions to joint learning by individuals remains unclear. Also challenging are the technological artifacts that mediate the experiences and have not been included in the scrutiny of traditional evaluation. And challenging because of the many evaluation traditions that converge in the variety of potential evaluators involved in the project (YCI staff, youth leaders, participants, etc.). All of these aspects lie beyond the present scope of program and policy evaluation.

Evidence 3: Issues Observed

Issues observed at YCI Summer Academy regarding YCI as a whole
- *Is the YCI summer academy helping youth to address their needs?*
- *Are the Inquiry Units/activities designed for the summer academy promoting interconnectness among the different sites where youth learn?*
- *How appropriate was time spent in action vs. time spent in reflection?*
- *What was the role of technology? What are the consequences of using Open Source vs. commercial products in the YCI Toolkit?*
- *How effective was collaborative work? Did learning proceed in a connected way?*
- *How, and how effectively, were youth involved?*
- *What was the role of sponsorship for participants?*
- *How successful were the timing and agenda?*
- *How did graduate assistants assess their workload: time spent in preparation and implementation?*
- *Other particular issues*
    - *Organizational: How well did the YCI Summer Academy work as part of 2009 Illini academies?*

Issues observed at Cass County Workshops regarding YCI as a whole
- *Is the workshop helping youth to address their needs?*
- *Is the workshop actively engaging youth in their community?*

- *Did the developed Inquiry Units promote interconnectness among the different sites where youth learn?*
- *How appropriate was time spent in action vs. time spent in reflection?*
- *What was the role of technology? What are the consequences of using Open Source vs. commercial products in the YCI Toolkit?*
- *How effective was collaborative work? Did learning proceed in a connected way?*
- *How, and how effectively, were youth involved?*
- *How successful were the timing and agenda?*
- *How did graduate assistants assess their workload: time spent in preparation and implementation?*
- *Other particular Issues*
    - *Are there any similarities between Virginia High School and other sites within the YCI?*
    - *Is the role YCI is playing within the Virginia community different from the role played in other communities?*
    - *How successful was the implementation of the workshop?*
    - *Does it make sense to have youth coming from other communities?*

Emerging Issues
- *Rural vs. Urban*
- *Local vs. Distant*
- *African American community vs. White rural community*
- *School vs. Out of school*
- *Different organizational traits*
- *Different values/perspectives among the YCI staff*

There is a further challenge coming from the change in the evaluand promoted by YCI. This kind of complex project encourages sophisticated ways of learning in which its evaluation often needs to shift from the classroom or individual to the collaborative activity, in context. This constitutes a difficulty for current approaches to education evaluation since much of its tradition particularized the school and classroom and other fixed spatial and temporal settings. This change in evaluand should acknowledge the interconnectedness of formal and informal learning spheres, aiming at providing better understanding of how these new ways of learning happen.

The last challenge has to do with agency issues. In these days, the balance of agency, the mediation of learning, has shifted in many domains of our lives. There is little need to be a passive learner when one can become a codesigner of knowledge, collaborating with others. YCI is a good example of it. In this sense, evaluation should respond to agency changes by focusing more on the active roles played by participants and community leaders, deepening the understanding of their interactions (both face-to-face and computer-mediated). Therefore, the evaluation of YCI and other projects with the same characteristics should give focus to the mediator's role (graduate research assistants, staff, youth leaders, etc.) as a key dynamizing element of the multiple and sometimes dissonant information to be found in the extended settings in which participants learn. In the same way, the evaluation of YCI should also include the recognition and valuing of learner differences, the connections between an individual's own thinking and collective intelligence, and the mix of representational modes needed to describe education.

All of these show the prospect and challenge of YCI in regards to program evaluation. In the same way, they indicate opportunities. In this chapter we are not claiming that more evaluation necessarily means better learning or improvement in the project, but we have come to believe that without more responsive and situated evaluation, it will be difficult to promote learning in the desired ways. Aligning the issues discussed above, more practical and action-oriented guidance could be useful to potential evaluators of YCI. The final act of this play-script is devoted to putting forth ideas on how to overcome some of the difficulties addressed so far.

Final Act: A Needle in a Haystack

Evaluating complex projects like YCI requires instruments of some sort to help evaluators find the needle in a haystack. For such endeavors we suggest the use of the Evaluand-oriented Responsive Evaluation Model (EREM) (Jorrín-Abellán & Stake, 2009). EREM is an evaluand-oriented model focused on the evaluation object rather than on who is evaluating or even on the ultimate purpose of the evaluation. It promotes deep understanding of the innovation being evaluated, getting closely acquainted with its functioning. The aim of the model is to provide clear, understandable, and action-oriented guidance to practitioners involved in the evaluation of these complex environments. It spans the different evaluands that could be assessed in these settings and is framed within the Responsive Evaluation (Stake, 2003) approach. It is oriented to the activity, the uniqueness and the plurality of the activity to be evaluated, promoting responsiveness to key issues and problems recognized by participants at the site, as well as stakeholders elsewhere.

Evaluating this kind of project requires a great deal of effort in the design stage of the evaluation. The model I propose could help to minimize the complexity involved in the decision-making process that encompasses the design phase (and beyond) of an evaluation.

The model contains three facets representing the most visible manifestations (perspective, ground, and method) to deepen the understanding of the evaluand; four question-oriented practical courses (pathways) identifying main sub-evaluands; a diagram for planning the evaluation; and a set of recommendations for writing the evaluation report. More details on the EREM model can be found in Jorrín-Abellán and Stake (2009) and Jorrín-Abellán et al. (2009).

A graphical representation of an evaluation design for YCI, developed by following the step-by-step criteria provided by EREM is available on request. The design takes into account the special conditions in which YCI exists (Ground) and defines a set of issues (Perspective) to drive the evaluation process. Issues are suggested in the model as conceptual organizers for the evaluation study, rather than as hypotheses or objectives. An issue can be understood as a troubling choice, tension, an organizational perplexity or a problem (Stake, 2006). As conceptual organizers of the evaluation, issues help evaluators focus on informative tensions within the evaluand. The design also encourages the use of a concrete set of data-gathering techniques (Method) including, observations, interviews and the analysis of the artifacts created by youth, according to the availability of the evaluators. Another relevant aspect within the Method facet has to do with the selection of the informants. Some of the technologies used to support YCI practices (the YCI site, wiki, and blog) are included not only as tools but as informants. These peculiar informants could help to gather rich data more easily, contributing to the feasibility of the evaluation.

This multifaceted and multilevel evaluation design could help to better understand the roots and evolution of YCI by deepening attention in only a few aspects that, in effect, condition the whole project. If desired, the model could also be applied at different levels of coalescence across YCI at the same time, assuming for instance a particular site or activity as the evaluand. This way, each collaborating site and even each activity would be analyzed following the same evaluation framework, thus contributing to the evaluation of the project as a whole. A complementary approach is the *practice profile* of inquiry presented in Bruce and Casey (2011).

To bridge the gap between the presented design and real practice, we can use as examples the two scenes shown at the beginning of this chapter. Each of them can be seen as a way to portray a particular activity within YCI, highlighting an event in the form of a vignette. Potential evaluators could use this strategy to analyze a small number of issues regarding YCI as a whole, across sites, and within specific activities that were conducted. These processes should be planned in advance, having in mind the particularities in which every site exists, the availability of potential evaluators, the issues found by participants, and their potential contribution to a better understanding of YCI functioning.

Applause

In this chapter I have reflected on the importance of a responsive and multilevel evaluation model to cope with the evaluation challenges posed by YCI as a social, informal, and ubiquitous educational setting that blurs the traditional fixed boundaries of formal evaluation.

Although a variety of means have been used to evaluate YCI, further work could be done to assess the project as a whole. I have made a proposal by using the Evaluand-oriented Responsive Evaluation Model. The model is intended to promote mutual understanding among the different backgrounds and perspectives traditionally involved in the evaluation of these scenarios. It tries to provide categorical criteria for most of them. At the same time, the model can guide the evaluation of YCI as a holistic and interconnected situation, showing that the effects of such a complex setting cannot be assumed to lie along a single continuum. The approach strengthens the idea of conducting evaluand-oriented evaluations instead of encapsulating evaluations on the particular field of whomever is evaluating. The model can be worked into a practical tool providing question-oriented pathways and real examples, especially to help novice evaluators conduct an evaluation. The proposed model also aims to help in the planning stage of the evaluation by providing a graphic representation of connections to be made in the evaluation of YCI. My proposal is not intended to be a complete and prescriptive model, but more a cautionary device.

With this intention, we are currently providing access to the EREM as a web-based tool. The development here also has the aim of generating an online community of practice among evaluators. Users are likely to benefit from expertise achieved by other evaluators at the same time they play an active role in refining this model. The web-based tool is accessible at http://pandora.tel.uva.es/cscl-erem.

13. "It Takes a Community": Community Inquiry as Emancipatory Scholarship, Indigenous Agency, Performative Inquiry, and Democracy Education

Angela M. Slates

with

Ann Peterson Bishop

I advocate change that envisions a democracy founded in a social justice that is not yet. –Norman K. Denzin

This chapter explores the praxis of community inquiry juxtaposed against school-based prevention programs. As an African American female scholar and researcher who once attended school in a rural public school district with faint success, I have a particular focus on children of color, because it is predominantly children of color who are classified as truant, suspended, and underachieving on a macro level. This declares to us all that the United States is failing children of color at an alarming rate.

What can be done? We must confront the "deficit model" (Bak, 2001; Darder, 1991) that claims children of color, with their defective parents and lack of interest in education, are the problem. The deficit model shifts our critical gaze away from the traditional systems of education that reproduce and maintain the status quo by supporting curricula that marginalize the voices, histories, experiences, and values of students of color, while at the same time emphasizing traditions and canons of European culture.

Community inquiry provided the basic framework for the many activities encompassed by the Youth Community Informatics (YCI) project, for which I served as a research assistant in its final months. Here, I point to community inquiry as a tool for indigenous agency, emancipatory scholarship, performative inquiry, and democracy education—facets of an educational system that fights against the deficit model. My purpose is to interrogate the ways that community inquiry as praxis can be emancipatory for youth in marginalized communities. With a belief that understanding can create change, I advocate the praxis of YCI to help young people of color understand, in a broader sense, the sociopolitical systems that oppress them and their families. YCI also works to improve on their condition by educating them about the institutions that affect their daily lives and assisting them in finding solutions while enhancing their technological skills, all of which enhances their ability to be agents of change within their indigenous community space and culture.

The urgency of a pedagogical shift in youth education cannot remain a theoretical construct relegated to graduate studies classrooms, scholarly journals, and the privileged discourse of higher education. This chapter discusses how community inquiry praxis can be developed to assist people of color in receiving a quality education that is congruent with the cultural, family, and communal values that encourage self-improvement through indigenous agency.

An integral component of this shift consists of changing the ways in which we see, hear, feel, and understand children of color. In America, we are not a race-neutral society; there is no authenticity to the ideology of colorblindness. Research indicates that color *is* phenotypically the first thing we notice about another human being on first contact, followed by racial group categorization and spontaneous stereotyping, which is historically and consistently negative for people of color. This stereotyping of human beings is then used to perpetuate a skin color–coded caste system that is historically rooted and ratified within the sociopolitical structures of America. It is this pervasive act of seeing and reacting to, yet not acknowledging, color that serves to conceal and reinforce a multitude of personal and institutional micro-aggressions often experienced by African American, Latino/Latina, and Native American students within and outside of public school institutions.

So, although the systematic act of racialization and stereotyping in the United States is an age-old ritual that today goes unacknowledged by most, it is this act of covert stereotyping that many social science researchers believe to be a central contributor to the negative educational experiences and outcomes of many students of color. Along with exclusionary practices, disinterest, and silencing of the lived experiences of these students, stereotyping renders their reality irrelevant, leaving many students feeling irrelevant.

Thus, young people of color are pushed to the periphery of the traditional educational experience, and oppressive sociopolitical structures are reproduced from one generation to the next. Systemic exclusionary educational practices result in frustrated students, and the systematic grouping of learning disorders and behavior disorders with school-based prevention programs. While such programs may serve to accommodate some student issues, the fact remains that high dropout rates, truancy, suspensions, and excessive amounts of students of color in special education classes persists. I concur with Potts (2003) that it is primarily because most environmental prevention programs seek to modify childrearing techniques or classroom management strategies, as opposed to seeking change at the community or societal level:

> Data and positive facts on school failure, violence, and substance abuse do not tell the whole story of the cultural experience[s] of children . . . nor of the structures and processes that sustain these circumstances. Children and adolescents . . . only become "at risk" under specific historical circumstances, and as a result of specific social relationships marked by racism and oppression. However in most school-based

prevention programs, the only targets of change are the individual behaviors, attitudes, and interpersonal skills of children.

The time has come for youth voices, youth experiences, and popular culture to become a centralized component of how indigenous communities engage the American K–12 educational system. If we can do this, we will be on the path to instituting indigenous values and ideas into a curriculum that supports the advancement of community goals.

YCI as Indigenous Agency

The term *indigenous* is predominantly associated with Native Americans in the United States. I use it, however, more broadly, with respect to original peoples and spaces beset with colonialism. Indigenous knowledge is, thus, local or traditional knowledge, the right to claim knowledge and resources that exist within one's own culture and within one's own geographically located space, and those rights that exist in recognition of that culture and space (Battiste, 2002). When we speak of indigenous knowledge, we are sensitive to the sustained effects of colonialism, racism, oppression, and hierarchal caste systems based on race and culture that adversely affect learning. With the term *agency* then defined as the ability of social actors to make independent choices, indigenous agency then becomes self-representation, defining itself within the framework of community inquiry as *individuals claiming the self, the community, the space, the resources, the knowledge, and the culture that is their own.*

Can we find examples of indigenous agency in the YCI project? I believe there are many. For example, in Chapter 11, we learned about the extension of library services to incarcerated youth. Through the work of the Peer Ambassadors, and with the support of other groups in the community, indigenous agency is promoted among those held in the juvenile detention center. The ELSEY project helps the young people gain a voice in the institution holding them by incorporating their views in library policymaking and including their perspectives in the library's contents. The voices of incarcerated youth are heard explicitly in ELSEY's reading and writing programs. In addition, ELSEY is striving to increase the power of youth in the broader community by connecting them with libraries beyond the walls of the detention center.

Indigenous agency operates in the community inquiry program described by Alex Jean-Charles in Chapter 3, where young black Caribbean males claimed their culture by protesting the stereotypes associated with AIDS sufferers. The young men in Chicago, further, gained agency by conducting research on surveillance in their community, developing their understanding of surveillance as a tool of power, and producing a video to share their findings and views with local families, neighbors, and institutions.

YCI as Emancipatory Scholarship

> The term "research" is inextricably linked to European imperialism and colonialism.
> The word itself "research" is probably one of the dirtiest words in the indigenous
> world's vocabulary.—Norman K. Denzin

Community inquiry as emancipatory scholarship (Simons & Usher, 2000;
Truman, Mertens, & Humphries, 2000) seeks to be distinguished from
conventional research, research that some community members and scholars
identify as "drive-by research." Drive-by research is disconnected, and static,
described by University of Illinois's Will Patterson (2010, in conversation) as

> research of no consequence. Meaning it has no redeeming social value for
> marginalized communities . . . research that people in these [marginalized]
> communities cannot afford, and therefore continues to contribute to the strained
> relationship between higher education organizations and distressed communities.

Fluid, open, and responsive, the practice of community inquiry as a tool
for emancipatory scholarship does not group participants according to
assessment scores or national statistics, nor does it measure participants by
how accurately they followed the steps of an assignment. Instead, it is inspired
by whether participants feel a strong and authentic sense of development and
evolution in their practice, gain an understanding of their practice, and have
an authentic connection to the situation in which they practice. Typically
undertaken as a collaborative effort between participants, community
members, community organizations, and a college or university, this distinct
inquiry practice is delineated by a process involving a spiral of self-reflection:
asking questions, investigating solutions, creating new knowledge as
information is collected, engaging in discussions that evolve from the
discoveries and experiences of the practice, and reflecting on new-found
knowledge. Through a shared ownership of the community inquiry practice,
community inquiry as emancipatory scholarship exploits the opportunity to
create forums where people who may have otherwise never connected can join
together as co-participants in a struggle toward recovery. Thus, all of those who
participate (including university members) can release themselves from the
constraints of irrational, unproductive, unjust, and unsatisfying social
structures that limit self-development and self-determination.

It is through this community-based democratic process of developing self-
awareness through analysis of community, culture, history, and social issues
that participants have an opportunity to explore the ways in which their lived
experience is affected by broader societal structures, those structures that
shape and constrain the cultural, economic, and political conditions of those
whom they love the most; those broader societal structures that remain
concealed and unacknowledged through traditional K–12 educational
practices.

In emancipatory research, participants make use of community inquiry practice as a tool for healing and empowerment, acknowledging some of their more urgent issues, seeing themselves as agents to bring about positive change, doing something in the world around them, correcting some of the problems and making the world a better place to live in. I believe that emancipatory scholarship is a fair characterization of YCI work. A number of the chapters convey the personal perspectives of various participants, including teachers, community members, program directors, youth, and university members. Through their lenses, we see the ways in which the project helped them to grow and develop a deeper understanding of the world around them, its injustices and institutional failures, along with inklings of redress. In Chapter 5, middle school teacher Shameem Rakha recounts the professional and personal impact of participation in the Youth Media Workshop:

> Working with the students in Youth Media Workshop helped me to realize that many of my assumptions, understandings, and teaching methods were inadequate. Spending time with these young women, two times (and often more) a week, learning with them about their history and lives, hearing their hopes (often dashed), and dreams (again, dashed) changed me. I learned the wealth of the history of these students. I learned of the wealth of the history of our community, of the African American community, in particular. This not only led me to further understand my own complicated racial identity, but to determine to change my pedagogy to better reflect the gifts and meet the needs of my African American students.

Chris Ritzo shows the emancipatory effect experienced by youth in the Teen Tech program in East St. Louis (Chapter 7):

> It was apparent that they were very been used to being given specific, task-based instruction in the classroom and in extracurricular programs. In our first few activities, teens were slow to contribute to group discussions, to make guesses in answer to questions, or to take a leadership role themselves in the activities. Part of their hesitance was surely getting used to a new, unfamiliar face. But slowly they began to see the adults from YCI and Teen Tech as facilitators in *their* learning and recognized the need to lead and direct their own learning in the inquiry process.

In describing her experiences with African American youth in a teen community mapping project (Chapter 10), Chaebong Nam provides us with several insights about the nature of emancipatory scholarship. Most helpful, perhaps, is her portrayal of how adult participants learned that shifting power to the youth can result in improved research practice. The E2Y project strongly encouraged active youth participation, but was driven by adult university-community partners. There was not much room for the youth to participate in decision-making, especially at the earlier stages. Yet, as London (2007) notes, the power relationship between youth and adults can change. In this case, the youth gradually developed the big picture of the project and provided good suggestions for improvement.

As these examples remind us, emancipatory scholarship is not meant to be a utopian form of intervention, not meant to be a form of intervention at all, but meant to be a transformative way of connecting the participants' lived experiences to their community, the world, language, social relationships of power, injustice, dissatisfaction, ways of relating to others, critical insights, the potential of different perspectives, reaching out, reaching in, and the emancipatory means by which to assassinate the deficit model.

YCI as Performative Inquiry

Understanding the ways in which performative inquiry (Pelias, 2008) has historically been and continues to be a political platform for education in communities of color assists us in understanding the interconnection of community inquiry and youth voices as a tool for such work. In YCI, youth voices, youth experiences, and popular culture become a significant component in the education, in the process of understanding one's place in the world and what to do about it. Incorporating the historical moment, morally informed performance, counter-narratives, and personal expressions connected to one's lived experience, performative inquiry uses arts-based disciplines to help recover the meaning of struggle, resistance, conflict, brutal violence, terror, injustice, oppression, and death within communities of color, the nation, and the world. Performative inquiry in education "contributes to an epistemological and political pluralism that challenges existing ways of knowing and representing the world."

It is this type of oppositional performance with pedagogies of dissent that people of color have historically used to demonstrate their own experiential knowledge and condition. Through music, monologues, poetry, vocal performance, choreopoems, and stage plays, performative inquiry has been a staple in indigenous communities in the quest toward freedom and emancipation. From the old Negro spirituals of slavery, to Maya Angelou's 1969 legendary poem *I Know Why the Caged Bird Sings*, to Ntozake Shange's 1975 famed choreopoem *For Colored Girls Who Have Considered Suicide When the Rainbow Is Enuf*, to some of the most beloved African American musical performers of the century, categorized as rhythm and blues (performers such as Billie Holiday, Marvin Gaye, Stevie Wonder, Prince, Janet Jackson, and Michael Jackson), performative inquiry aims at healing, empowering, and de-essentializing the "other," while working toward dismantling the unjust, sociopolitical structures of America. Performative inquiry also provides a lens to observe the rising popularity of the hip-hop generation throughout the 1980s and 1990s, with performers such as Public Enemy, KRS One, Eric B. and Rakim, Gang Starr, and Tupac Shakur. These artists represent many aspects of African American performance culture, which has merged with an urban aesthetic, one rooted in community-based performative inquiry.

Again, YCI can be seen to demonstrate the role of performative inquiry in enhancing both education and social justice. The TAP-In program (Chapter 6) incorporated community exhibits of youth digital photography as a means of teaching children the joys of artistic expression in a way that also enhanced their tech skills and increased their vision of themselves as active and capable community participants. At the Dr. Pedro Albizu Campos High School in Chicago's Paseo Boricua community, students wrote poetry about their lives and neighborhoods, and then performed and discussed their work in the classroom (Chapter 9). Poetry became a way for the youth to interrogate their circumstances and actions, to make sense of their experiences within a broader sociopolitical framework, and to find hope and meaning in their education. It is intriguing that Ivan Jorrín-Abellán foregrounds a theatrical metaphor in his consideration of YCI (Chapter 12), along with providing a closer look at the use of spoken word performance in one of YCI's annual symposia. Indeed, the collection of YCI Inquiry Units brought together as a curriculum (Chapter 15) is rich with infusions of music, poetry, and other arts in service of an education that both draws on and enriches the lives of young people of color.

YCI as Democracy Education

In 1916, John Dewey published his seminal book, titled simply *Democracy and Education*. How are these two social institutions connected? Mark Smith (2001a) begins his analysis with the claim "While our aims change with situations, all educators, it can be argued, share a larger purpose—to foster democracy." The connections between democratic practice and formal education have been explored in various ways (Goodlad, 1996; Guinier & Torres, 2002; Harber, 1992).

My own connection with YCI centered on the Youth Media Workshop, a project rooted in indigenous agency and emancipatory scholarship that brought together public media with educational institutions in Champaign-Urbana, Illinois (Chapter 5). So I will begin with that project as an example of democracy education. The Youth Media Workshop's goal was to teach African American youth how to make radio and television documentaries that link their generation, the hip-hop generation, to the civil rights and black power generations. Students were taught by a diverse team of media professionals from the public broadcasting station WILL AM-FM-TV, scholars and journalism students from the University, and local teachers and community leaders. Upon completion of the community inquiry project, the six young African American male filmmakers from Urbana High School premiered their documentary to an appreciative audience at Boardman's Art Theatre in downtown Champaign, then further went on to explain their project on radio talk shows on four different stations.

During the radio talk shows three of the student producers—Nick Green, Brian Mitchell, and Jay Walker—discussed the making of a video that was about the history and future of the legendary Douglass (community center) Center Drum Corps in Champaign, Illinois. They discussed how the video they created told the story of the drum corps during its heyday in the late 1960s and ask the question, "Who will carry on the tradition and provide this important social outlet for young black men and women today?" Mitchell told the audience about how the students hoped the video would help with efforts to revive the drum corps. "It's about small town living. It's about the history of drumming itself, the egos and pride of the drummers, the personalities of the drummers and the future of drumming." The 25-minute documentary includes recollections of former drum corps member and Champaign-Urbana community resident Terry Townsend, who reminisces during his interview about how the 1968 Douglass Center Drum Corps won first place in a national competition in New York City. Townsend recalls the sense of community pride people felt in the victory, how Walter Cronkite announced it on the CBS Evening News. When their bus pulled into town on their return, drum corps members discovered they were heroes, Townsend said. "When we got to Douglass Center, there was just a sea of people!"

During this process of community inquiry, students in the Youth Media Workshop learned to conduct library research; interview their families, peers, and community members; professionally edit audio and video into radio and TV programs; present their findings at public events and conferences; think analytically, problem solve, and lead group discussions with their peers; and contribute research to the fields of youth media and community inquiry. These culturally and community rich practices contributed to the participants' sense of pride. The young black men who created the drum corps documentary surely participated in democracy education, which gave them a strong and authentic sense of agency in both education and community affairs. Put another way, we can see the imprint of democracy education in the words of Kimberlie Kranich and Will Patterson, co-directors of the Youth Media Workshop, who describe its goals as "for young people to understand the significance of their history in order to pass it on to future generations to build better communities, to build stronger points of self-esteem, stronger identities and to be agents for change in society and mass media."

The public schools participating in the Youth Media Project ranged from primary to postsecondary, including Champaign's Franklin Middle School, where Shameem Rakha was a teacher; the Urbana High School; and the University of Illinois. Two other institutions stand out as exemplars for democracy education. One is the Dr. Pedro Albizu Campos High School in Chicago (Pedro Albizu, n.d.) already noted above and described in Chapters 9, 12, and 15, whose connection with community inquiry at the University of Illinois extends at least a decade before the YCI project (Bruce, 2008a). The second example is provided by Virginia High School (Chapters 2, 8, and 12) with the incorporation of community inquiry and mapping into their formal curriculum. Although Virginia's teachers and students do not include people of color, I include them here nonetheless because they, too, represent people on the periphery: those who live in a tiny rural town with few resources and limited educational opportunities and students with learning disabilities.

Conclusion

We live in pivotal times for American education. More and more youth slip through the cracks of the public school system every year. Although most educators and educational theorists would concede that there is no one comprehensive educational quick fix for American schools, what is also clear is that the current system of education in America is failing students at a distressing rate, particularly African American, Latino/Latina, and Native American students. The deficit model persists as an easy way out of accountability for teachers, administrations, and entire school districts nationwide. If African American, Latino/Latina, and Native American theoretical perspectives in higher education are working toward the advancement of colored people by "throwing out the lifeline to youth of color nationwide," then I ask the question to all of my colleagues, "What does it matter if young arms can't reach or benefit from the work?" Through exploring community inquiry as indigenous agency, emancipatory scholarship, performative inquiry, and democracy education, and experiencing these phenomena through the YCI project, I have learned that education that truly reaches young people of color, youth on the periphery, takes a whole community. I encourage readers to sample and experiment with the praxis of community inquiry. What do we have to lose?

14. Citizen Professional Toolkits: Empowering Communities Through Mass Amateurization

Martin Wolske
Eric Johnson
Paul Adams

Access to information and communications technology (ICT) is considered important for individuals to fully achieve educational and economic development goals. The creation of community-based public computing centers (PCCs) has been an important first step in reducing that digital divide by providing physical access to ICT. Also known as Community Technology Centers or Telecentres, PCCs provide a valuable means for diffusion of technology.

An often unstated premise is that such public access is only a stepping-stone (Viseu et al., 2006); that real computer use will not happen until low-income users have access in their homes (Bishop et al., 1999). For instance, Loader and Keeble (2004) note that the UK has historically viewed public access points only as a valuable safety net for those without access. As Bishop et al. (1999) note, it is certainly the case that PCCs typically limit access to certain hours and applications, and in many settings privacy is impossible and the spaces are uncomfortable for extended use. Many PCCs are set up to serve a maximum number of simultaneous users, in keeping with the digital divide framework. Further, efforts are often made to find ways to discourage unimportant (as defined by host organizations) computer use either directly through filters or indirectly through time limits. For instance, Gurstein (2003) finds important uses are often limited to passive access as opposed to active production of content. The research thus suggests that the result of emphasizing the distributive function of PCCs to bridge the digital divide can produce a more restrictive environment for users.

However, in South Korea, with high home computer and broadband penetration, public computing facilities such as cyber cafes still thrive as social hubs. And researchers such as Ceballos et al. (2006) suggest that the best telecentres are ones that become hubs for social change. This chapter, which is an updated version of a paper presented at the Community Informatics Research Network conference (Wolske et al., 2010), will first review a sample of literature that points toward the possible changing roles of PCCs. It will then consider a potential toolkit—based on the kit originally developed in the Youth Community Informatics project—that could be used to provide the technical tools needed to equip community members to more effectively serve as citizen professionals in support of community development goals.

Public Computing Centers:
From Diffusion of Technology to Hubs of Social Change

Fuchs (1998) points out that while diffusion of technology is often the initial motivator for creating telecentres, this need is reduced over time, at which point telecentres either need to transform to meet other "back of the market" needs, or dissolve. This need to adapt reflects not only a communal change but also an individual change as users of the telecentres go through a development process in which they (1) learn how they can harness the equipment and facilities available to meet their needs; (2) relearn information-seeking behavior using the new assets; and (3) learn how they can add to the value and breadth of available online knowledge. Gurstein (2003) further points out that achieving educational and economic development goals in an information society requires more than simple physical access to ICT. Instead, a framework of effective use is proposed, defined as "The capacity and opportunity to successfully integrate ICTs into the accomplishment of self- or collaboratively identified goals."

While PCCs as initial steppingstones for ICT access serves well as a framework emphasizing *physical diffusion* of ICT to meet development goals, a model of spatial hybridity best serves an *effective use* framework. Public and private physical spaces can each be used to foster public or private behaviors and activities, creating a complex range of interactions with ICT. For instance, public-in-public activities include both using a PCC to access training and to receive and give technical support, and also the use of the space to support collaboration with those co-located and also those online. By contrast, private-in-public activities using PCCs can include using the public space to gain privacy that might not be available at home or the workplace, as well as to gain access to specialized software in support of tasks done individually. These can be compared to activities done in private computing spaces such as a home or office, including public-in-private (e.g., participating in social media) and private-in-private (e.g., doing online banking) activities (Viseu et al., 2006).

In bringing together community members each with different backgrounds, insights, and skills, PCCs can serve as a place where knowledge acquired by one can be shared with others, an important aspect of any sustainable PCC. As such, the public-in-public hybridity of these centers enable them to become a gathering place for "communities of practice" (Wenger & Snyder, 2000), that is, groups of people who share a concern or a passion for something they do and who learn how to do it better as they interact regularly. PCCs also can serve to foster communities of inquiry, groups united by shared interest who work together to investigate and act to address common problems (Shields, 1999). Based on the theories and practices of Charles Peirce, John Dewey, and Jane Addams, a number of researchers have proposed that the inquiry cycle, especially as applied to communities of inquiry, provides an exceedingly rich environment for achieving educational and community development goals (Bruce & Bishop, 2002, 2008; Bishop & Bruce, 2007; Shields, 1999; Short et al., 1996; Wells, 2001).

The desire to build social capital is something most PCCs have in common. Ceballos (2006, p. 21) suggests that "the best telecentres are local gathering places; places where people come together to talk, tell stories and share knowledge." This leads the members of the community into conversations with each other to determine what is needed to improve the local quality of life. In so doing, not only do they become actively engaged in adapting the tools found in PCCs to their own local needs, they also become more connected with each other, thereby further strengthening the community. New technologies enable self-determined media production that is giving voice to communities: to share local stories; forge civic bonds; produce media that meets local needs; and localize and distribute knowledge. In this way, there is an increase in the communities' ability to paint a picture of the future as defined by the communities. PCCs thus become both hubs where community members enter together in communities of inquiry to determine what is needed to improve the quality of life and the centers where the tools necessary to effect that change are available for community use.

Berry, Kent, & Ken (1993) point out that participation in the political process is best fostered through regular face-to-face interactions. The strongest local governments are the ones that create mechanisms to encourage the formation and bi-directional flow of information with healthy neighborhood-based associations. Such associations help balance power between the elite and non-elite within the community and are shown to decrease tensions among those advocating for neighborhood or business interests. As local information hubs and gathering places, PCCs clearly have the potential to step beyond serving as only a channel for the delivery of government services to become also a platform that helps provide communities with the skills needed for a new type of citizenship, that is, places to negotiate the future of government creatively and inventively (Ceballos, 2006).

Equipping Public Computing Centers for New Roles

Emerging technologies are providing new tools for empowering individual and community engagement. The Horizon Report (Johnson, Levine, & Smith, 2009) points out that newly emerged and emerging technologies such as mobile and cloud computing are leading to a collective intelligence and mass amateurization that is redefining how we think about ambiguity. Cloud computing is the use of remote servers to provide online access to things such as storage (e.g., Box.net, Dropbox, Google Drive), collaborative document creation (e.g., Google Docs, Evernotes), and multimedia creation and sharing (e.g., YouTube and YouTube Editor, WeVideo, Animoto, Prezi). It is providing a unifying technological base for grassroots video and collaborative webs that are empowering citizen professionals at many levels. Cloud computing also enables enhanced mobile computing, providing the mechanism whereby computers taken into the field can be used as a tool to directly interface between community and rich datasets in the immediate setting of interest. The Horizon Report also reviews a number of ways in which individuals and communities are able to enhance storytelling, medical, and learning objectives through the growing availability of Geographic Information Systems (GIS) targeted at the consumer market, for instance using Google Maps and Google Earth.

One way that citizen professionals give voice to community goals and concerns is through techniques such as digital storytelling and photovoice. A range of studies indicates the value of these techniques for fostering community development goals. Digital storytelling is the process of oral storytelling with multimedia elements. Through efforts by Joe Lambert and the Center for Digital Storytelling, the KQED Digital Storytelling Initiative, and the StoryCorps project, an increasing number of people have been motivated to share their stories. Among other things, digital storytelling has been shown to be a valuable aid to begin personal reflections (Haven, 2007; Rule, 2010), to foster community building (Fields & Díaz, 2008; Haven, 2007), preserve history (Haven, 2007), enhance journalism (Barkin, 1984; Deuze, 2005; Knight Commission on the Information Needs of Communities in a Democracy, 2009), and support local business (Haven, 2007). Photovoice is a highly flexible methodology that builds on digital storytelling, enabling people to record and reflect their community, promote critical dialog about important community issues, and reach policymakers (Wang & Burris, 1997).

Another way to equip citizens to participate in communities of inquiry/practice is to provide the tools and skills necessary to gather and analyze the data needed for planning. Vaughan (2007) suggests: "The priority of the scientific community and government should be empowering citizens, developing the tools and approaches to bridge the gap between civil society and decision-makers." To increase democracy by levelling the playing field in the decision-making process, it is necessary to engage community members in a community-based participatory research model that increasingly empowers citizens to perform each step of the research cycle (Stoecker, 2013).

If PCCs are to become community centers empowering citizens through effective use of ICT as citizen scientists, citizen planners, or citizen journalists, it is necessary to revisit implementations of technology within these spaces. Viseu et al. (2006) found that facilities for simple diffusion of technology typically are set up as a dense cluster of shared terminals, located in an open space for easy monitoring. However, if a goal is to promote electronic commerce, terminals with personal storage space and privacy screens might be indicated. Support for civic engagement might require gathering spaces for face-to-face meetings in which the technology is unobtrusive, but readily available for presentations or side-research to supplement dialog. There are a growing number of examples in which community centers and libraries are redesigning space to create, for instance, innovative learning commons to foster development of twenty-first-century scholars and practitioners (Baker, 2008) and Makerspaces for people to come together to connect (Britton, 2012). Overall, new research using participatory and evidence-based design practices is helping to understand how intentional design of space for effective use can lead to changed social expectations of a space and to more sophisticated programming (Wolske et al., 2013).

Reconsideration of technology within space needs to also consider the role mobile computing now plays in our everyday lives. Nafus (2009) has presented data from Intel research arguing for "plastic" technologies, computers, and other technology that do not demand our conscious attention until needed, then easily defer to the events happening within the space. These data indicate the value of notebook, ultra-mobile PCs, and tablets for multiple uses. The Intel researchers found that even Internet workers rarely spend more than five minutes in a given session working on such computers as a result of ongoing external events that demand the core of the workers' attention. Weiser (1991) has gone so far as to suggest that the most profound technologies will be the ones that disappear. Taken from the ubiquitous computing framework, the argument is that as technology becomes easier and faster to use, as all ICTs integrate together in a unified whole, technology increasingly becomes a "pleasant and effective 'place' to get things done" (p. 100). Thus, the traditional computer lab will continue to serve a critical role in many public-in-public computing activities, particularly where full-sized screens and input devices facilitate extended work sessions and multiple windows. Mobile computers, however, will provide a more flexible mechanism for plastic technologies that readily move between public and private computing in public spaces, or can be moved aside completely to avoid disruption of non-technology-based interactions that are occurring at the moment.

The Citizen Professional Toolkits

An initial plan of YCI had been to help community partners build or upgrade their own, fixed PCCs. However, over the course of the project a new concept evolved as many of our partners identified a need for more flexible mobile PCC extensions to support communities of inquiry/practice engaged in their educational, economic, and community development goals. The design objective became to create a toolkit that includes many of the common tools used by professionals such as journalists, planners, and scientists. Design criteria include:

- ease of use to encourage adoption by citizens with a range of skills;
- room for growth as citizens gain comfort with the technology;
- sufficient quality to provide useful production for a range of presentation

mediums;
- portability to encourage use in the field and in different meeting spaces within a PCC;
- reasonable pricing for community organizations.

The components of the toolkit were selected to facilitate communities of inquiry/practice, whether functioning within traditional public computing facilities or in the field. Cameras, camcorders, microphones, GPS units, and the laptop were each chosen to support a range of citizen professional activities from community-based participatory research to photovoice and digital storytelling. Individual citizen professionals may check out a toolkit from a public computing facility, gather data and collect stories, and return to the facility to analyze data and report on findings within a broader group. Alternatively, a community of inquiry may take one or more toolkits into the field, thus creating a mobile extension to a fixed facility, in which multiple parts of the inquiry cycle may be performed within a community of inquiry as a whole.

Following extensive research using a range of technical reviews and interviews of practicing professionals, we purchased the equipment for 10 toolkits for initial field testing. Equipment was tested by masters students and staff at GSLIS. Initially, most toolkits were distributed as Mobile Media Toolkits, complete multimedia recording and production kits contained within a backpack weighing less than 16 pounds. However, the first pilot also included two toolkits that were integrated into a larger PCC installation at the Teen Tech project, an after-school program emphasizing development of technology and business skills for teens 14–18 years old (see Chapter 7). The installation at Teen Tech Team included both mobile and traditional desktop ICT.

Using field notes and interviews to provide key insights into how well the pilot version of the equipment functioned to meet stated objectives, we continued to refine development with additional partner sites. Over time we found that most sites preferred to use the toolkit as a starting point for a customized selection of individual items to meet their multimedia creation needs. For example, 4-H went on to develop its own version of the kit for use in youth video projects across the state. We came to see the portable toolkit as essentially a PCC in a backpack, which in turn led to broader thinking about what was really meant by "PCC." This led to further explorations regarding the location of computers within a physical space and the ways that participatory and evidence-based design techniques could be used to more strategically equip community centers with technology (Wolske et al., 2013). Further, we had a growing awareness that in at least some instances the concept of a computer lab with a bank of computers was not appropriate for equipping a site, but instead that computers should be located where work was being done (for instance, by locating a computer in each break-out room being used for mentoring) as well as the potential value of including mobile computing as a part of the overall plan for equipping an organization.

The following, then, is a review of the main components of the citizen professional toolkit that were tested over the project.

Computing Platform

With increased storage capacity; roaming Internet access; and the ability to record audio and video, to create and edit documents, spreadsheets, and even presentations, mobile devices such as smartphones have gained much of the functionality of laptop computers (Johnson et al., 2009). By 2020, it is predicted that the majority of Internet use will occur using mobile devices, according to a recent survey by the Pew Internet & American Life Project (Rainie & Anderson, 2008). But pricing plans for mobile devices remain high (Sadun, 2009). Further, input using the smartphone keyboard continues to limit its use for anything more than short writing exercises (Bender, 2009). While performance continues to increase, limited storage and memory, slower processor speeds, and single window displays will limit regular production of higher-quality, edited video, especially when including many special effects, on most mobile devices.

New ultra-mobile PCs (UMPC) or netbooks appear to provide a promising compromise between full-sized notebooks and the more limited capabilities of smartphones. These small-form-factor subnotebooks generally weigh less than 2.5 pounds and cost less than $400 USD. We found that the model chosen should provide a hard drive (as opposed to smaller solid-state drives) for large files such as video and at least 1 GB of memory, with 2 GB preferred. The 8.9" to 10" screens and 1024 x 600 resolution found on most UMPCs is less than ideal for extensive video editing, but is sufficient for simple editing functions while in the field. For situations in which video editing will be a regular activity, 14" laptops with at least 1366 x 768 pixel screen resolution and touchscreen capability promise even greater possibilities for video editing. The smaller netbooks did work exceedingly well as a platform in the field for note-taking and audio recordings. In addition, where roaming Internet access was available, the laptop provided a means for supplemental field research. When combined with a GPS receiver and maps, the laptop was able to provide driving directions. In all, the small form factor provides an ideal mobile computing platform for a range of citizen science activities at a cost lower than many tablet computers and other mobile devices, especially when such mobile devices required a monthly service plan.

For more extensive video editing, an in-house docking station that includes an external monitor, keyboard, and mouse should be considered. Indeed, for more advanced editing, especially with special effects, a multimedia desktop should be considered. In our first full implementation within a PCC at Teen Tech Team, a more traditional lab configuration with five desktop stations, two docking stations, and a Network Attached Storage (NAS) was used to provide a mechanism for easily transferring files between devices and to allow for easy access of recorded video footage into multiple projects being developed simultaneously. This illustrates the value of a hybrid model of ICT implementation that combines traditional and mobile technologies into one configuration.

The tested configuration included the MSI Wind: U100-432US UMPC with Windows XP Home. Pinnacle Studio Moviebox Ultimate 12 was the primary software used for video editing, although Adobe Premiere Elements has also been successfully used in other projects. The open source program Audacity was used for direct audio recording and editing. The open source application GIMP provided advanced photo editing in addition to the built-in photo editing capabilities that come with Windows XP. Later, Adobe Photoshop Elements was also used on some devices for easy, feature-rich photo editing. Both the open source application Open Office and Microsoft Office were provided for document editing. The programs Google Earth and ESRI Arc GIS workstation were provided for GIS applications.

Video and Audio Recording

Early video recordings were made using a simple-to-use flash storage camcorder with integrated USB device. Testing was performed with the Flip Video Ultra. Extensive field testing has found this device to be easy to use by all testers because of its one-button operation. Accessing video was likewise easy once the software included on the device was installed to a computer, as the camcorder would appear as a storage device. Because Flip cameras produce MPEGs that can be played on any computer, it was reasoned any computer with basic video editing software (iMovie in Mac, Windows Movie Maker, Kino on Linux) could be used to create short clips. However, because not all computers provide the needed administrative access to install the included software, it was not possible to use all computers to access and edit video.

Given its ease of use and relatively low cost, the Flip camcorders have become a mainstay for basic training in digital storytelling and citizen journalism. For instance, while completing a project with 22 fourth graders at an elementary school, Flip cameras were used to teach the students how to record and interview each other. The students were intrigued and genuinely excited to use this type of technology. Many found the cameras self-explanatory and many needed little direction on how to use them. However, their audio recording quality is inadequate for all but the quietest recording environments. Video quality is also somewhat limited, particularly when significant edits are made or when video is to be projected to large screens.

For this reason, newer kits included a DV tape-based camcorder with microphone input jack for improved audio recordings in noisy environments. For quieter environments, these camcorders provide a capable built-in stereo microphone. The DV tapes provide both a high-quality video and also a tested archiving mechanism, ideal for citizen journalism and digital storytelling activities. After extensive field-testing, though, these camcorders weren't as popular for introductory use in spite of their improved audio and video capabilities because of the difficulties of importing video to computer.

Given the early findings emphasizing the need for high-quality audio recordings for effective storytelling/citizen journalism, each toolkit included several different microphones. A wireless microphone kit that included both an omni-directional lapel microphone and uni-directional handheld microphone option provided input to either the DV-based camcorder or the laptop. This was particularly useful for interviews in noisy environments. It also allows the videographer to capture not only head shots of the person being interviewed but also surrounding images without concern for losing audio from the interviewee. A small passive mixer and wired lapel mic were included in some kits to allow for simultaneous recordings of both the interviewee and the interviewer. However, complexity of setup meant the passive mixer option was rarely used. Instead, a USB-based headset included with the toolkit was used in combination with the laptop to record voiceovers by the interviewer and to add questions during video editing. This has the added advantage of allowing the interviewer to ask the question more succinctly for final production than what might be necessary to effectively inform the interviewee while in the field. A USB-based omni-directional microphone was also included in the kit to provide a mechanism for recording audio from group discussions directly to the UMPC. This microphone was also used to facilitate group discussions using Voice-over-IP applications such as Skype.

Interestingly, Teen Tech Team used the DV-based camcorders, not only for video recordings but also as a portable audio-recording device. In this way, they have been able to capture a range of unique environmental sounds that they subsequently use to enhance their multimedia productions, as the Pinnacle software allows for easy disassociation of the video and audio tracks. This is a great illustration of how citizens will often find novel ways to re-purpose ICT to meet their own needs from the technology.

Other Components

A number of different digital cameras have been tested to date. Initially, a Canon Powershot S3 IS was tested as a highly rated high-end point-and-shoot camera. However, less expensive but more portable point-and-shoot cameras such as the Canon Powershot SD1100IS and the Panasonic LZ8 have proven more popular for most uses. Both can be easily carried in a pocket and provide excellent quality still pictures. The Panasonic LZ8 has two features that show some further promise: it has been highly rated for its ability to include simple shot modes along with manual settings to allow exploration in creativity for budding professional photographers; and it has a slide switch to turn the camera on and off, which seems to reduce accidental power on when being transported in a pocket or backpack. The newer SD4000IS has since also been tested and proven a great camera for both still and video pictures. The sound recording with video has been a higher quality than that on the Flip Video, and as such is an excellent single-device alternative for both still and video photography. Likewise, as camera and video capabilities improve on mobile devices, these will increasingly become a valuable alternative that also includes editing and cloud storage capabilities. However, to date mobile devices do not include optical zoom capabilities and limited exposure controls. As such, we find it valuable to continue to include at least a reasonable point-and-shoot camera within our kits.

Toolkit Use Scenarios

Depending on exactly which components were included within a kit, the backpack-based mobile media toolkits cost around $1,600 USD and weighed less than 16 pounds. These kits were tested in a range of applications. Youth from the Teen Tech Team after school program used the toolkits to produce video on the topic "Violence in My Community." The adult leader of the program described how working together to produce a video telling their own story brought the teens together as a team in a way that working with ICT in the past had not. Shy students began to come out of their corners to engage with other youth. Some students who were not comfortable working with other ICT found the video a more comfortable technology with which to work. Together, they began finding a way to give voice to their communal understanding of the world around them.

They were rewarded for their efforts with an opportunity to use the newest version of the toolkit to begin working with the local community cable access channel as youth reporter interns. This positive result from participatory action research is consistent with that seen in other projects and settings. For instance, when rural Chinese women began using the photovoice methodology to foster better social services for health care, the participants found that "it contributed to and enhanced self-esteem and peer status . . . many shy participants gradually learned to express their thoughts boldly and confidently during group discussions" (Wang, 1998).

Geotagging of data proved valuable for a range of activities. Much of our current research builds upon work with 4-H, a youth empowerment group that teaches through hands-on experiential learning and is found in the United States and 80 other countries worldwide. Most toolkits included a Garmin eTrex Legend GPS receiver. These were used for a range of geomapping activities. For instance, one middle school used the receivers to map the location of gravestones in a local cemetery (see Chapter 4). In E2Y, another YCI project (see Chapter 10), the receivers were used to map local assets for youth. And in the first YCI Summer Academy, they were used to map information sources, including traditional sources such as libraries and nontraditional sources such as historical signs and bus stops. Some toolkits also included the Amod AGL 3080 photo tracker. This simple GPS receiver has an on/off switch and a waypoint button. When activated, it synchronizes with satellites then begins recording location to internal flash storage every 1, 5, or 10 seconds as preconfigured. When connected to a computer, the device is available as a flash storage device, and recordings are stored as text files with data encoded using open standards, simplifying access to data. These devices were tested with citizens in Africa during summer 2009 to track their daily and weekly walking patterns, data that were important in providing community development planning information.

Technology adoption is a complex mix of technical design and social processes (Rogers, 1995; Williams & Edge, 1996). Tying community development goals to particular products—either software or hardware—brings a significant risk of compromised goals in some way. If we are to work toward a more just society, Virginia Eubanks (2011) stresses the importance of approaches to technology that recognize the expertise of all participants and engage in a participatory decision-making approach. Throughout the Youth Community Informatics project, various participants struggled with different technologies, which affected their levels of participation and types of contributions. But rather than using a deficit-based model that works to address gaps in knowledge, the project applied Dewey's (1938) principles for education to the technological aspects of the project. By using technologies that allowed for greater flexibility, we were better able to account for the purpose and past experience of the participants along with an understanding of the current conditions to construct a more effective learning environment for activities. For example, some partners used YouTube while others were in schools where YouTube was banned. Still others were already using different video sharing services and it was better to change our training to make use of the tool they were most comfortable with. In yet other cases the focus ended up on still images through sites such as Flickr or Wordpress, avoiding the complications of video altogether to better target the intended audience. It became evident that successful implementation of the project required continuous experimentation with various hardware and software collaboration tools to assure that community goals were the primary driver for how a project unfolded, not the technology. Where there did not seem to be sufficient buy-in for a particular tool, other solutions were explored. For instance, the Teen Tech Team project chose to use a mix of backpack and fixed PCC installations, while others chose to work exclusively with one or another for their activities.

Conclusion

By using components that can easily be taken into the field, it became possible to create a mobile public computing facility for the wide variety of projects and programs encompassed by YCI. In this way, the PCC can be located wherever ICT is needed at the moment. An outdoor classroom or research laboratory is quickly created as components are unloaded from backpacks. A backpack can easily be transported to the office of an official to perform an interview, then brought back to a central PCC for extended production using the additional facilities of a docking station and fixed desktops. Backpacks can be taken to a library or other community center when needed to supplement existing computers that might be valuable for certain types of research and text production but might not have all the needed hardware and software to enable multimedia production. Including mobile computing platforms in PCCs also provides an easy mechanism to allow citizens to quickly supplement face-to-face dialog with information garnered during meetings that was collected using netbooks to perform online research. The netbook also provides a mechanism for inclusion of remote participants. Yet its portability simultaneously allows it to be quickly put aside to continue the dialog without interference from technology. Indeed, it is interesting to reflect how closely each of these examples matches the way many professional researchers work on a daily basis today using plastic technologies (Nafus, 2009).

As the initial role of technology diffusion is met, the traditional public computing center needs to move on to new roles if it is to be sustained (Fuchs, 1998). Emerging technologies and ways in which professionals are using technology can help us understand new types of technologies and new ways of implementing existing technologies to better empower citizens in their move toward "mass amateurization" (Johnson et al., 2009). In this chapter we have reviewed alternative frameworks for public and private activities within both public and private spaces, and ways in which mobile and fixed installations can work together to provide more effective use of technologies if PCCs are to thrive as places advancing community development goals (Nafus, 2009; Viseu et al., 2006). We proposed a set of mobile technologies that we have found useful in YCI as either a stand-alone or a supplemental toolkit for community centers in which technology is provided for community use that can facilitate further mass amateurization. As the capabilities of mobile devices continue to increase, we expect to see even greater opportunities for creating hybrid spaces that harness plastic technologies that adapt to the ever-changing ways we come together in community spaces to engage in communities of practice and inquiry.

15. Youth Community Informatics Curriculum

Lisa Bouillion Diaz

Five years from its inception, a range of youth, communities, and countries have participated in Youth Community Informatics projects. We worked together to capture the insights and inspiration from these activities within a document we called the Youth Community Informatics curriculum (Diaz, Nam, & Rakha, 2011). It is here that I would like to outline some of the guiding principles and insights that emerged from this work. As I am only one of many collaborators on the YCI curriculum, my analysis here is necessarily reflective of my perspective as a learning scientist and my experience within the 4-H context of YCI practice.

The 4-H program is a national youth development program that is implemented and supported by a network of more than 100 land-grant universities across the country. I help provide program direction for the University of Illinois Extension 4-H program that reaches more than 200,000 youth. Someone most familiar with images of 4-Hers showing animals at a county fair might ask what interest this organization could have with the YCI initiative. One hundred years ago, land-grant universities were trying to bring cutting-edge agricultural research to farmers, with limited success. The 4-H youth program grew out of the seed of inspiration that youth who are exposed to new ideas and encouraged to actively investigate real-world problems might go home and share their insights with family members. And as parents saw their children experimenting with new agricultural techniques and having great success, they became interested themselves in learning more.

This success anchored youth voice and leadership at the heart of the 4-H program (e.g., Lerner, Dowling, & Anderson, 2003). One hundred years later, the projects in 4-H have grown to include a much broader scope of inquiry, including filmmaking, community mapping, sustainable energy, robotics, computer science, environmental studies, and much more. Across all topics, youth are consistently positioned in roles as inquirers, activists, leaders, and contributors. The vision for youth community informatics is a natural extension to our work within 4-H, and thus, 4-H staff, clubs, and members were active contributors to the work conducted in YCI.

The Role of Curriculum

Our vision for a youth community informatics curriculum was a document that would inspire and guide possibilities, and in that sense be "educative" (Ball & Cohen, 1996). Fidelity to a model of "best practice" was never our aim. Instead, we assumed a "law of adaptation" (McLaughlin, 1976, 1996) in which core concepts and practices are necessarily adapted and personalized within different contexts. Therefore, we expected that a curriculum would need to make visible a range of possible YCI goals and endeavors, and provide case study examples showing how those activities were enacted within different contexts of practice.

In all of the modules, we show the framework of inquiry *in practice* (outlined elsewhere in this volume). The inquiry model used here (Ask, Investigate, Create, Discuss, Reflect) is similar to the five-step experiential learning model used within 4-H (experience, share, process, generalize, apply). The key difference is in the inquiry model's emphasis on questions. In 2006, 4-H at the national level identified STEM (science, technology, engineering, mathematics) as a mission mandate, motivating the inclusion of a scientific inquiry model in which questioning is viewed as integral to the experiential learning process. I share this in the hopes that readers will see how the inquiry cycle represented in these curriculum modules can be applied within contexts that use different but complementary models of (or approaches to) learning. YCI and 4-H share the assumption that the learning process is nonlinear, emergent, and iterative. The specifics of what we call each stage seem less important and our hope is that the information in the YCI curriculum will be useful across multiple contexts.

Initially, our curriculum focus was on specific technologies. YCI envisioned technology as an important tool for both inquiry and action. Therefore, a first set of curriculum modules grew out of an effort to teach various skills such as mapping with geographic information tools and video production. But we knew that technology literacy was more than learning technical skills. Informed by a framework developed by the National Academies Press (Pearson & Young, 2002), our goals included helping youth understand the value and role of different technologies within practices of social inquiry and community change. The titles of the curriculum modules were therefore intentionally changed from titles such as "Geographic Information System Tools" to "Youth as Community Mapper," and from "Blogging and Social Media Tools" to "Youth as Author: Tell Your Stories."

As we began to document cases of youth community informatics work, we found that youth had different motivations for engaging with YCI projects. Representing these different entry points was viewed as critical to choosing an organizational structure for the YCI curriculum. The modules are currently organized into two sections. In the "Youth as Social Activist" section, the modules capture cases of youth as curators (see Figure 15.1), social networkers, journalists, videographers, mappers, authors, community planners, librarians, spoken word artists, and citizen scientists. These modules might be the first choice for youth who are eager to learn and use a new technology, such as making a video. In the "Youth as Social Inquirer" section, modules share inquiries into topics such as community violence, poverty, unemployment, racism, crime, racial segregation, substance abuse, school drop-outs, and physical health. These modules might be the first choice for youth who have a vested interest in a specific community issue that they want to better understand and/or influence.

All *social inquiry* modules invite consideration of a complimentary *social action* module, and vice versa. In some cases a project may start with social action that motivates further inquiry (e.g., when social action fails or produces unexpected results), and in other cases it is inquiry into a social issue that inspires social action. And in many cases, those processes are revisited, cyclical, and iterative. The hope was that this organization would help to make visible multiple paths of action related to any single inquiry. That is, the information and insight constructed through an inquiry into the topic of community health might inspire one group to make a map using GIS tools to show how access to fresh foods and vegetables is disproportionally scarce within low-income communities and advocate with the city council to create spaces for community gardens. Alternately, another group might be inspired to create an educational video for families to promote healthy eating habits.

As already outlined, the YCI curriculum includes both generalizable possibilities and richly contextualized examples of their enactment. Our assumption is that the measure of success in these YCI activities is locally defined and necessarily aligned to the unique fabric of needs, opportunities, and values in each community context. The inclusion of "case studies" within the curriculum is meant to capture more contextual details, thereby supporting the purposeful adaptation of someone else's good idea and success within a new context. We recognize that these case studies face the limitation of space constraints and our imposed value in choosing which details to share.

Curriculum Uses—Current and Imagined

The curriculum is currently available online (Diaz, Nam, & Rakha, 2011). The intent was to create a living document in which an online community of YCI practitioners (youth and adult) could freely contribute to this compendium of practice. Our hope was to use online tools (e.g., moodle, wiki) to create a community of practice (Wenger, 1998) in which the curriculum resource continues to grow with the experience and insights shared among its members.

We have learned (or been reminded) that online communities are much like those based in offline worlds. They require motivation and an impetus to gather together. And they often thrive only when individuals step forward who convene us, help to articulate and remind us of the shared purpose that binds us, and keep us focused on the collective goals. As YCI collaborators from the original grant period have since moved in different directions, the online community has faded.

And yet the distributed YCI work and practice continues to grow. For example, Ann Peterson Bishop, one of original YCI co-principal investigators, is working with immigrant youth and public libraries in Seattle to design better ways to support the community information sharing activities of teens (see the InfoMe project at http://infome.uw.edu). Nama Budhathoki has co-founded Kathmandu Living Labs, an institution for harnessing youths' local knowledge, developing open data and promoting civic technologies in Nepal. Within the University of Illinois's 4-H program we have hired 13 educators with assigned responsibilities within metro regions of our state that have populations of 100,000 or more. Program priorities include STEM literacy and youth civic engagement, which align naturally to YCI. We expect to use the YCI curriculum as a resource within our work with youth who are influencing change in their communities. Similarly, many of those associated with YCI are expanding and evolving the project's original ideas and activities. We expect to continue learning from youth perspectives and are open to being led down new paths of inquiry. We invite you to join this journey.

YOUTH AS CURATOR: DESIGN A PUBLIC EXHIBIT

Brief Description

As a curator, you will explore how the creation of a public exhibit can be a way to create change around the issue of your social inquiry. You will learn how to do research using primary sources and artifacts such as books, maps, artwork, and music to create a physical display. It is your job to find historical objects within the community to help tell the story of the social justice issue you investigated. For instance, when investigating the issue of racial segregation, the community archive may have a map showing historical borders dividing races within the community, which may be used to help people think about this issue historically and today. We often see such exhibits in museums, libraries, and sometimes in the lobbies of businesses such as banks. As part of this inquiry, you need to identify which organizations within the community currently host or archive historical objects. Within this inquiry, you may partner with one of these organizations to develop your exhibit. For this project to be successful, a willing collaboration between a participating cultural institution (museum, library, or historical society) and a youth group must be established. The goals should be adapted to the specific resources of the institution and your group. You can then learn about the participating cultural institution. This may include behind-the-scenes tours, introductions to staff, or guided tours of existing exhibits. As a curator, you will then work to research and select the final objects that will be put on display. You should help create the thematic organization, work to draft the accompanying text, and design the exhibit layout. Parameters and limitations for the exhibition should be clearly defined with the participating cultural institution.

Goals of Activities

• Learn how to do research using primary sources, while gaining experience with museum and library studies.
• Think critically about this issue within the context of your local history and social reality.
• Create an exhibit in a public space that will empower others to take action on your issue of interest.

Inquiry Cycle

?**Ask:** How do historical materials reflect your identity and enable you to better understand your history? What organizations exist that have information on your topic of interest? Where might your story best be told? What resources (maps, objects, etc.) are available that will help you tell others about your topic of interest?

?**Investigate:** You should investigate possible locations for your exhibit. You should think critically about how you might best present your findings in a way that inspires others to take action on this issue. After investigating your issue of choice (see Youth as Social Inquirer section), you should locate objects that can be used to tell the story of your research and findings. You can think about ways to tell your story or the story of your findings. You may do this by viewing similar exhibits and analyzing them. What makes these exhibits interesting? How do they tell a story? Do they move people to do something? If so, how?

Continued on next page

Continued from previous page

?Create: You will collaborate with the cultural institution where your exhibit will be located to select exhibit themes, find artifacts (physical objects) that you want to display, create and finalize an object list, and write object descriptions. You should gather objects for your exhibit and put them with your descriptions in a way that is visually interesting.

?Discuss: You may engage in a discussion about the nature of history and the role of primary sources. Discuss what primary sources are, how primary sources tell stories, how we decide to trust or distrust historical sources, and how history determines the present. You may also want to discuss what makes exhibits powerful, and whether the exhibit you created was powerful and why.

?Reflect: Create an object list of at least ten items that could serve to represent your life to someone living a hundred years from now. Additionally, ask family, friends, or teachers to select three of these objects and find out how those objects are viewed by those close to you. In other words, what do these objects reveal about you, and what remains hidden (undisclosed)? What story do they tell about you and your life?

{Inquiry in Action: The Newberry Library Project in Paseo Boricua, Chicago, IL}

In spring of 2008, Dr. Pedro Albizu Campos High School (PACHS) and the Newberry Library initiated a collaboration, with assistance from the University of Illinois's Graduate School of Library and Information Science. This collaboration culminated in an exhibition of materials at the library relating to the culture and history of Puerto Rico. The project was incorporated into the PACHS Puerto Rican history and culture class as well as the Spanish class, and aimed to teach students primary research skills while empowering them to serve as curators of an exhibition of Puerto Rican materials at a prominent cultural institution in the city of Chicago.

[Ask]

What books are available at the library about Puerto Rico and Puerto Rican history?
What maps of Puerto Rico are available at the library?
What other resources on Puerto Rico and Puerto Rican history are available at the library?
What is included in an exhibition?
What is the purpose of an exhibition?

[Investigate]

Students were brought to the library where they searched the archives, shelves, and stacks for materials relating to Puerto Rico and Puerto Rican history. They worked with a librarian to located resources. Students then assessed and discussed the materials. Students and leaders discussed how the exhibition should be organized, which brought to light more questions such as: What is a public exhibit? Who writes history? How is history documented and inherited, and what ultimately are the consequences? How and when do exhibitions present an opportunity to address these questions?

[Create]

Students became familiar with the library's on-line catalog and began to research their own specific items of interest. The students wrote about their objects in both English and Spanish. They put their exhibit together and it was shown at the Newberry Library in June of that year.

[Discuss]

What did you learn about our own history by doing this project? What did you learn by telling the story of our own history? What did you learn about libraries through this project? What did you learn about creating an actual exhibit?

[Reflect]

How might exhibits and processes such as these be used to inform the public about history and the creation of history? How might projects such as these be expanded to involve more students in the future? How might telling history in this way empower youth?

Figure 15.1. Sample Curriculum Unit

References

Aber, J. L. (1993). *The effects of poor neighborhoods on children, youth and families: Theory, research and policy implications.* Background memorandum prepared for the Social Science Research Council Policy Conference on Persistent Urban Poverty, Nov. 9–10, Washington, DC.

Addams, J. (1912). *Twenty years at Hull-House with autobiographical notes.* New York: Macmillan.

Addams, J. (2002/1892). The subjective necessity for social settlement. In J. B. Elshtain (ed.), *The Jane Addams reader* (pp. 14–28). New York: Basic.

Addams, J. (1915). *Democracy and social ethics.* New York: Macmillan.

Alvermann, D. (Ed.). (2010). *Adolescents' online literacies.* New York: Peter Lang.

Antrop-González, R. (2003). "This school is my sanctuary": The Pedro Albizu Campos Alternative High School. *Centro Journal, 15*(2), 232–255.

Association of Specialized and Cooperative Library Agencies (1999). Library standards for juvenile correctional facilities. Chicago: ASCLA.

Austin, J. (2012). *Critical issues in juvenile detention libraries.* YALSA. Retrieved from: http://www.yalsa.ala.org/jrlya/2012/07/critical-issues-in-juvenile-detention-center-libraries

Bak, H. J. (2001). Education and public attitudes toward science: Implications for the "deficit model" of education and support for science and technology. *Social Science Quarterly, 82*(4), 779–795.

Baker, L. (2008). *Learning infused libraries: Honest talk about what it really takes to create a learning commons.* LOEX 2008, Retrieved from http://www.slideshare.net/bakerl/learning-infused-libraries-honest-talk-about-what-it-really-takes-to-create-a-learning-commons

Ball, D. L., & Cohen, D. K. (1996). Reform by the book: What is—or might be—the role of curriculum materials in teacher learning and instructional reform? *Educational Researcher, 25*(4), pp. 6–8+14.

Barkin, S. M. (1984). The journalist as storyteller: An interdisciplinary perspective. *American Journalism, 1*(2): 27–33.

Barton, W. H., & Butts, J. A. (2008). *Building on strength: Positive youth development in juvenile justice programs.* Chicago: University of Chicago Press.

Battiste, M. (2002). *Indigenous knowledge and pedagogy in First Nations education: A literature review with recommendations.* Ottawa: Apamuwek Institute.

Bender, W. (2009). *Beyond the XO laptop: Walter Bender on OLPC and sugar on a stick, Tech & Learning.* Retrieved from http://www.techlearning.com/article/16348

Benkler, Y. (2006). *The wealth of networks: How social production transforms markets and freedom.* New Haven: Yale University Press.

Benson, C., & Christian, S. (2002). *Writing to make a difference: Classroom projects for community change.* New York: Teachers College Press.

Benson, L., Puckett, J. L., & Harkavy, I. (2007). *Dewey's dream: Universities and democracies in an age of education reform.* Philadelphia: Temple University Press.

Berry, M., Kent, P., & Ken, T. (1993). *The rebirth of urban democracy.* Washington, DC: Brookings.

Berry, P., Cavallaro, A., & Vázquez, E. (2009). *(Re)voicing teaching and learning in Paseo Boricua* [Video]. Retrieved from http://www.pedroalbizucamposhs.org/revoicing-teaching-and-learning-in-paseo-boricua-video/

Berry, P., Cavallaro, A., Vázquez, E., DeJesús, C. R., & Garcia, N. (2014, in press). Sustaining narratives of hope: Literacy, multimodality, and the Dr. Pedro Albizu Campos High School. *English Education.*

Bishop, A., & Bruce, B. C. (2007). Community inquiry [Homepage of *Liberating Voices! A Pattern Language for Communication Revolution*], [Online]. Retrieved from http://www.publicsphereproject.org/patterns/print-pattern.php?begin=122

Bishop, A. P., Bruce, B. C., & Jeong, S. (2009, March). Beyond service learning: Toward community schools and reflective community learners. In L. Roy, K. Jensen, & A. Hershey Meyers (Eds.), *Service learning: Linking library education and practice* (pp. 16-31). Chicago: ALA Editions.

Bishop, A., Tidline, T. J., Shoemaker, S., & Salela, P. (1999). Public libraries and networked information services in low-income communities. *Library and Information Science Research, 21*(3), 361-390.

Boal, A. (1996). *The rainbow of desire : The Boal method of theatre and therapy* (Reprinted. ed.). London: Routledge.

Bodart, J. R. (2008). It's all about the kids: Presenting options and opening doors. *Young Adult Library Services, 7*(1), 35-45.

Boss, S., & Krauss, J. (2008). *Reinventing project-based learning: Your field guide to real-world projects in the digital age.* Washington, DC: International Society for Technology in Education.

Bouillion-Diaz, L., Ritzo, C., & Ayad, M. (2009, May). Youth Community Informatics: Engagement through technology-supported inquiry into community issues. In *Proceedings of the Children, Youth & Families at Risk (CYFAR) Conference,* Baltimore, MD.

boyd, d., Palfrey, J., & Sacco, D. (Eds.). (2012). *The Kinder & Braver World Project: Research series.* Cambridge, MA: Born This Way Foundation & the Berkman Center for Internet and Society at Harvard University.

boyd, d. (2007). Why youth (heart) social network sites: The role of networked publics in teenage social life. In D. Buckingham (ed.), *Youth, identity, and digital media* (pp. 119-142). Cambridge, MA: MIT Press.

Britton, L. (2012). The makings of maker spaces. *Library Journal, 137*(16), 20-23.

Brooks-Gunn, J., Duncan, G. J., Klebanov, P. K., & Sealand, N. (1993). Do neighborhoods influence child and adolescent development? *American Journal of Psychology, 99,* 353-395.

Bruce, B. C. (Ed.). (2003). *Literacy in the information age: Inquiries into meaning making with new technologies.* Newark, DE: International Reading Association.

Bruce, B. C. (2008a). From Hull House to Paseo Boricua: The theory and practice of community inquiry. In B. Dicher & A. Luduşan (Ed.), *Philosophy of pragmatism*

(II): Salient inquiries (pp. 181–198). Cluj-Napoca, Romania: Editura Fundaţiei pentru Studii Europene (European Studies Foundation Publishing House).

Bruce, B. C. (2008b). Ubiquitous learning, ubiquitous computing, and lived experience. In W. Cope & M. Kalantzis (eds.), *Ubiquitous learning* (pp. 21–30). Champaign, IL: University of Illinois Press.

Bruce, B. C. (2009). "Building an airplane in the air": The life of the inquiry group. In J. Falk & B. Drayton (eds.), *Creating and sustaining online professional learning communities* (pp. 47–67). New York: Teachers College Press.

Bruce, B. C., & Bishop, A. P. (2002, May). Using the web to support inquiry-based literacy development. *Journal of Adolescent and Adult Literacy, 45*(8), 706–714.

Bruce, B. C., & Bishop, A. P. (2008). New literacies and community inquiry. In J. Coiro, M. Knobel, C. Lankshear, & D. Leu (Eds.), *Handbook of research on new literacies* (pp. 699–742). New York: Routledge.

Bruce, B. C., & Bishop, A. P. (2011, September). *Community informatics for youth: Using the Extension Network to recruit future LIS professionals: RE-03-07-0007-07.* Final report to the U.S. Institute of Museum and Library Services. Champaign, IL: Graduate School of Library and information Sciences, University of Illinois. Retrieved from http://hdl.handle.net/2142/28563

Bruce, B. C., & Bloch, N. (2013). Pragmatism and community inquiry: A case study of community-based learning. *Education and Culture: The Journal of the John Dewey Society, 29*(1), 27-45.

Bruce, B. C., & Davidson, J. (1996). An inquiry model for literacy across the curriculum. *Journal of Curriculum Studies, 28*(3), 281–300.

Bruce, B. C., & Drayton, B. (Eds.) (2013, June). *Progressive education: Educating for democracy and the process of authority* [Special issue], *International Journal of Progressive Education, 9*(2).

Bruce, B. C., & Lin, C. (2009). Voices of youth: Podcasting as a means for inquiry-based community engagement. *E-learning and Digital Media, 6*(2), 230–241.

Bruce, B. C., & Levin, J. A. (1997). Educational technology: Media for inquiry, communication, construction, and expression. *Journal of Educational Computing Research, 17*(1), 79–102.

Bruce, B. C., & Levin, J. A. (2003). Roles for new technologies in language arts: Inquiry, communication, construction, and expression. In J. Flood, D. Lapp, J. R. Squire, & J. R. Jensen (Eds.), *Handbook of research on teaching the English language arts* (2nd ed., pp. 649–657). Mahwah, NJ: Lawrence Erlbaum.

Bruce, B. C., & Pecore, J. (Eds.) (2013, February). *Progressive education: Antecedents of educating for democracy* [Special issue]. *International Journal of Progressive Education, 9*(1).

Buckingham, D. (2007). *Beyond technology: Children's learning in the age of digital culture.* Malden, MA: Polity.

Budhathoki, N. R., Nedovic-Budic, Z., & Bruce, B. C. (2010). An interdisciplinary frame for understanding volunteered geographic information. *Geomatica, the Journal of Geospatial Information Science, Technology, and Practice, 64*(1).

Calhoun, C. (Ed.). (1992). *Habermas and the public sphere.* Cambridge, MA: MIT Press.

Casey, L., & Bruce, B. C. (2011). The practice profile of inquiry: Connecting digital literacy and pedagogy. *E-Learning and Digital Media*, 8(1), 76–85.

Ceballos, F., et al. (2006). *From the ground up: The evolution of the telecentre movement.* Ottawa, ON, CA: Telecenter.org. Retrieved from http://idl-bnc.idrc.ca/dspace/handle/123456789/27550

Center for Digital Inclusion. (2012). *Mission statement.* Retrieved from http://cdi.lis.illinois.edu/cdi/?page_id=45

Certeau, M. d. (1984). *The practice of everyday life.* Berkeley: University of California Press.

Choksi, B. (1997). *Evaluating the use of information technology in the East St. Louis Action Research Project (ESLARP).* Retrieved from http://lrs.ed.uiuc.edu/Students/b-choksi/ESLARP/

Cisneros, S. (2009). *The house on Mango Street (25th anniv. ed.).* New York: Vintage.

City of Virginia. (n.d.). History of Virginia. Retrieved from http://www.casscomm.com/~cityofva/history.htm

Clark, G. (1994). Rescuing the discourse of community. *College Composition and Communication*, 45(1), pp. 61–74.

Cohen, A. P. (1985). *The symbolic construction of community.* London: Tavistock.

Cohen, J. (1999). Social and emotional learning past and present: A psychoeducational dialogue. In J. Cohen (Ed.), *Educating minds and hearts: Social emotional learning and the passage into adolescence* (pp. 2-23). New York: Teachers College.

Coiro, J., Knobel, M., Lankshear, C., & Leu, D. J. (Eds.). (2008). *Handbook of research on new literacies.* New York: Routledge.

Coleman, J. S. (1988). Social capital in the creation of human capital. *American Journal of Sociology*, 94, Supplement: Organizations and institutions: Sociological and economic approaches to the analysis of social structure, S95–S120.

Coleman, J. S. (1990). *Foundations of social theory.* Cambridge, MA: Harvard University Press.

Computer Village. (2009). Retrieved from http://www.cvillage.org/

Danticat, E. (1994). *Breath, eyes, memory.* New York: Vintage.

Darder, A. (1991). *Culture and power in the classroom: A critical foundation for bicultural education.* Westport: Greenwood.

Delpit, L. (1995). *Other people's children: Cultural conflict in the classroom.* New York: New.

Deuze, M. (2005). Towards professional participatory storytelling in journalism and advertising. *First Monday*, 10(7)

Dewey, J. (1900). *The school and society.* Chicago: University of Chicago Press.

Dewey, J. (1902). The school as social center. *The Elementary School Teacher*, 3(2), 73–86.

Dewey, J. (1916). *Democracy and education.* New York: Courier Dover.

Dewey, J. (1920). *Reconstruction in philosophy.* New York: Holt.

Dewey, J. (1927). *The public and its problems.* New York: Holt.

Dewey, J. (1934). *A common faith.* New Haven, CT: Yale University Press.

Dewey, J. (1937). The challenge of democracy to education. *Progressive Education 14*, 79–85.

Dewey, J. (1938). *Experience and education*. New York: Macmillan.

Dewey, J. (1939). *Theory of valuation*. Chicago: University of Chicago Press.

Dewey, J. (2005). *Art as experience*. New York: Perigee.

Diaz, L. B., Nam, C., & Rakha, S. (Eds.) (2011). *Community as curriculum: Integrating inquiry and social action with technology*. Retrieved from http://hdl.handle.net/2142/29967

Dillon, S. (2006, March 26). Schools cut back subjects to push reading and math. *The New York Times*. Retrieved from http://www.nytimes.com

DiMaggio, P., & Hargittai, E. (2001). *From the "digital divide" to "digital inequality": Studying Internet use as penetration increases*. Working Paper No. 15. Princeton, NJ: Center for Arts and Cultural Policy Studies, Princeton University. Retrieved from http://www.princeton.edu/~artspol/workpap

Dittmann, K. (2007). Between the lines: Girls in detention escape into books. *The Monthly, 37*(7). Retrieved from http://www.themonthly.com/feature-04-07.html

Dreyfus, H. L., & Rabinow, P. (1983). *Michel Foucault, beyond structuralism and hermeneutics*. Chicago, IL: University of Chicago Press.

Earl, J., & Kimport, K. (2012). *Digitally enabled social change: Activism in the Internet age*. Cambridge, MA: MIT Press.

East St. Louis Action Research Project, ESLARP (2009). *Teen Tech team*. Retrieved from http://www.eslarp.uiuc.edu/view/teen-tech-team.aspx

Eglash, R., Crossiant, J., Di Chiro, G., & Fouché, R. (Eds.). (2004). *Appropriating technology: Vernacular science and social power*. Minneapolis: University of Minnesota Press.

Ehrenreich, B. (2007, February). Pathologies of hope. *Harper's Magazine, 314*(1881), 9–11.

Ellison, R. (1995). *Invisible man* (2nd Vintage ed.). New York: Vintage.

Ellul, J. (1964). *The technological society*. New York: Knopf.

Enfield, R. P. (2001). *Head, heart, hands and health: "Experience and education" by Dewey's criteria?* Paper presented at the Annual Meeting of the American Educational Research Association, Seattle.

Eubanks, V. (2011). *Digital dead end: Fighting for social justice in the information age*. Cambridge, MA: MIT Press.

Extending Library Services to Empower Youth (ELSEY). (n.d.) Retrieved from http://elseyjdc.wordpress.com

Farmer, P. (2006). AIDS and accusation: Haiti and the geography of blame. *Comparative studies of health systems and medical care, 33*. Berkeley: University of California Press.

Fields, A. M., & Díaz, K. R. (2008). *Fostering community through digital storytelling: A guide for academic libraries*. Westport, CT: Libraries Unlimited.

Flores-Gonzalez, N., Rodriguez, M., & Rodriguez-Muniz, M. (2006). From hip-hop to humanization: Batey Urbano as a space for Latino youth culture and community action. In S. Ginwright, P. Noguera, & J. Cammarota (eds.), *Beyond resistance! Youth activism and community change* (pp. 175-196). New York: Routledge.

Flower, L. (2008). *Community literacy and the rhetoric of public engagement.* Carbondale, IL: Southern Illinois University Press.

Foucault, M. (1977). *Discipline and punish: The birth of the prison.* New York: Pantheon.

Foucault, M. (2003). *"Society must be defended": Lectures at the Collège de France, 1975-1976.* New York: Macmillan.

Foucault, M., & Gordon, C. (1980). *Power/knowledge: Selected interviews and other writings, 1972-1977.* New York: Pantheon.

Foucault, M., Gutman, H., Hutton, P. H., & Martin, L. H. (1988). *Technologies of the self: A seminar with Michel Foucault.* Amherst: University of Massachusetts Press.

Foucault, M., & Rabinow, P. (1984). *The Foucault reader.* New York: Pantheon.

Franz, G., & Papert, S. (1988, Spring). Computer as material: Messing about with time. *Teachers College Record, 89*(3), 408-417.

Freire, P. (1970/2000). *Pedagogy of the oppressed* (30th anniv. ed.). New York: Continuum.

Freire, P., & Macedo, D. (1987). *Literacy: Reading the word and the world.* Westport, CT: Bergin & Garvey.

Fuchs, R. P. (1998). *Little engines that did—case histories from the global telecentre movement.* Retrieved from http://www.idrc.ca/fr/ev-10630-201-1-DO_TOPIC.html

Gamberg, R., Kwak, W., Hutchings, M., & Altheim, J. (1988). *Learning and loving it: Theme studies in the classroom.* Portsmouth, NH: Heinemann.

Ginwright, S., Noguera, P., & Cammarota, J. (2006). *Beyond resistance! Youth activism and community change: New democratic possibilities for practice and policy for America's youth.* New York: Routledge.

Gonzales, N. A., Cauce, A. M., Friedman, R. J., & Mason, C. A. (1996). Family, peer, and neighborhood influences on academic achievement among African-American adolescents: One-year prospective effects. *American Journal of Community Psychology, 24,* 365-387.

Goodchild, M. F. (2007). Citizens as voluntary sensors: Spatial data infrastructure in the world of web 2.0. *International Journal of Spatial Data Infrastructures Research, 2,* 24-32.

Goodlad, J. (1996). Democracy, education, and community. In R. Soder, (Ed.), *Democracy, education, and the schools* (pp. 87-124). San Francisco: Jossey-Bass.

Graduate School of Library and Information Science. (2010). Full course catalog. Retrieved from http://www.lis.illinois.edu/academics/courses/

Graduate School of Library and Information Science. (2009). *Mission.* Retrieved from http://www.lis.illinois.edu/about-gslis/overview#mission

Graff, H. J. (1979). *The literacy myth: Literacy and social structure in the nineteenth-century city.* New York: Academic Press.

Graff, H. J., & Duffy, J. (2009). Literacy myths. In N. H. Hornberger (Ed.), *Encyclopedia of language and education* (pp. 42-52). New York: Springer, 2008.

Grahame, K. (1913). *The wind in the willows.* New York: Grosset & Dunlap.

Graves, D. H. (1983). *Writing: Teachers and children at work.* Portsmouth, NH: Heinemann.

Green, H., Facer, K., & Rudd, T., with Dillon, P., & Humphreys, P. (2005). Personalisation and digital technologies. Bristol: NESTA futurelab. http://www.futurelab.org.uk/resources/documents/opening_education/Personalisation_report.pdf

Guinier, L., & Torres, G. (2002). *The miner's canary: Enlisting race, resisting power, transforming democracy.* Cambridge, MA: Harvard University Press.

Gurstein, M. (2003). Effective Use: A community informatics strategy beyond the digital divide. *First Monday, 8*(12–1), December 2003.

Hanifan, L. J. (1916). The rural school community center. Annals of the *American Academy of Political and Social Science, 67,* 130–138.

Harber, C. (1992). *Democratic learning and learning democracy: Education for active citizenship.* Ticknall: Education Now.

Harper, E. H., & Dunham, A. (1959). *Community organization in action. Basic literature and critical comments.* New York: Association.

Haven, K. F. (2007). *Story proof: The science behind the startling power of story.* Westport, CT: Libraries Unlimited.

Hawkins, D. (1965). Messing about in science. *Science and Children, 2*(5), 5–9.

Hayes, M. (2007). *From state policy to classroom practice: Improving literacy instruction for all students.* Alexandria, VA: National Association of State Boards of Education.

Haythornthwaite, C., & Kazmer, M. M. (Eds.) (2004). *Learning, culture and community in online education: Research and practice.* New York: Peter Lang.

Haythornthwaite, C., & Kendall, L. (2010). Internet and community. *American Behavioral Scientist, 53,* 1083–1094.

Heath, S. B. (2001). Three's not a crowd: Plans, roles, and focus. *Educational Researcher, 30*(7), 10–17.

Heidegger, M. (1977). *The question concerning technology, and other essays.* New York: Garland.

Henry, P. (2000). *Caliban's reason: Introducing Afro-Caribbean philosophy.* New York: Routledge.

Hogan, M., & Bruce, B. C. (Eds.) (2013, October). *Progressive education: What's next?* [Special issue], *International Journal of Progressive Education, 9*(3).

Holland, J., Reynolds, T., & Weller, S. (2007). Transitions, networks and communities: The significance of social capital in the lives of children and young people. *Journal of youth studies, 10*(1), 97–116.

Horton, M., & Freire, P. (1990). *We make the road by walking.* Philadelphia, PA: Temple University Press.

Hull, G., & Katz, M.-L. (2006). Crafting an agentive self: Case studies in digital storytelling. *Research in the Teaching of English, 41*(1), 43–81.

Ito, M., et al. (Eds.). (2010). *Hanging out, messing around, and geeking out: Kids living and learning with new media.* Cambridge, MA: MIT Press. http://mitpress.mit.edu/books/hanging-out-messing-around-and-geeking-out

Jean-Charles, A. (2010). *Youth expression with video surveillance technology.* Ph.D. dissertation, University of Illinois. Retrieved from http://hdl.handle.net/2142/16930

Jenkins, H. (2006). *Convergence culture.* New York: New York University Press.

Jenkins, H. (2009). *Confronting the challenges of participatory culture. Media education for the 21st century.* Cambridge, MA: MIT Press.

John Dewey Project on Progressive Education. (2002). *A brief overview of Progressive Education.* Retrieved from http://www.uvm.edu/~dewey/articles/proged.html

Johnson, L., Levine, A., & Smith, R. (2009). *The 2009 horizon report.* Austin, TX: The New Media Consortium.

Jones, P. (2001). Why we are kids' best assets. *School Library Journal, 47*(11), 44–47.

Jorrín-Abellán, I. M., & Stake, R. E. (2009). Does ubiquitous learning call for ubiquitous forms of formal evaluation?: An evaluand-oriented responsive evaluation model. *Ubiquitous Learning: An International Journal, 1*(3). Melbourne, Australia: Common Ground.

Jorrín-Abellán, I. M., Stake, R. E., & Martínez-Mones, A. (2009, June). The needlework in evaluating a CSCL system: The evaluand-oriented responsive evaluation model. In *Proceedings of the 9th International conference CSCL, 68–72,* Rodhes, Greece.

Jorrín-Abellán, I. M., Rubia-Avi, B., Anguita-Martínez, R., Gómez-Sánchez, E., & Martínez-Mones, A. (2008). Bouncing between the dark and bright sides: Can technology help qualitative research? *Qualitative Inquiry, 14*(7), 1187–1204.

Kafai, Y. B., & Resnick, M. (1996). *Constructionism in practice: Designing, thinking, and learning in a digital world.* Mahwah, NJ: Lawrence Erlbaum.

Kapitzke, C., & Bruce, B. C. (2006). *Libr@ries: Changing information space and practice.* Hillsdale, NJ: Lawrence Erlbaum.

Kendzior, S. (2011). Digital distrust: Uzbek cynicism and solidarity in the Internet Age. *American Ethnologist, 38*(3), 559–575.

Knight Commission on the Information Needs of Communities in a Democracy. (2009). *Informing communities: Sustaining democracy in the digital age.* Washington, DC: Aspen Institute.

Kozol, J. (1991). *Savage inequalities: Children in America's schools.* New York: HarperCollins.

Kretzmann, J., & McKnight, J. P. (1996). Assets-based community development. *National Civic Review, 85*(4), 23.

Lacan, J., & Fink, B. (2006). *Ecrits: The first complete edition in English.* New York: Norton.

Ladson-Billings, G., & Donnor, J. (2005). The moral activist role of critical race theory scholarship. In N. Denzin & Y. Lincoln (Eds.), *The Sage handbook of qualitative research (3rd ed.).* Thousand Oaks, CA: Sage.

Laurence, A. (2000, November). [Web log message]. Retrieved from http://www.free williamsburg.com/still_fresh/edwidge.html

Ledwith, M (2005). *Community development: A critical approach.* Bristol: Policy.

Lerner, R. M, Dowling, E. M., & Anderson, P. M. (2003). Positive youth development: Thriving as the basis of personhood and civic society. Applied Developmental Science, 7(3), 172–180.

Levin, J. A., & Bruce, B. C. (2003). Technology as media: A learner centered perspective. In Y. Zhao (Ed.), What should teachers know about technology? Perspectives and practices. Information Age (pp. 45–51).

Li, Y., & Ranieri, M. (2010). Are "digital natives" really digitally competent?–A study on Chinese teenagers. British Journal of Educational Technology, 41(6), 1029–1042...104

Linden, R. M. (2002). Working across boundaries: Making collaboration work in government and non-profit organizations. San Francisco: Jossey-Bass.

Llewellyn, G. (1998). The teenage liberation handbook: How to quit school and get a real life and education. Eugene, OR: Lowry House.

Loader, B. D., & Keeble, L. (2004). Challenging the digital divide? A literature review of community informatics initiatives. York: The Joseph Rowntree Foundation.

Loader, B., & Mercea, D. (Eds.). (2012). Social media and democracy: Innovations in participatory politics. New York: Routledge.

London, J. K. (2007). Power and pitfalls of youth participation in community-based action research. Children, Youth & Environments, 17(2), 406–432.

Longo, N. V. (2005, April). Recognizing the role of community in civic education: Lessons from Hull House, Highlander Folk School, and the Neighborhood Learning Community. CIRCLE Working Paper No. 30. Medford, MA: The Center for Information and Research on Civic Learning and Engagement.

Longo, N. V. (2007). Why community matters: Connecting education with civic life. New York: SUNY Press.

Lucas, I. (1971). Puerto Rican dropouts in Chicago: Numbers and motivation. Chicago: Council on Urban Education.

Lyon, G. E. (1999). Where I'm from: Where poems come from. Spring, TX: Absey.

Martin, D. (2000). Mathematics success and failure among African American youth: The roles of sociohistorical context, community forces, school influence, and individual agency. Mahwah, NJ: Lawrence Erlbaum.

Marx, K. (1986). Economic and philosophic manuscripts of 1844. New York: International.

McKechnie, L. (2006). Becoming a reader: Childhood years. In C. Ross, L. McKechnie, & P. Rothbauer (Eds.), Reading matters: What the research reveals about reading, libraries, and community (pp. 63–81). Westport, CT: Libraries Unlimited.

McKoy, D., & Vincent, J. (2007). Engaging schools in urban revitalization: The Y-PLAN (Youth-Plan, Learn, Act, Now). Journal of Planning Education and Research, 26, 389–403.

McLaren, P. (1989). Critical pedagogy: A look at the major concepts. In A. Darder, M. P. Baltodano, & R. D. Torres (eds.), The critical pedagogy reader (2nd ed., pp. 61–83). New York: Routledge.

McLaughlin, M. (1976). Implementation as mutual adaptation: Change in classroom organization. The Teachers College Record, 77(3), 339–351.

McLaughlin, M. W. (1996). The Rand change agent study revisited: Macro perspectives and micro realities. *Educational Researcher, 19*(9), 11-16.

Meyer Reimer, K., & Bruce, B. C. (1994). Building teacher-researcher collaboration: Dilemmas and strategies. *Educational Action Research, 2*(2), 211-221.

Miller, C. C. (2006). A beast in the field: The Google Maps mashup as GIS/2. *Cartographica: The International Journal for Geographic Information and Geovisualization, 41*(3).

Mix IT Up!. (n.d.). Retrieved from http://mixituplis.wordpress.com

Moll, L. C., Amanti, C., Neff, D., & González, N. (1992). Funds of knowledge for teaching: Using a qualitative approach to connect homes and classrooms. *Theory into Practice, 31*(2), 132-141.

Morville, P. (2005). *Ambient findability: What we find changes who we become.* California: O'Reilly Media.

Nafus, D. (2009). *From multitasking to plastic time: The busyness (or not) of technology use.* Seminar presented January 23, 2009, Abstract accessed July 2009 at https://apps.lis.illinois.edu/wiki/display/sp09lis590ul/Schedule

Nam, C. (2012, October). Implications of community activism among urban minority young people for education for engaged and critical citizenship. *International Journal of Progressive Education, 8*(3), 62-76.

Nam, C. (in press). Crossing through the invisible gate, Mapping our neighborhood: The Empowering and Engaging Youth Project (E2Y). *Journal of Community Engagement and Scholarship.*

Nam, C., & Bishop, A. P. (2011). This is the real me: A community informatics researcher joins the Barrio Arts, Culture, and Communication Academy in a health information campaign. *Proceedings of iConference 2011, ACM Digital Library,* pp. 371-378.

Nam, C., Ritzo, C., & Bruce, B. C. (2009, May). *Approaching evaluation in Youth Community Informatics.* 5th International Congress of Qualitative Inquiry. Urbana-Champaign, IL.

National Writing Project, Berdan, K., Boulton, I., & Eidman-Aadahl, E. (Eds.). (2006). *Writing for a change: Boosting literacy and learning through social action.* San Francisco: Jossey-Bass.

Oakes, J., Rogers, J., & Lipton, M. (2006). *Learning power: Organizing for education and justice.* New York: Teachers College Press.

Office of Juvenile Justice and Delinquency Prevention. (2008). *Statistical briefing book.* Retrieved from http://www.ojjdp.gov/ojstatbb/

Office of Juvenile Justice and Delinquency Prevention. (2009). *Juvenile justice 2008.* Juvenile Justice Bulletin.

Orwell, G. (2008). *1984: A novel.* New York: Signet Classic.

PACHS Day Program. (n.d.). Pedro Albizu Campos High School Website. Retrieved from http://www.pedroalbizucamposhs.org/programs/pachs/

PACHS, our school history. (n.d.). *Pedro Albizu Campos High School website.* Retrieved from http://www.pedroalbizucamposhs.org/about/dr-pedro-albizu-campos-high-school/PACHS

Patterson, W., & Kranich, K. (2007). *Transforming education through alternative media: Public broadcasting as an accessing point to engage potentially at-risk African American youth in the development of educational and social enrichment media.* Chicago: American Educational Research Association.

Pea, B. (1995). *The Prairienet companion: The essential new user's guide to Prairienet.* Champaign, IL: Andrew Pea.

Pearson, G., & Young, A. T. (2002). *Technically speaking: Why all Americans need to know more about technology.* National Academies Press.

Pedro Albizu Campos High School website. (n.d.) Retrieved from http://www.pedro albizucamposhs.org/

Peirce, C. S. (1877). *The fixation of belief.* Wikisource. Retrieved from http://en.wikisource.org/wiki/The_Fixation_of_Belief

Pelias, R. J. (2008). Performative inquiry: Embodiment and its challenges. In *Handbook of the arts in qualitative research: Perspectives, methodologies, examples, and issues* (pp. 185–193). Thousand Oaks, CA: Sage.

Potts, R. G. (2003). Emancipatory education versus school-based prevention in African American communities. *American Journal of Community Psychology, 31*(1–2), 173–183.

Prairienet Community Network. (2012). *About Prairienet.* Retrieved from http://www.prairienet.org/about

Putnam, R. (2000). *Bowling alone: The collapse and revival of American community.* New York: Simon and Schuster.

Rainie, L., & Anderson, J. (2008). *The future of the Internet III.* Retrieved from http://www.pewinternet.org/Reports/2008/The-Future-of-the-Internet-III.aspx

Reardon, K. (1999). A sustainable community/university partnership. *Liberal Education, Summer, 99,* 85:3.

Reardon, K. (2005, April). Empowerment planning in East St. Louis, Illinois: A peoples' response to the deindustrialization blues. *City, 9*(1).

Ritzo, C., Nam, C., & Bruce, B. C. (2009). Building a strong web: Connecting information spaces across communities. *Library Trends, 57*(4), 82–94.

Rogers, E. (1995). *Diffusion of innovations* (4th ed.). New York: Free.

Ross, A. (2012, October). *Education for active citizenship* [Special issue]. *International Journal of Progressive Education, 8*(3).

Rothbauer, P. M. (2006). Young adults and reading. In C. S. Ross, L. McKechnie, & P. M. Rothbauer, *Reading matters: What the research reveals about reading, libraries, and community* (pp. 101–132). Westport, CT: Libraries Unlimited.

Rule, L. (2010, March/April). Digital storytelling has never been so easy or so powerful. *Knowledge Quest, 38*(4), 56–57.

Sadun, E. (2009). Consumers, not providers, ready for ubiquitous cellular data. Retrieved from http://arstechnica.com/telecom/news/2009/03/going-ubiquitous-with-cellular-data.ars

Schutz, A. (2006). Home is a prison in the global city: The tragic failure of school-based community engagement strategies. *Review of Educational Research, 76*(4), 691–743.

Shields, P. (1999). *The community of inquiry: Insights for public administration from Jane Addams, John Dewey and Charles S. Peirce*. Public Administration Theory Network. Retrieved from http://ecommons.txstate.edu/polsfacp/3

Shor, I. (1992). *Empowering education: Critical teaching for social change*. Chicago, IL: University of Chicago Press.

Shor, I. (1999). What is critical literacy? In A. Darder, M. P. Baltodano, & R. D. Torres (eds.), *The critical pedagogy reader (2nd ed.)* (pp. 282–304). New York: Routledge.

Shor, I., & Freire. P. (1987). *A pedagogy for liberation: Dialogues on transforming education*. New York: Bergin and Garvey.

Short, K. G., Schroeder, J., Laird, J., Kauffman, G., Ferguson, M. J., & Crawford, K. M. (1996). *Learning together through inquiry: From Columbus to integrated curriculum*. Portland, ME: Stenhouse.

Siegel, F., & Kramer, L. (2007). *YouthWorks facilitator guide*. Urbana: University of Illinois Press.

Simons, H., & Usher, R. (2000). *Situated ethics in educational research*. New York: Routledge.

Smith, M. K. (2001a). Education for democracy. In M. K. Smith, M. E. Doyle, & T. Jeffs (eds.), *infed: the encyclopedia of informal education*. Retrieved from http://www.infed.org/biblio/b-dem.htm

Smith, M. K. (2001b). Community. In M. K. Smith, M. E. Doyle, & T. Jeffs (eds.), *infed: the encyclopedia of informal education*. Retrieved from http://www.infed.org/community/community.htm

Smith, M. K. (2001c, September). Young people, informal education and association. In M. K. Smith, M. E. Doyle, & T. Jeffs (eds.), *infed: the encyclopedia of informal education*. Retrieved from http://www.infed.org/youthwork/ypandassoc.htm

Sorensen, J., & Lawson, L. (2012). Evolution in partnership: Lessons from the East St Louis Action Research Project. *Action Research, 10*, 150.

Stake, R. E. (2003). *Standards-based and responsive evaluation*. London. Sage.

Stake, R. E. (2006). *Multiple case study analysis*. New York: Guilford.

Stoecker, R. (2013). *Research methods for community change: A project-based approach (2nd ed.)*. Thousand Oaks, CA: Sage.

Swanson, T. I. (2010). Information is personal: Critical information literacy and personal epistemology. In M. T. Accardi, E. Drabinski, & A. Kumbier (eds.), *Critical library instruction: Theories and methods*. Duluth, MN: Library Juice.

Tarantola, D., & Mann, J. (1993, January 1). Medical ethics and the Nazi legacy. *World & I, 8*, 358.

Tenenbaum, S. (1951). *William Heard Kilpatrick: Trail blazer in education*. New York: Harper & Brothers.

Theatre of the Oppressed Website. (n.d.) Retrieved from http://www.theatreofthe oppressed.org/

Theising, A. (2003). *Made in USA: East St. Louis, the rise and fall of an industrial river town*. St. Louis: Virginia.

Truman, C., Mertens, D. M., & Humphries, B. (2000). *Research and inequality*. New York: Routledge.

Tully, J. (2008). *Public philosophy in a new key [two volumes]*. Cambridge: Cambridge University Press.

Urban, W. J., & Wagoner, J. L. (2009). *American education: A history*. New York: Routledge.

Urbana Free Library. (2009). *An extraordinary public library*. Retrieved from http://urbanafreelibrary.org/about/

Vacca, J. (2008). Crime can be prevented if schools teach juvenile offenders to read. *Children and Youth Services Review, 30*, 1055-1062.

Vaughan, H. (2007). *Citizen science as a catalyst in bridging the gap between science and decision-makers*. Citizen Science Toolkit Conference. Retrieved from http://www.birds.cornell.edu/citscitoolkit/conference/proceeding-pdfs/Vaughan%202007%20CS%20Conference.pdf

Venable, B. (2005). At risk and in-need: Reaching juvenile offenders through art. *Art Education, 58*(4), 48-53.

Villanueva, V. (2009). Colonial memory and the crimes of rhetoric: Pedro Albizu Campos. *College English, 71*(6), 630-638.

Viseu, A., Clement, A., Aspinall, J., & Kennedy, T. M. (2006, October). The interplay of public and private spaces in Internet access. *Information, Communication & Society, 9*(5), 633-656.

Volunteer Virginia. (n.d.). Retrieved from http://www.facebook.com/pages/ Virginia-IL/Volunteer-Virginia/170775759367

Wald, J., & Losen, D. J. (2003). Defining and redirecting a school-to-prison pipeline. *New Directions for Youth Development, 99*, 9-15.

Wang, C., & Burris, G., (1997). Photovoice: Concept, methodology, and use for participatory needs. *Health Education & Behavior, 24*(3), 369-387.

Wang, C., et al. (1998). *Photovoice as a participator health promotion strategy*. Retrieved from http://heapro.oxfordjournals.org/cgi/reprint/13/1/75.pdf

Warschauer, M. (2003). *Technology and social inclusion: Rethinking the digital divide*. Cambridge, MA: MIT press.

Weiser, M. (1991). The computer for the 21st century. *Scientific American, 265*(3), 94-104.

Wells, G. (2001). *Dialogic inquiry*. New York: Cambridge University Press.

Wenger, E. (1998). *Community of practice: Learning, meaning, and identity*. Cambridge: Harvard University Press.

Wenger, E. (2006, June). *Communities of practice. A brief introduction*. Retrieved from http://www.ewenger.com/theory/

Wenger, E. C., & Snyder, W. M. (2000, Jan./Feb.). Communities of practice: The organizational frontier. *Harvard Business Review*, 139-145.

Williams, R., & Edge, D. (1996). The social shaping of technology. *Research Policy, 25*, 865-899.

Williams-Garcia, R. (1995). *Like sisters on the homefront*. New York: Lodestar Books.

Williamson, T., Alperovitz, G., & Imbroscio, D. (2002). *Making a place for community: Local politics in a global era.* New York: Routledge.

Wolske, M., Gibbs, D., Kehoe, A., Jones, V., & Irish, S. (2013). Outcome of applying evidence-based design to public computing centers: A preliminary study. *Journal of Community Informatics, 9*(1). http://go.illinois.edu/PCCRedesignPaper

Wolske, M., Johnson, E., & Adams, P. (2010, January). *Citizen professional toolkits: Empowering communities through mass amateurization.* Centre for Community Networking Research, Coulfield School of IT, Monash University. Retrieved from http://hdl.handle.net/2142/16299

Yosso, T. (2005). Whose culture has capital? A critical race theory discussion of community cultural wealth. *Race, Ethnicity and Education, 8*(1), 69-91.

Contributors

Note: GSLIS here refers to the Graduate School of Library and Information Science at the University of Illinois at Urbana-Champaign.

Mike Adams is an instructor with Computer Village, a community-based not-for-profit corporation in St. Louis, Missouri. Mr. Adams is the primary volunteer organizer of Teen Tech East St. Louis.

Paul Adams worked at GSLIS for 14 years as director of community networking (Prairienet). He led student teams to Sao Tome, employing service learning and action research for social entrepreneurship.

Jeanie Austin is a PhD student and has been a juvenile detention center librarian since fall 2009.

Jeff Bennett has been a social studies teacher at Virginia High School in Illinois for 19 years.

Patrick W. Berry is an assistant professor of writing and rhetoric at Syracuse University. His research focuses on literacy narratives, digital media and production, and community outreach.

Ann Peterson Bishop is an associate professor emerita in GSLIS. She focuses on community-based research methods, social justice in the information professions, and studies of digital information use and users.

Bertram (Chip) Bruce is professor emeritus in GSLIS. His interests include environments to support inquiry-based learning, collaboration in knowledge making, and new literacy practices. Recently, he edited a series of special issues for the *International Journal of Progressive Education*.

Nama R. Budhathoki earned his doctorate from the University of Illinois. He is the Co-Founder and Director of Kathmandu Living Labs, and is also a consultant at the World Bank. His interest and expertise lie at the intersection of digital media, civic engagement, and collective action, with particular focus on crowd-sourcing and social media.

Sally K. Carter is the director and founder of Tap In Leadership Academy. Sally has constructed a program that serves as a vehicle for sustainable, meaningful collaboration between the university and the community in which it exists. Sally graduated with an MBA from Kaplan University.

Alexandra Cavallaro is currently a PhD student and teaching assistant in the Center for Writing Studies in the English Department at the University of Illinois at Urbana-Champaign. Her research focuses on LGBTQ literacies and rhetorics.

Joe Coyle is a juvenile detention center librarian and runs a writing program in Champaign-Urbana that serves young people in the juvenile justice system.

Carlos R. DeJesús served as Assistant Principal at Pedro Albizu Campos High School (PACHS). He is presently the Managing Director of Housing at Heartland Human Care Services of the Heartland Alliance, working to end homelessness in Chicago. Carlos has dedicated his professional life to working with and for his community, in the areas of food security, education, housing, health, and mental health.

Lisa Bouillion Diaz is an adjunct assistant professor and extension specialist at the University of Illinois. She is trained as a learning scientist and received her doctoral degree from Northwestern University. Her work focuses on the use of digital and information technologies to support learning opportunities for youth across school and community settings.

Robin Fisher was an agriculture and science teacher at Virginia High School in Illinois during the time of the project there.

Naomi García studied at the Pedro Albizu Campos High School (PACHS). She is a poet and spoken-word artist and has been an active member of PACHS and a contributor to the Youth Community Informatics initiative.

Alex Jean-Charles is an assistant professor of STEM and Educational Technology at SUNY Oneonta, New York. His areas of interest are the social construction of technology, human (youth) interaction with new media technology, identity, and technology literacies.

Iván M. Jorrín-Abellán is associate professor at the University of Valladolid (Spain). His research focuses on educational implications of computer-supported collaborative learning scenarios, with special attention to new ways of evaluating these particular settings.

Ching-Chiu Lin is a postdoctoral research fellow in the Department of Curriculum and Pedagogy at the University of British Columbia. Lin's research interests lie in issues of technology and community in art education.

Karyn M. Mendoza is a clinical supervisor for the Orange County Bar Foundation, supervising therapists who provide mental health services to "at-risk" youth and their families. She was formerly youth development educator for 4-H at the University of Illinois at Urbana-Champaign.

Rae-Anne Montague is assistant professor at the University of Hawaii Library and Information Science Program and coordinator of the School Library Media Program. Her academic interests include LIS education, multimodal learning, and social justice. Rae has worked as an educator in Canada, Mexico, and the United States.

Jill Murphy has taught sixth-grade math at Iroquois West in Onarga, Illinois, for 17 years. She has been geocaching since 2003 when her husband, Gregg, brought home the first GPS for the family. Since then she has geocached in many U.S. states and Mexico.

Chaebong Nam is currently a research fellow at Soongsil University in Korea. She received her PhD in Education from the University of Illinois at Urbana-Champaign, with a focus on community engagement, community-based learning, and new media learning.

William Patterson is co-director of The Youth Media Workshop. He is associate director of the African-American Studies and Research Program at the University of Illinois and founder of Innovative Ed Consulting, Inc., a marketing and educational consulting firm that assists at-risk youth in creating their own media.

Kimberly Rahn taught an at-risk bilingual pre-K program for 7 years at Iroquois West Elementary in Danforth, Illinois. Then she spent the next 10 years working for University of Illinois Extension as a youth development educator. She graduated from Olivet Nazarene University and Illinois State University.

Shameem Rakha graduated from the University of Illinois with a PhD in Educational Policy Studies. Her dissertation examines culturally competent teaching practices in an after-school program and how these practices can be generalized in the school setting to more fully engage students of color. She is a National Board Certified Teacher and has served as a public school elementary and middle school teacher for 17 years.

Chris Ritzo is a staff technologist with the New America Foundation's Open Technology Institute. Chris's past work in librarianship, information management, communications, community media production, K–12 education, and higher education informs his work as a community-focused technologist.

Angela M. Slates is a doctoral student in Education Policy and Organizational Leadership at the University of Illinois at Urbana-Champaign. Her focus is on urban education imperatives for African American and Latino/Latina students in science, technology, engineering, arts, and mathematics education (STEAM).

Elaine Vázquez taught English at the Pedro Albizu Campos High School (PACHS) and is currently employed with the San Francisco Unified School District as an English Department Head and teacher, helping teachers and administrators reform instruction and school climate in ways that address equity gaps at her school site, Raoul Wallenberg Traditional High School.

Martin Wolske is a senior research scientist at GSLIS. His research interests focus on engagement pedagogy; participatory, evidence-based design of public computing spaces to support communities of inquiry; and popular education approaches to digital media literacy training.

Index

new

literacies

q

AND DIGITAL EPISTEMOLOGIES

Colin Lankshear & Michele Knobel

General Editors

New literacies emerge and evolve apace as people from all walks of life engage with new technologies, shifting values and institutional change, and increasingly assume 'postmodern' orientations toward their everyday worlds. Despite many efforts to take account of such changes, educational institutions largely remain out of touch with the range of new ways of making and sharing meanings that increasingly mediate and shape the lives of the young people they teach and the futures they face. This series aims to explore some key dimensions of the changes occurring within social practices of literacy and the educational challenges they present, with a view to informing educational practice in helpful ways. It asks what are new literacies, how do they impact on life in schools, homes, communities, workplaces, sites of leisure, and other key settings of human cultural engagement, and what significance do new literacies have for how people learn and how they understand and construct knowledge. It aims to challenge established and 'official' ways of framing literacy, and to ask what it means for literacies to be powerful, effective, and enabling under current and foreseeable conditions. Collectively, the works in this series will help to reorient literacy debates and literacy education agendas.

For further information about the series and submitting manuscripts, please contact:

Michele Knobel & Colin Lankshear
Montclair State University
Dept. of Education and Human Services
3173 University Hall
Montclair, NJ 07043
michele@coatepec.net

To order other books in this series, please contact our Customer Service Department at:

(800) 770-LANG (within the U.S.)
(212) 647-7706 (outside the U.S.)
(212) 647-7707 FAX

Or browse online by series at:
www.peterlang.com